best music coach

THE BEST MUSIC THEORY BOOK FOR BEGINNERS

How to Create Soul-Stirring Songs
with Remarkable Rhythms and Captivating Chords

3

How This Series Works

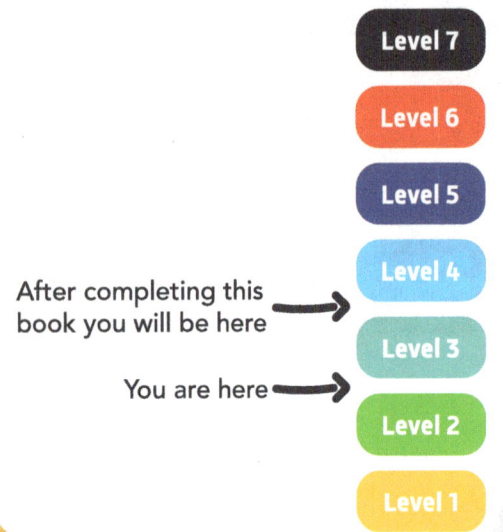

- Level 7
- Level 6
- Level 5
- Level 4 ← After completing this book you will be here
- Level 3
- Level 2 ← You are here
- Level 1

Claim your free 10-day trial to #1 music courses + software

Copyright ©2023 Best Music Coach LLC

First Edition 2023

All rights reserved. Printed in the United States of America. No part of this book may be used or reproduced in any manner whatsoever without written permission.

ISBN: 978-1-957835-11-2

@bestmusiccoach
www.bestmusiccoach.com
facebook.com/bestmusiccoach
youtube.com/bestmusiccoach
twitter.com/bestmusiccoach
instagram.com/bestmusiccoach

Book Design by Adam Hay Studio
Editing by Emily Flanagan

Welcome to Best Music Coach!

A note to adult students and parents of younger students

I am thrilled that you chose this book and our coaches to guide you or your family on your music journey. We are here to answer all your musical questions and to empower you, our students, readers, and coaches, to discover and achieve your musical goals.

This book is for musicians, music students, and anyone who is interested in understanding more about music—even a perfect beginner who has never played an instrument or a parent of a student who wants to understand and help their child!

For best results with this book, work with a qualified music theory coach in weekly sessions of 30 minutes (ages 5-10) or 60 minutes (ages 11-adult).

A quick note for the intrepid "I'll do it myself" folks reading this: This book is clear enough that you can teach yourself, but you will see measurably faster growth and progress with a coach.

Dan Spencer
Lead Coach

learn the rules, follow the rules, break the rules, make music. the music in your heart may not conform to the rules you will learn in this book, or it may follow the rules without exception. rules provide a structure to be creative in. all ways of making music are fine. go make music and express yourself with passion.

Contents

11. Rhythm 11: Compound Meter
12. What is Compound Meter?
13. How to Count Compound Meter
14. Compound Time Signatures
15. Dotted Whole Note
15. Rhythmic Value Hierarchy: Compound vs. Simple Meter
16. How to Divide the Beat into Three Equal Parts: Count
17. Compound Meter: Count In
18. Clap and Count Compound Meter
20. Review: Rhythm 11

21. Rhythm 12: Strong and Weak Beats: Compound Meter
22. Compound Meter: Strong and Weak Beats
23. Metric Hierarchy: Compound vs. Simple Meter
24. Strong and Weak Beats: $\frac{6}{8}$
24. Strong and Weak Beats: $\frac{9}{8}$
25. Strong and Weak Beats: $\frac{12}{8}$
25. New Drum Notation
26. Review: Rhythm 12

27. Rhythm 13: Advanced Rests
28. Dotted Whole Rest
28. Dotted Half Rest
29. Rhythmic Value Hierarchy 2: Compound vs. Simple Meter
29. Whole Rests Return
30. Clap and Count with Rests
31. Multi-Measure Rests
32. Tacet
32. Review: Rhythm 13

33. Rhythm 14: How to Write Music in Compound Meter
34. How to Write Eighth Notes in Compound Meter
36. Measure Math 5
38. How to Write Notes and Rests in a Measure: Compound Meter
41. How to Space Notes on the Staff: Compound Meter
42. Review: Rhythm 14

43. How to Write Slash and Beat Notation
44. Slash Notation
46. Beat Notation

47. Articulation Marks 2
48. Accent
49. Articulation Combination
49. Articulation Location
50. Review: Articulation Marks 2

51. Rhythm 15: Syncopation
52. Syncopation
53. Syncopation: Simple Meter
56. Syncopation: Compound Meter
59. How to Write Syncopation
59. Syncopation Example
60. Review: Rhythm 15

Contents

61. Rhythm 16: Turnkey Triplets + Sassy Swing & Shuffle
- 62. Eighth Note Triplets
- 64. Swing Eighth Notes
- 66. Shuffle: Eighth Notes
- 68. Review: Rhythm 16

69. Rhythm 17: Multiple Endings
- 70. Multiple Endings
- 72. Review: Rhythm 17

73. Dynamic Marks 2, Performance Marks, & Tempo Marks
- 74. Dynamics 2
- 75. Rit., Rall., A tempo
- 77. Tempo and Metronome Marks
- 78. Review: Dynamic Marks 2

79. Pitch and Notes 9: New Keys & Notes
- 80. New Accidental Notes 3
- 80. Key Signatures 3
- 82. How to Remember the Number of Accidentals in a Key: 7
- 83. Accidentals and Key Signatures: The Full Picture
- 84. Parallel Keys and Scales
- 85. Circle of Fifths & Circle of Fourths
- 86. Accidentals 2
- 88. Review: Pitch and Notes 9

89. Pitch and Notes 10: Compound Intervals
- 90. Compound Intervals
- 90. Compound Interval Numbers = 7
- 91. Interval Quality: Compound
- 92. How to Talk and Think About Compound Intervals
- 93. How to Write Compound Intervals
- 94. Augmented and Diminished Intervals: Anything Goes
- 94. Review: Pitch and Notes 10

95. Harmony 5: Seventh Chords 2
- 96. Seventh Chord Quality 2
- 97. A New Look at Roman Numerals
- 98. Roman Numerals: Berklee Way
- 99. SD = RN
- 99. More Roman Numerals for Seventh Chords
- 100. Harmonic Minor Scale Harmonized to the Seventh
- 101. Real Melodic Minor Scale Harmonized to the Seventh
- 102. Inversions 2: Seventh Chords
- 104. Review: Harmony 5

105. Harmony 6: sus, ADD, Extended, Omit, and Advanced Inversions
- 106. More Chord Tones
- 107. ADD Chords
- 109. Extended Chords
- 109. Tensions
- 110. Alterations
- 112. The Octave Puzzle
- 113. sus Chords
- 115. Omit Chords
- 116. Advanced Slash Chords
- 117. A New Look at Inversions
- 118. Review: Harmony 6

119. Harmony 7: Harmonized Scales Summary

- 120. All Major Scales
- 121. All Natural Minor Scales
- 122. All Major Pentatonic Scales
- 122. All Minor Pentatonic Scales
- 123. All Harmonic Minor Scales
- 124. All Real Melodic Minor Scales

125. Analysis 5: Harmonic Function 1

- 126. Harmonic Function
- 126. Tonal Center
- 127. Tonic Area (T)
- 129. Dominant Area (D)
- 132. T - D - T
- 137. Subdominant Area (SD)
- 140. T - SD - D - T
- 144. Review: Analysis 5

145. Pitch and Notes 11: Melody

- 146. Melody
- 146. What Makes a "Good" Melody?
- 147. Motif
- 149. Motivic Development
- 149. 1. Repetition
- 149. 2. Transposition
- 150. 3. Sequence
- 150. 4. Variation
- 151. 5. Fragmentation
- 151. 6. Interval Alteration
- 152. 7. Rhythm Alteration
- 152. 8. Inversion
- 152. 9. Retrograde
- 153. 10. Augmentation
- 154. 11. Diminution
- 155. 12. Extension
- 155. 13. Truncation
- 156. Phrase
- 156. Basic Phrase
- 157. Antecedent and Consequent
- 157. Subphrase
- 158. Review: Pitch and Notes 11

159. Analysis 6: Cadences 1

- 160. Cadences
- 160. Music in Two Ways: Cadences
- 161. Perfect Authentic Cadence: **V**
- 162. Imperfect Authentic Cadence: **V**
- 163. Theory and Art Meet
- 164. Leading Tone Imperfect Authentic Cadence: **VII°**
- 167. Plagal Cadence
- 169. Half Cadence
- 170. Deceptive Cadence
- 171. SD - D Cadence
- 174. sus Chord Extra Tension Before Resolution
- 175. When a Phrase Does Not Line Up with Measures
- 176. Review: Analysis 6

177. Analysis 7: Borrowed Chords Bonanza

- 178. Roman Numeral Reality Check
- 178. How to Recognize and Analyze a Key Change
- 179. Borrowed Chords from Parallel Keys
- 180. Secondary Dominants
- 183. Borrowed SD - D
- 185. More Borrowed Chords
- 187. Tritone Substitution
- 190. Review: Analysis 7

191. Analysis 8: Phrase & Advanced Lead Sheet Analysis
- 192. Musical Form Hierarchy
- 192. Advanced Lead Sheet Analysis
- 193. How to Write a Cadence & Harmonic Function Analysis
- 198. How to Perform a Phrase Analysis
- 202. Form Analysis 2
- 204. Review: Analysis 8

205. Analysis 9: The Blues
- 206. The Blues
- 206. 12-Bar Blues Harmony
- 208. 12-Bar Minor Blues Harmony
- 210. Blues with a B Section
- 211. 12-Bar Jazz-Blues
- 212. Blues Melody
- 214. Review: Analysis 9

215. How to Write Music 3: Cycles of Tension, Resolution, & Reharmonization
- 216. Melody Making Maps
- 217. Chord-Melody Relationship
- 218. Types of Tension and Resolution
- 219. Cycles of Tension and Resolution
- 220. Harmonic Rhythm
- 221. Phrase Rhythm
- 221. Reharmonization
- 222. How to Begin Reharmonization
- 224. Level 1 Reharmonization
- 226. Level 2 Reharmonization
- 228. Level 3 Reharmonization
- 230. How to Show There Is No Chord
- 230. Review: How to Write Music 3

231. How to Write Music 4: Art
- 232. What Makes "Good" Art?
- 232. What Is Needed to Create Art?
- 233. The Dichotomy of Art
- 233. There Are Answers, but There Are No Answers
- 234. How to Write a Song 2
- 238. Ideas: Mix and Match
- 239. What Is the Next Step?

How to Scan QR Codes

1

2

3

1. On an iPhone, open the camera. On an Android, download and open a QR code-scanner application.

2. Hold your phone so you can see the QR code on the screen, with the screen in focus.

3. On iPhones, tap the banner that asks you if you want to open the QR code. On Android, tap the button that asks you to open the QR code. Try it out with the code at below this writing.

Get a 10 day free trial to the bite-sized course that walks you through this book! Scan the QR code to claim your free trial

Music Theory: Introduction

What Is Music Theory?

The study and understanding of the elements and structure of music. It is the key to understanding the "how" and the "why" behind all music you hear or play.

Why Learn Music Theory?

Learn Pieces of Music Faster on Any Instrument or Voice
Just like using a GPS app will get to your destination faster, music theory shows you the way to the end of a piece of music, speeding memorization, because you understand what is actually going on. With this, you will be able to play and sing music more accurately, with a deeper intellectual and emotional understanding and interpretation.

Get Better at Writing Music
Anytime you write songs (songwriting), compositions (composing), or produce music (music production), you are using music theory. You now have a clear path to easily use music theory to create. There is even a chapter dedicated to take everything you learn here and use it to write music. Writing and creating music is a journey, and this is the **first step**.

Strengthen Your Relationship to All the Music in Your Life
Music theory will help you understand and relate to all music you hear.

What You Will Need

1. This book.
2. Music notation software
3. Free notation software: musescore
4. Paid notation software: noteflight, sibelius, or finale.

How This Book Works

Free Audio and Video Examples and Flashcards

This book comes with video examples of exercises and songs. Any time you see the icon (23) it is showing the video example number for you to listen to or watch to help you understand the song or exercise. All video examples can be found by scanning the QR code below with your device or at

bestmusiccoach.com/books

1. Click on "Music Theory."
2. Click on "The Best Music Theory Books for Beginners **Series**."
3. Click on "The Best Music Theory Books for Beginners **3**."
4. Click on "Free Examples" then create a free account—click "Login to Enroll."

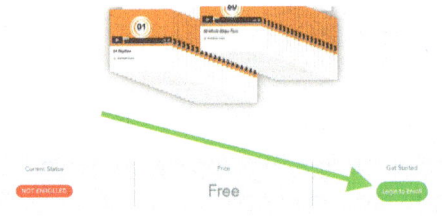

How to Read Timestamps

The timestamp shows how many seconds or minutes into music examples begin, and when it ends.

03:29 – 05:00
minutes:seconds — minutes:seconds
Example starts at three minutes and twenty-nine seconds | Example ends at five minutes and zero seconds

I am here for you.
Get free lessons and community
facebook.com/groups/musicmakersofficial

Rhythm 11: Compound Meter

In this chapter you will discover how to understand, write, and perform notes in compound time signatures.

What Is Compound Meter?

- Compound meters have 3 beat divisions in every beat.
- Compound meters can be duple, triple, and quadruple, like simple meters.
- The top number of compound time signatures shows the **beat division**, not the **beat unit (beat)**.
- If the top number of the time signature is 6, there are 6 beat divisions and 2 beats.
- If the top number of the time signature is 9, there are 9 beat divisions and 3 beats.
- If the top number of the time signature is 12, there are 12 beat divisions and 4 beats.
- Because each beat has 3 beat divisions, the beat unit will be a dotted note.

Duple Compound Meter

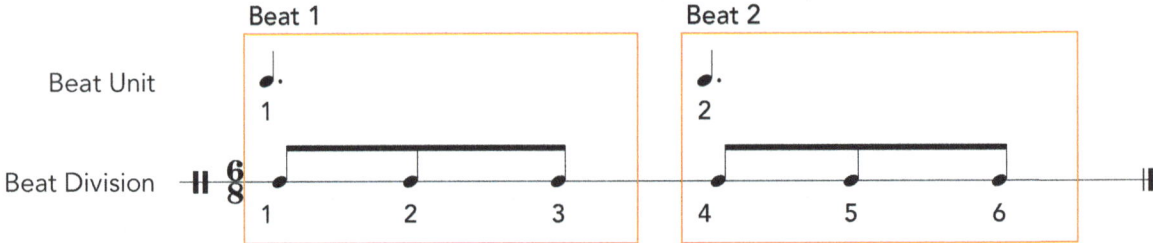

Triple Compound Meter

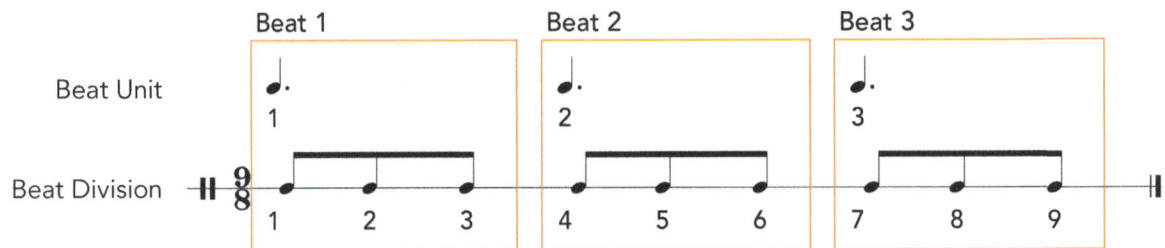

Quadruple Compound Meter

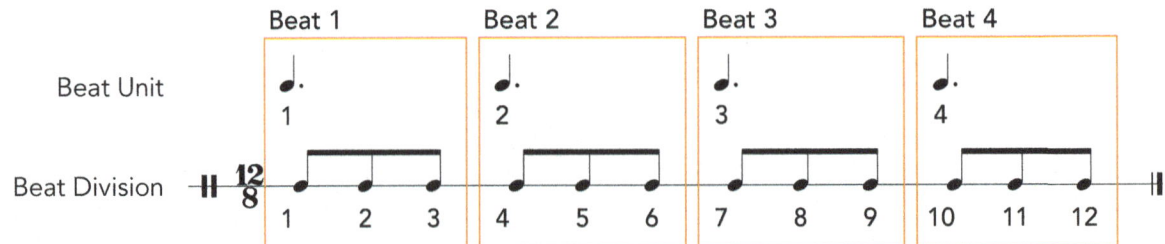

How to Count Compound Meter

- Each beat is divided into three equal parts.
- The first beat division lands on count 1, 2, 3, or 4, with the dotted quarter note.
- The second beat division lands 1/3 into the empty space between counts 1, 2, 3, or 4. This is the "ti" of 1, 2, 3, or 4. ("ti" like tea)
- The third beat division lands 2/3 into the empty space between counts 1, 2, 3, or 4. This is the "da" of 1, 2, 3, or 4. ("da" like dahlia)

Count Duple Compound Meter

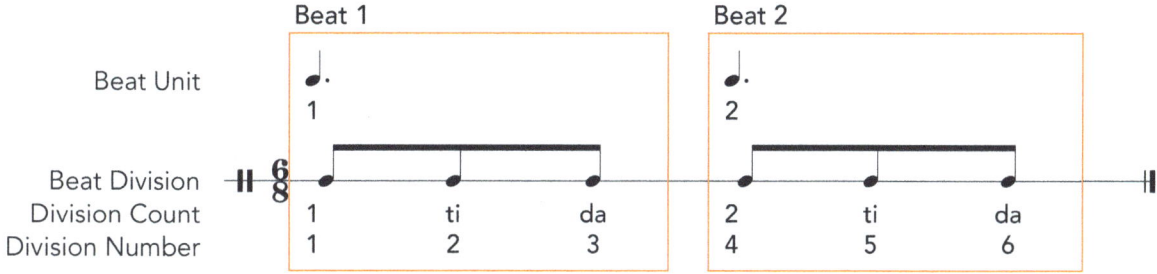

Count Triple Compound Meter

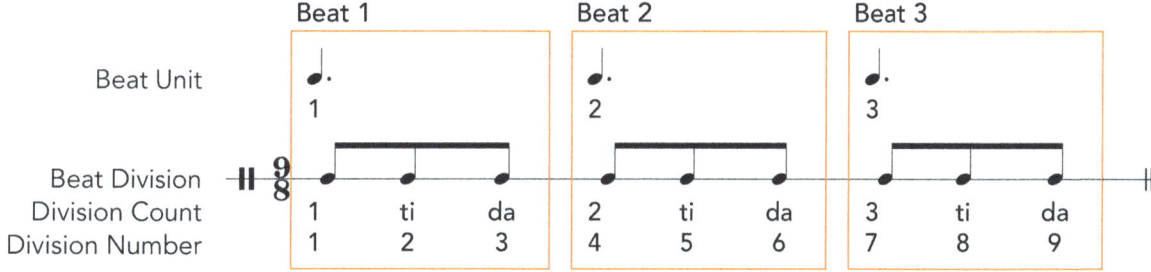

Count Quadruple Compound Meter

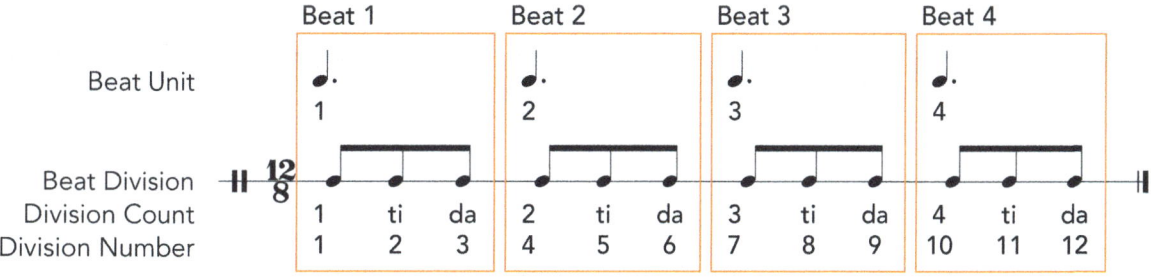

Rhythm 11: Compound Meter

Compound Time Signatures

The top number of a compound time signature shows how many **beat divisions** there are per measure. The bottom number as a fraction is the name of the note rhythmic value that "gets" the **beat division**. Look at the chart below.

Bottom Number	8
Bottom Number as a Fraction	⅛
Name of the Fraction	Eighth
Note Value that is the Beat Division	Eighth note

Top: Number of beat divisions per measure? **12/8** 12 beat divisions per measure.
Bottom: Type of note that is the beat division? Eighth note is the beat division.

Compound Duple

6/8 (divisions per measure, eighth note is the division)

Measure: 1st | 2nd
Count: 1 ti da 2 ti da | 1 ti da 2 ti da

Compound Triple

9/8 (divisions per measure, eighth note is the division)

Measure: 1st | 2nd
Count: 1 ti da 2 ti da 3 ti da | 1 ti da 2 ti da 3 ti da

Compound Quadruple

12/8 (divisions per measure, eighth note is the division)

Measure: 1st | 2nd
Count: 1 ti da 2 ti da 3 ti da 4 ti da | 1 ti da 2 ti da 3 ti da 4 ti da

Dotted Whole Note

Dotted notes are worth 1 ½ times the written note's rhythmic value.

open notehead 𝅝 • **dot**

The written note value + ½ of the written note value = dotted note value. Dotted whole notes fill up an entire measure of $\frac{12}{8}$. In simple meter, a dotted whole note would get six beats! Because the beat unit in compound meters is a dotted quarter note, the dotted whole note gets 4 beats. See the rhythmic value hierarchy below for a complete overview of compound and simple meters.

Rhythmic Value Hierarchy: Compound vs. Simple Meter

Simple Meter

𝅝			
1 &	2 &	3 &	4 &
𝅗𝅥		𝅗𝅥	
1 &	2 &	3 &	4 &
♩	♩	♩	♩
1 &	2 &	3 &	4 &
♫♫	♫♫	♫♫	♫♫
1 &	2 &	3 &	4 &

Compound Meter

𝅝.			
1 ti da	2 ti da	3 ti da	4 ti da
𝅗𝅥.		𝅗𝅥.	
1 ti da	2 ti da	3 ti da	4 ti da
♩.	♩.	♩.	♩.
1 ti da	2 ti da	3 ti da	4 ti da
♫♪	♫♪	♫♪	♫♪
1 ti da	2 ti da	3 ti da	4 ti da

Rhythm 11: Compound Meter

How to Divide the Beat into Three Equal Parts: Count

Rhythm 11: Compound Meter

① Count

6/8

1. Start a metronome at 60 BPM. Listen to the metronome until you can hear the pattern. When you feel you can anticipate the timing between the clicks:
2. Count "1, 2" aloud with each number you speak happening at the same time as a click. Be as precise as possible and speak exactly with the clicking sound, not before or after.
3. Now repeat the count over and over again, like counting in 2/4.
4. When this count is comfortable, add in the "ti" and "da." The most common mistake at this point is to count the "ti" and "da" too quickly or too slowly.
5. If you can't quite get it right, it may help to say "blueberry." Blue lands precisely on the click and ber-ry takes up the space in between the clicks.

② Count

9/8

1. Start a metronome at 60 BPM. Listen to the metronome until you can hear the pattern. When you feel you can anticipate the timing between the clicks:
2. Count "1, 2, 3" aloud with each number you speak happening at the same time as a click. Be as precise as possible and speak exactly with the clicking sound, not before or after.
3. Now repeat the count over and over again, like counting in 3/4.
4. When this count is comfortable, add in the "ti" and "da." The most common mistake at this point is to count the "ti" and "da" too quickly or too slowly.
5. If you can't quite get it right, it may help to say "blueberry." Blue lands precisely on the click and ber-ry takes up the space in between the clicks.

③ Count

12/8

1. Start a metronome at 60 BPM. Listen to the metronome until you can hear the pattern. When you feel you can anticipate the timing between the clicks:
2. Count "1, 2, 3, 4" aloud with each number you speak happening at the same time as a click. Speak exactly with the clicking sound, not before or after.
3. Now repeat the count over and over again, like counting in 4/4.
4. When this count is comfortable, add in the "ti" and "da." The most common mistake at this point is to count the "ti" and "da" too quickly or too slowly.
5. If you can't quite get it right, it may help to say "blueberry." Blue lands precisely on the click and ber-ry takes up the space in between the clicks.

Compound Meter: Count In

The count in is giving the beat with spoken words or sounds. This is like: "On your mark, get set, go!" so musicians can start making music at the same time and speed together.

 Count In: Application

Give yourself a count in before performing the exercises in this book or your own compositions.

 Count In

6/8

1. Listen to the metronome until you can hear the pattern and anticipate when the next click will happen before moving forward. When you feel you can anticipate the timing between the clicks:
2. Count "1 ti da, 2 ti da" aloud with each number you speak happening at the same time as a click.
3. Try to be as precise as possible and speak exactly with the clicking sound, not before or after.

 Count In

9/8

1. Listen to the metronome until you can hear the pattern and anticipate when the next click will happen before moving forward. When you feel you can anticipate the timing between the clicks:
2. Count "1 ti da, 2 ti da, 3 ti da" aloud with each number you speak happening at the same time as a click.
3. Try to be as precise as possible and speak exactly with the clicking sound, not before or after.

 Count In

12/8

1. Listen to the metronome until you can hear the pattern and anticipate when the next click will happen before moving forward. When you feel you can anticipate the timing between the clicks:
2. Count "1 ti da, 2 ti da, 3 ti da, 4 ti da" aloud with each number you speak happening at the same time as a click.
3. Try to be as precise as possible and speak exactly with the clicking sound, not before or after.

Clap and Count Compound Meter

Clap and Count 1

Clap and Count 2

Clap and Count 3

Clap and Count 4

Clap and Count 5

Clap and Count 6

Common Compound Meters

Dotted quarter note gets the beat

Compound duple: 6/8

Compound triple: 9/8

Compound quadruple: 12/8

Rhythm 11: Compound Meter

Review

- Compound meter
- How to count compound meter
    Division "ti"
    Division "da"
- Compound time signatures
    Compound duple
    Compound triple
    Compound quadruple
- Dotted whole notes
- Compound vs. simple meter
- How to count compound meter with a metronome
    Compound duple
    Compound triple
    Compound quadruple
- How to give a count in for compound meter
    Compound duple
    Compound triple
    Compound quadruple

New Words You Should Know

1. Compound meter
2. ti
3. da

Rhythm 12: Strong and Weak Beats: Compound Meter

See more connections between simple and compound meters and unlock the concept of "metric hierarchy."

Compound Meter: Strong and Weak Beats

Metric Hierarchy

The order of strong and weak beats is called metric hierarchy. "Hierarchy" means a way of organizing things in an ordered series. In this case, the hierarchy is organized by which beats are "strongest" and "weakest." Metric hierarchy is the term for talking about the idea of stronger and weaker beats.

Compound Meter: Strong Beats, Weak Beats, and Beat Division Colors

Because compound meters have 3 equal divisions of each beat, there are 2 divisions with the counts of "ti" and "da."

Metric Hierarchy: Compound vs. Simple Meter

Even though there are three beat divisions in compound meters, the order of strong and weak beats is the same between simple and compound duple, simple and compound triple, and simple and compound quadruple meters.

Simple Meter

Compound Meter

Simple Duple Meter

(Strongest Weakest)

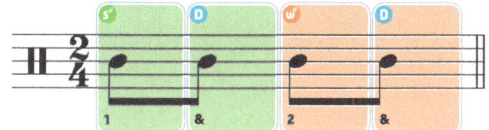

Compound Duple Meter

(Strongest Weakest)

Simple Triple Meter

(Strongest, Weak, Weakest)

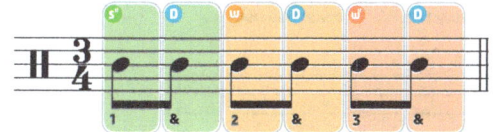

Compound Triple Meter

(Strongest, Weak, Weakest)

Simple Quadruple Meter

(Strongest, Weak, Strong, Weakest)

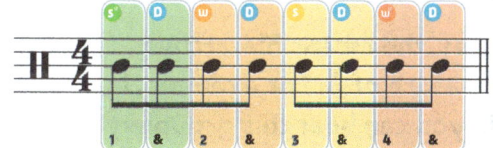

Compound Quadruple Meter

(Strongest, Weak, Strong, Weakest)

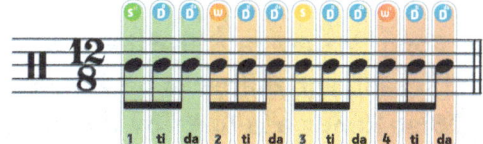

Strong and Weak Beats: 6/8

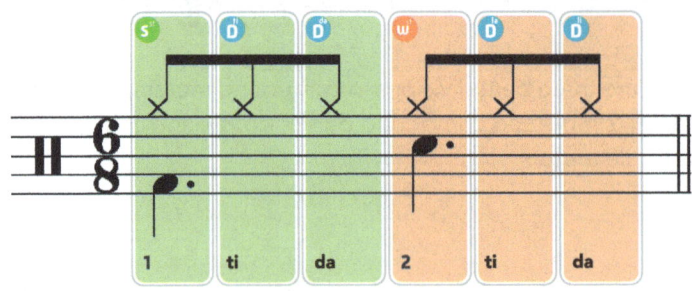

LISTEN

House of the Rising Sun	The Animals
From the Inside	Linkin Park
Nothing Else Matters	Metallica
Hallelujah	Leonard Cohen
Can't Help Falling In Love	Elvis Presley

Strong and Weak Beats: 9/8

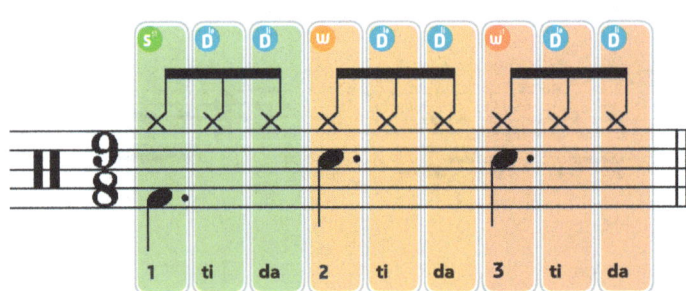

LISTEN

Weird Song #1	Chase
Prelude and Fugue in C major, BWV 547	J. S. Bach

> Songs in 9/8 are rare. In other music cultures, the metric hierarchy is different, and there can be 4 beats in a measure of 9/8. For example, in "Blue Rondo a la Turk" by Dave Brubeck, you can hear this grouping of eighth notes: 2+2+2+3 followed by a measure of 3+3+3. This is 4 beats per measure and then 3 beats per measure, alternating back and forth for the duration of the song...all in 9/8!

Strong and Weak Beats: 12/8

12/8

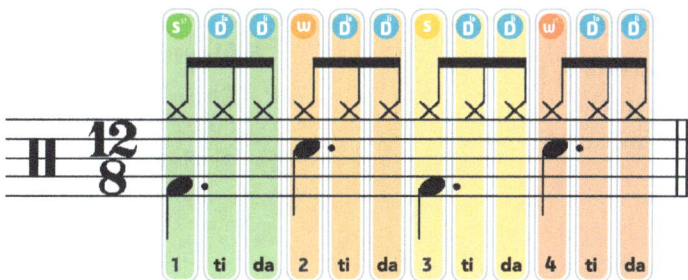

LISTEN

Blue Ain't Your Color	Keith Urban
Gravity	John Mayer
Perfect	Ed Sheeran
bury a friend	Billie Eilish
Oh! Darling	The Beatles

New Drum Notation

Here is a quick bonus guide to add more pizzazz to drum parts you write in notation. There are more nuanced and specific notations which fall under the skill of arranging. This book is about music theory, so we won't do a deep dive into every instrument and its possible notations.

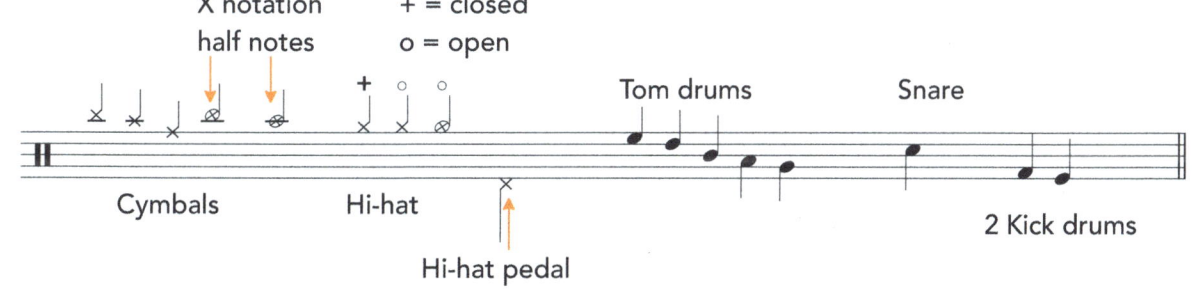

best music coach | the best music theory book for beginners 3

Rhythm 12: Strong and Weak Beats: Compound Meter

Review

- **Compound meter**
    Strong beats
    Weak beats
    Beat divisions

- $\frac{6}{8}$
    Strong beats
    Weak beats
    Beat divisions

- $\frac{9}{8}$
    Strong beats
    Weak beats
    Beat divisions

- $\frac{12}{8}$
    Strong beats
    Weak beats
    Beat divisions

New Words You Should Know

1. Metric hierarchy

Rhythm 13: Advanced Rests

With compound meter comes the need for more dotted rests...and some fun rest extras!

Rhythm 13: Advanced Rests

Dotted Whole Rest

dot

In compound time signatures, the dotted whole rest "gets" 4 beats of silence.

How to Write a Dotted Whole Rest

> **How to Write Dotted Whole Rests**
> 1. Write a whole rest.
> 2. Write a small dot to the right of the whole rest in Space 4.

1.   2.

> **A whole rest (with no dot) may be used in any time signature and any meter to show a full measure of rest.**

Dotted Half Rest

dot

In compound time signatures, the dotted half rest "gets" 2 beats of silence.

How to Write a Dotted Half Rest

> **How to Write Dotted Half Rests**
> 1. Write a half rest.
> 2. Write a small dot to the right of the half rest in Space 3.

1.   2.

Rhythmic Value Hierarchy 2: Compound vs. Simple Meter

Simple Meter				
𝄽				
1 &	2 &	3 &	4 &	
𝄽		𝄽		
1 &	2 &	3 &	4 &	
𝄽	𝄽	𝄽	𝄽	
1 &	2 &	3 &	4 &	
𝄿𝄿	𝄿𝄿	𝄿𝄿	𝄿𝄿	
1 &	2 &	3 &	4 &	

Compound Meter			
𝄽.			
1 ti da	2 ti da	3 ti da	4 ti da
𝄽.		𝄽.	
1 ti da	2 ti da	3 ti da	4 ti da
𝄽.	𝄽.	𝄽.	𝄽.
1 ti da	2 ti da	3 ti da	4 ti da
𝄿𝄿𝄿	𝄿𝄿𝄿	𝄿𝄿𝄿	𝄿𝄿𝄿
1 ti da	2 ti da	3 ti da	4 ti da

Rhythm 13: Advanced Rests

Whole Rests Return

In the compound vs. simple meter on this page you can see that the whole rest in simple meter is compared to a dotted whole rest in compound meter.

This **is** correct.

Just like 3/4, you can use **also** a whole rest in all compound time signatures to show a measure of silence.

Just like 3/4, you will write/find/read the whole rest in the middle of the measure of compound time signatures, instead of "on" beat/count 1.

Correct   **Correct**   **Correct**   **Correct**   **Correct**

(12/8 with dotted whole rest | whole rest)   (9/8 with whole rest)   (6/8 with dotted whole rest | whole rest)

Clap and Count with Rests

Rhythm 13: Advanced Rests

Clap and Count 7

Clap and Count 8

Clap and Count 9

Clap and Count 10

Multi-Measure Rests

- Shows multiple measures of silence. Also called "multi-bar rests."
- Use when

    There are more than 4 measures of rest in a row.
    It makes the music fit on one page.
    It creates an easier page turn for the musician.
    It makes the music easier to read or play.
    There is more than 1 measure of rest at the beginning of a piece of music.

- If the music has repeat signs and/or marks, include the extra measures created by the repeat signs and marks in the multi-measure rest.

How to Write Multi-Measure Rests in One Measure

1. In one measure, write a thick line on Line 3 with two vertical lines on either end with the number of measures of rest above the staff.

How to Write Multi-Measure Rests in One Line

1. On one line, write a thick line on Line 3 with two vertical lines on either end with the number of measures of rest above the staff.

Rhythm 13: Advanced Rests

Tacet

- When an instrument or voice does not participate in any way during a song or piece.
- Write the song title, song duration in time code (minutes : seconds), and "Tacet" on the page for that instrument or voice part.

This Is The Best Song Ever
Music by Your Favorite Artists
Duration– 3:10

Tacet

Review

- Dotted whole rest
    - How to think about dotted whole rests
    - How to write dotted whole rests
- Dotted half rest
    - How to think about dotted half rests
    - How to write dotted half rests
- Compound vs. simple meter rests
- Multi-measure rests
    - How to write multi-measure rests in one measure
    - How to write multi-measure rests in one line
- Tacet

New Words You Should Know

1. Dotted whole rest
2. Dotted half rest
3. Multi-measure rests
4. Tacet

Rhythm 14: How to Write Music in Compound Meter

All things measure math, plus color-coded note and rest placements for compound meters.

How to Write Eighth Notes in Compound Meter

Triple Eighth Notes (three connected by a beam)
    1. Write closed noteheads   **2.** Write stems   **3.** Write beams

> Beam direction, angle, and tilt rules are all the same as eighth notes in simple meter.

Beam Rules: Review

Beam Rules: Stem Direction

1. The note furthest away from Line 3 of the staff shows if all the other notes will be stem up or stem down in the beam group. If the majority should be up/down, go with the majority for all stem directions.

2. Only break Rule **1.** if one note is much higher or lower than the rest of the notes.

Beam Rules: Angle

1. Angled beams use up to 1 staff space, and sometimes cross over 1 staff line.
Stem up: angle the beam up to the right. Stem down: angle the beam down to the right.

2. You can shorten the stem length for beam notes up to 2 ½ staff spaces (shorter than the normal 4 staff lines) to keep the angle of the beam in one staff space.

3. (Optional) When all the notes are on ledger lines, the beam can get a slight angle.

Beam Rules: Tilt Direction

1. The tilt direction of the beam follows the interval created by the first and last notes in the beam. Ascending interval: tilt up. Descending interval: tilt down. Unison: no tilt.

2. When only one note is different in a beam and it is the furthest away from the beam, the beam is straight.

3. When the first or last note is different and closest to the beam, the beam is angled.

4. When there are equal numbers of notes, the beam is straight or slightly angled.

Eighth Notes In Compound Meter

Compound Meter Eighth Note Rules:

1. Two single eighth notes **can** be used in the same beat when separated by a rest.
2. If there are two eighth notes **in a row** in the same beat connect them with a beam.
3. Double eighth notes can be used in any beat, if there is an eighth rest.
4. Beam groups show the beat. The exception are quadruple eighths in 4/4.

The same rhythm is written in both the incorrect and correct examples. The only change is the beaming of the eighth notes to follow rules **1.**, **2.**, and **3**.

Incorrect 1

Correct 1

Incorrect 2

Correct 2

Incorrect 3

Correct 3

Measure Math 5

> **Compound Meter Measure Math**
> 1. The dotted half note gets 2 beats. In simple meter dotted half notes get 3 beats.
> 2. The dotted quarter note gets 1 beat. In simple meter dotted quarter notes get 1 ½ beats.
> 3. The single eighth note gets 1/3 beat. In simple meter single eighth notes get 1/2 a beat.

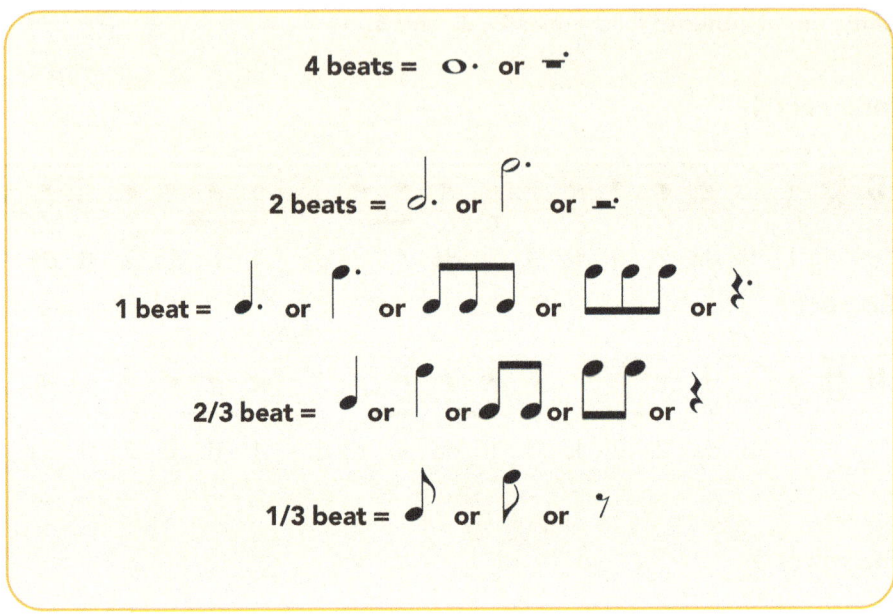

Measure Math 6/8

Incorrect

Correct

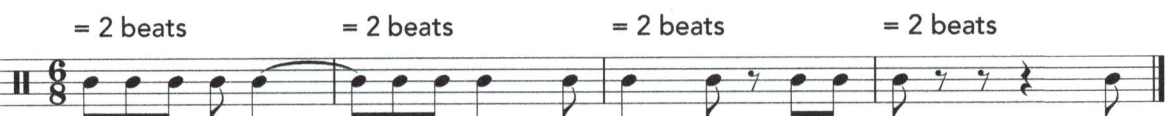

Measure Math 9/8

Incorrect

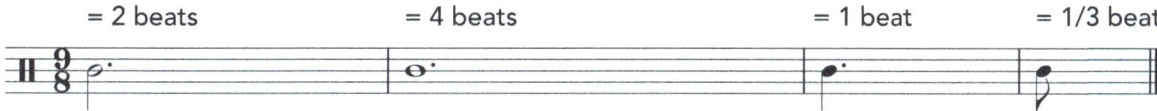

Correct

Measure Math 12/8

Incorrect

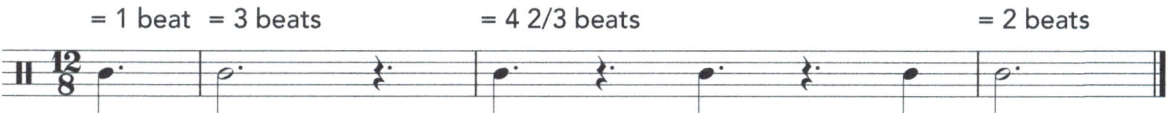

Correct

How to Write Notes and Rests in a Measure: Compound Meter

Where to Write Notes and Rests 3
Memorize the colors and which type of beats the different notations can be written on.

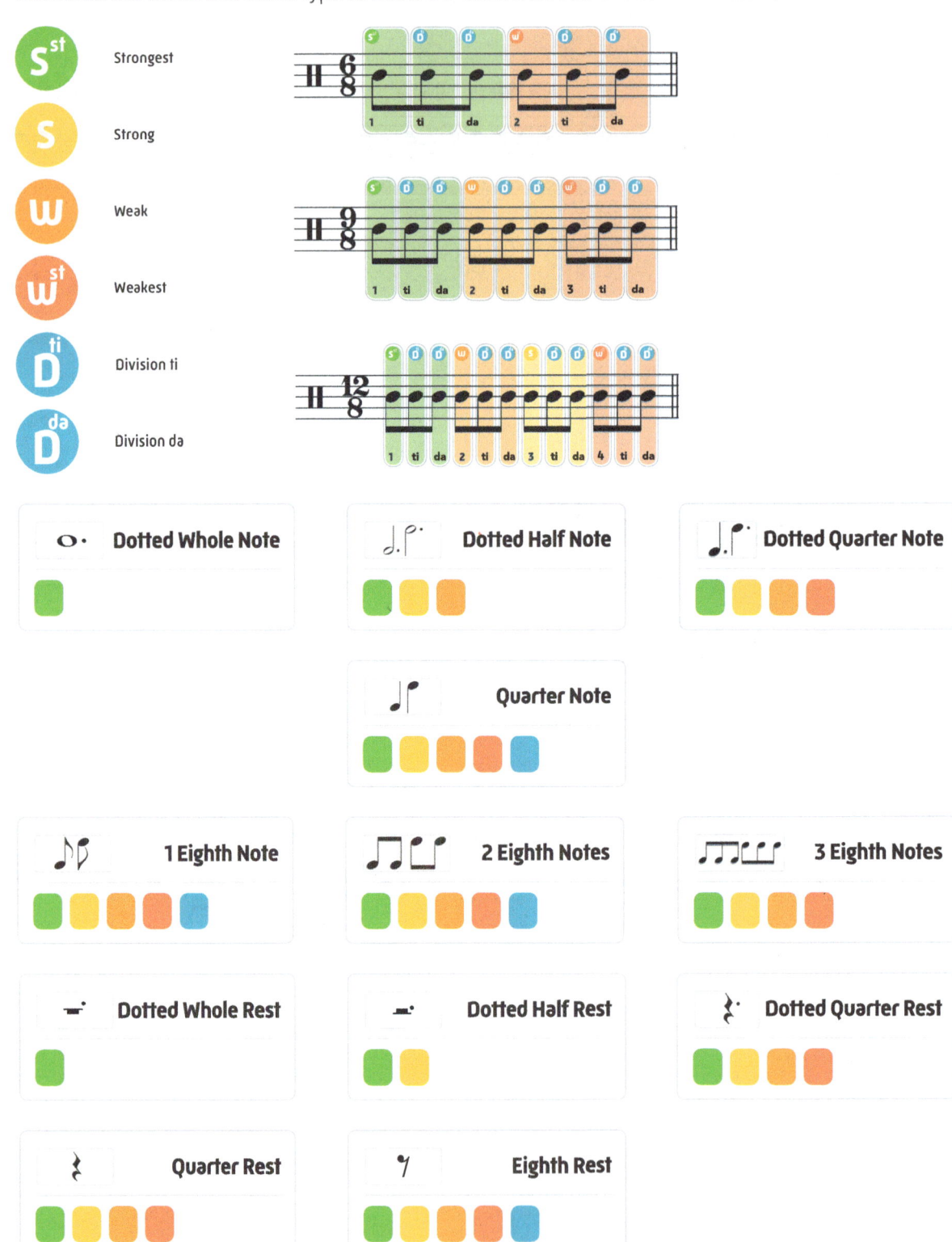

Rhythm 14: How to Write Music in Compound Meter

38 best music coach | the best music theory book for beginners 3

How to Write Compound Meter: Rests

> **Compound Meter Rest Rules**
> 1. A rest starting on a strong beat can last into a weak beat.
> 2. A rest starting on a weak beat cannot last into the next beat(s). Use two separate rests.
> 3. When possible, combine smaller rests into larger rests as long as this does not break the previous two rules (not pictured on this page).
> 4. Each beat is like a mini measure of $\frac{3}{4}$. A rest starting on any downbeat (1, 2, 3, 4) can last into the next beat divisions, as long as this does not break the previous three rules.
> 5. Each beat is like a mini measure of $\frac{3}{4}$. A rest starting on a "ti" or "da" division will be broken up into smaller rests to show the beat divisions.
> 6. A whole rest shows a measure of silence in all time signatures.
> 7. Whole rests are written in the middle of measures for all time signatures besides $\frac{4}{4}$.

1.

2.

4.

5.

6., 7.

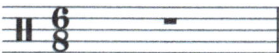  

Where are whole notes, half notes, whole rests, and half rests? They are not used in compound meter to make the music easier to read.

How to Write Compound Meter: Notes

> **Compound Meter Note Rules**
> 1. Notes that start on a beat division cannot continue into the next beat. Use ties.
> 2. Notes that start on a down beat can last into the next beats, but only if they take up the entire beat(s) that follow. Notes cannot end on a down beat or beat divisions ti and da.
> 3. Do not use whole or half notes **without** dots. This breaks Rule 2 (not pictured below).
> 4. In 12/8 there is an invisible divide between beats 2 and 3 that only the dotted whole and half notes and rests can cross, exactly like the invisible divide in 4/4.
> 5. You can use everything you have learned in Books 1 and 2 including articulations, performance, and dynamic marks.
> 6. Tempo marks in compound meter is the speed that the dotted quarter note equals.

1.

2.

4.

5.

6.

♩.=80

How to Space Notes on the Staff: Compound Meter

Note Spacing

Each note and rest should line up with a beat or division of the measure.

Incorrect 1

Correct 1

Incorrect 2

Correct 2

Incorrect 3

Correct 3

Rhythm 14: How to Write Music in Compound Meter

Review

- How to write eighth notes in compound meter
    - Beam rules
    - How to group eighth notes in compound meter
- Measure math: compound meter
- How to write notes and rests in measures in compound meter
- How to space notes on the staff for compound meter

New Words You Should Know

1. Triple eighth notes

How to Write Slash and Beat Notation

A chapter to prepare you for writing, understanding, and analyzing full lead sheets and instrument-specific music, parts, and songs.

Slash Notation

This notation is used for showing the rhythm of chords. It is not named for the famous rock guitarist Slash, though he is pretty cool. Slash notation can be an easy way to show musicians a rhythm to play while they are playing chords without telling them exactly how to spell the chord, which can get great results from experienced instrumentalists.

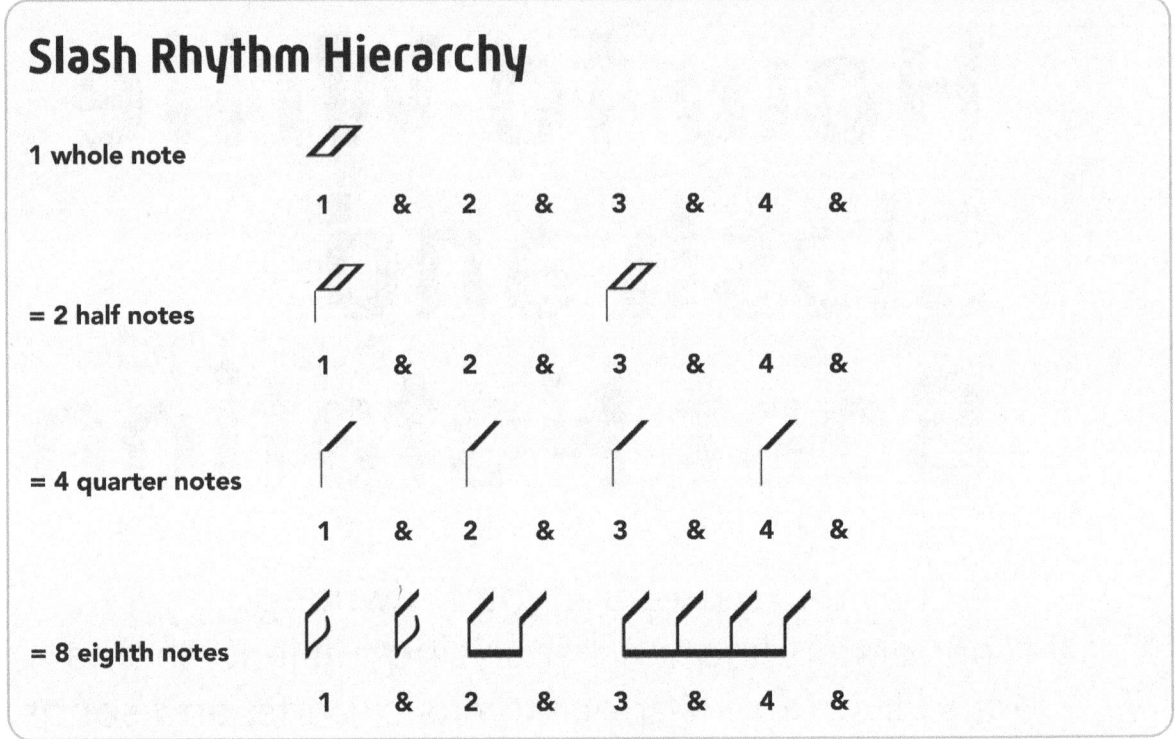

Where You Will Find And Use Slash Notation

Guitar/Ukulele Music

Slashes in guitar/ukulele/strummed chordophone music show where to strum (attack) the instrument within the measure using lead sheet-style chords above the measure. The musician does not need to read pitch notation. They look at the rhythm and chord symbol. This can make their job a lot easier.

My Second Song

Best Music Coach

⊓=strum down   V=strum up
sim. = repeat the same pattern of strumming directions

Single Slashes

Slashes without stems from Line 2 to 4 of the staff are used to tell a musician to improvise or decide what happens in that measure.

Improvise = Ad Lib.

Performer plays a solo over the measures and chords indicated. Write "Ad Lib."

Performer Decides = Slashes Only

Performer decides where attacks will be. The performer will also pick the style they play.

How to Write Slash Notation

> **How to Write Slash Notation**
> 1. Write a forward slanted line from Line 2 to Line 4 of the staff. Performer decides or Ad Lib., leave as slashes without a step.
> 2. Add stems, beams, and flags where needed. Stems are down.
> 3. For whole notes and half notes, write a second slanted line and connect the two lines at the top and bottom to make a rectangle.

1.   2.   3.

Beat Notation

Beat notation is used to show rhythms for all accompanying instruments to play in lead sheets. This is very useful when the melody is on the staff and you also want instruments to play specific rhythms.

Beat Notation vs. Slash Notation

Beat notation shows whole and half notes with a diamond shape.

Slash Notation

Beat Notation

Where You Will Find And Use Beat Notation

Above the Staff: Beat Notation

Beat notation above the staff shows the rhythm to use to play the chord(s) in that measure. This way of writing rhythms for lead sheets allows the performer to decide how they will play their instrument within the context of the rhythm. Because all instruments will "hit" these rhythms together, they are also called "hits" or "rhythm hits." Instruments in a band or group playing the same rhythms together creates a big effect, especially when all instruments were doing different things before the "hits."

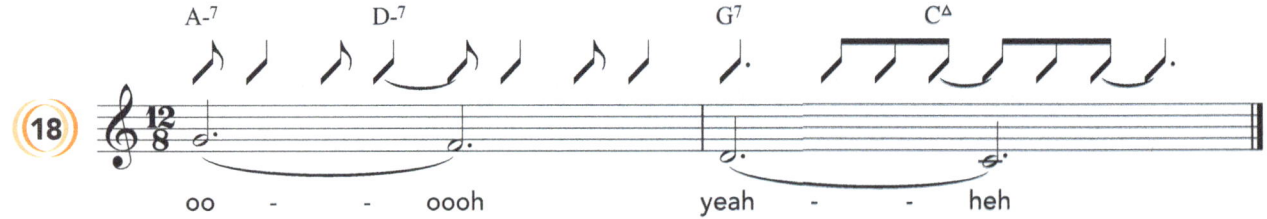

How to Write Beat Notation

1. Write all beat notation above the staff and under chord symbols.
2. Write small diagonal lines with stems for quarter notes and beams for eighth notes.
3. Write small diamonds with stems for half notes and small diamonds for whole notes.

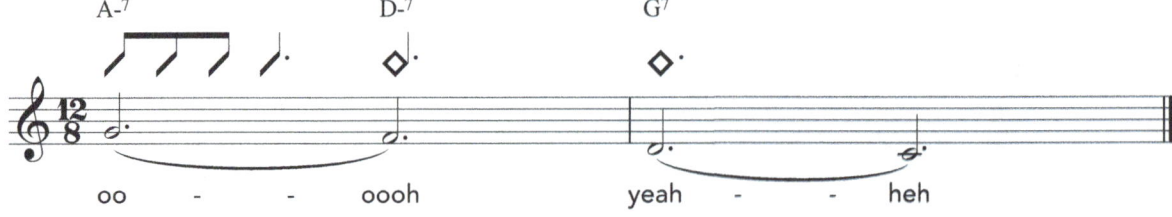

Articulation Marks 2

In this chapter you will learn how to read, write, and understand more articulation marks.

Accent

Accent

> Accent marks kinda look like a mini diminuendo. They also are the mathematical symbol for "more than" or "greater than."

Why Not Write a Dynamic Mark?

Accents are not a big change in volume. Accents are an emphasis on a note to make it stand out from the other notes before or after the accented note through a small increase in volume. An accent can also result in a change in timber, because many instrument and voices sound different at different levels of volume.

(19)

Accent Rules:

1. Accent marks go directly above stem down notehead(s) and below stem up notehead(s) they apply to.

How to Write Accented Notes

1. Pick a note you wish to make accented.

2. Write the accent directly above the notehead for stem down notes and directly below the notehead for stem up notes. Write the accent one staff space above or below the notehead, and that same amount of space for ledger line notes. Write the accent above the staff for stem down and below the staff for stem up slurs or ties.

1.

2.

Clap and Count Accents

Clap and Count 11

Clap and Count 12

Clap and Count 13

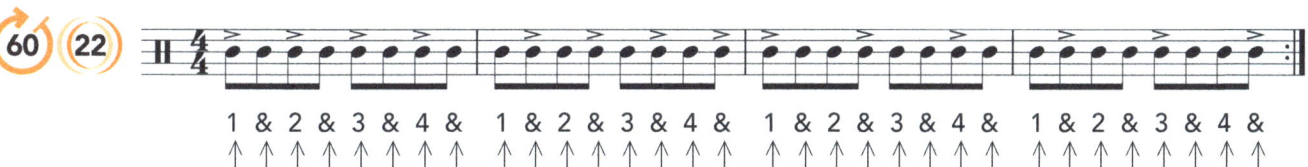

Articulation Combination

Combining different articulations creates many different textures. Think of articulations as parts of a salad. Salads that are only lettuce have one texture and flavor. If you add in dressing, cheese, croutons, and other vegetables, the salad becomes a lot more interesting. Music is the same way.

You do not have to use articulations. When you work with high-level musicians, you can hand them a lead sheet with no articulations. As the musicians "do their thing" the lead sheet will come to life in ways you might never have magined with articulations and other creative additions. To get any musician to accurately execute your **exact** vision for music, you must write every single articulation you want, or be willing to talk through every note and phrase.

Articulation Location

Generally, you will only find slurs and staccati in lead sheets. These slurs show which notes the singer should connect together, and also something called a "phrase" (more on that later in this book!).

In any music where all the notes are written out, you will find and use articulation marks.

Looking at old music on websites like **imslp.org** can lead you to find inspiration and ideas for your own music. It can also be a playground for music analysis!

Articulation Marks 2

Listen to this fantastic example of articulations from Beethoven!

(23) **Piano Concerto No. 2 in B-flat Major, Op. 19, mm. 1-5** Ludwig van Beethoven

Review

- Accent
    - Accent rules
    - How to write accents
- How to combine articulations

New Words You Should Know

1. Accent

Rhythm 15: Syncopation

In this chapter you will learn about how to read, write, and understand syncopation and the different ways syncopation can happen.

Syncopation

- Syncopation is the word that describes any moment in music when the expected pattern of strong beats, weak beats, and beat divisions is interrupted.
- This interruption and displacement of strength can happen in many ways. Here are a few:

  Emphasis on notes that start on weaker beats or beat divisions
  Dotted notes in simple meter
  Ties that move emphasis to weaker beats or beat divisions
  Rests that move emphasis to weaker beats or beat divisions
  Accent articulation marks that move emphasis to weaker beats or beat divisions

- Syncopation creates new and different types of rhythmic tension and resolution. The tension comes from emphasizing the weak and weakest beats. The resolution is when the music returns to the usual pattern of Strong and Weak beats.
- Syncopation can happen above the beat unit level (with half and whole notes).
- Syncopation can happen at the beat unit level (quarter notes).
- Syncopation can happen at the beat division level (eighth notes).

Syncopation: Hear The Difference

The black noteheads are not syncopated. The red noteheads are syncopated. Can you hear the difference between not syncopated and syncopated?

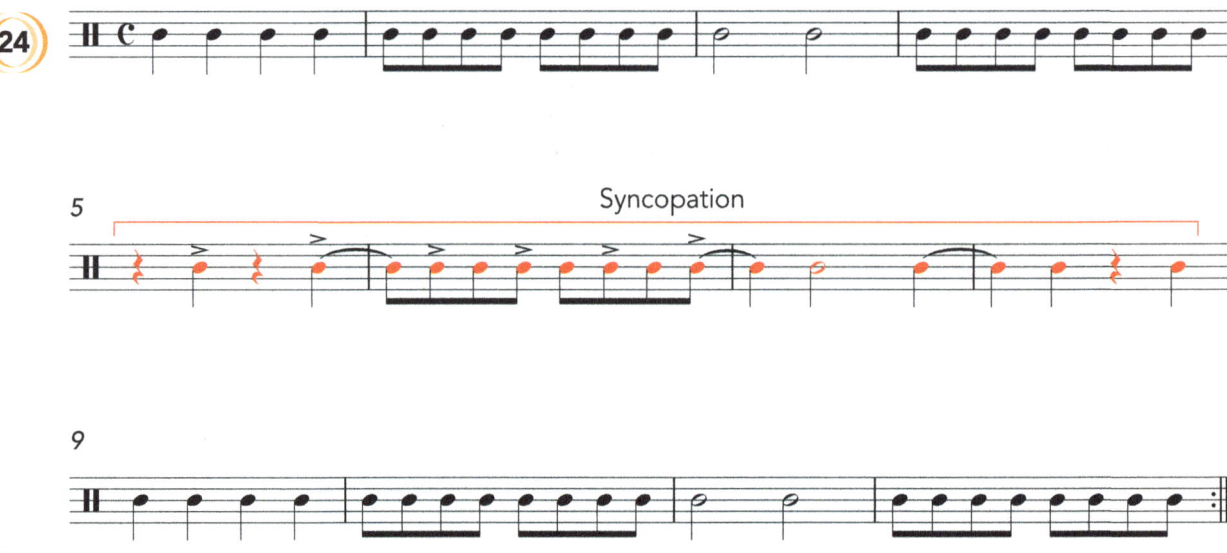

Syncopation: Simple Meter

Beat Unit Syncopation: Simple Meter

The Strong beats are avoided by giving emphasis to weaker beats. Syncopation is red. The black notation gives you a foundation with which to compare the syncopation in mm. 2-3. **Clap all examples.**

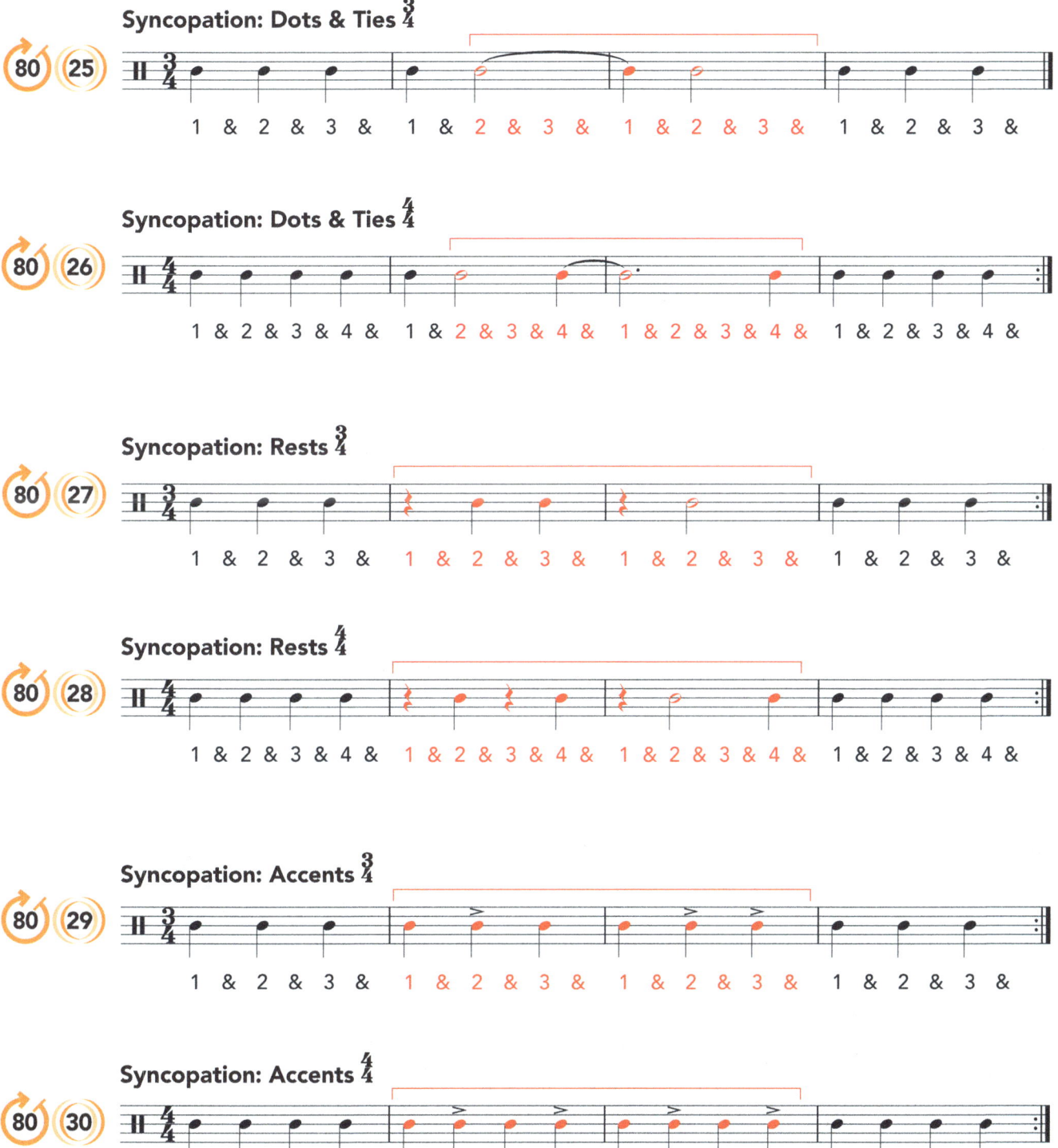

Beat Division Syncopation: Simple Meter

Attacks on strong beats are avoided by giving emphasis to weaker beats and beat divisions. Syncopation is red. These examples break the rules of using quarter notes on &s on purpose to make it easier to read and perform. When you can "see" the meter clearly (where the beats are), it makes it easier to perform. This is acceptable rule breaking. **Clap all examples.**

Beat Unit & Division Syncopation: Simple Meter

Attacks on strong beats are avoided by giving emphasis to weaker beats. Syncopation is red. The black notation gives you a foundation with which to compare the syncopation in mm. 2-3. Some rules are broken to make the music easier to read. This is acceptable rule breaking. **Clap all examples.**

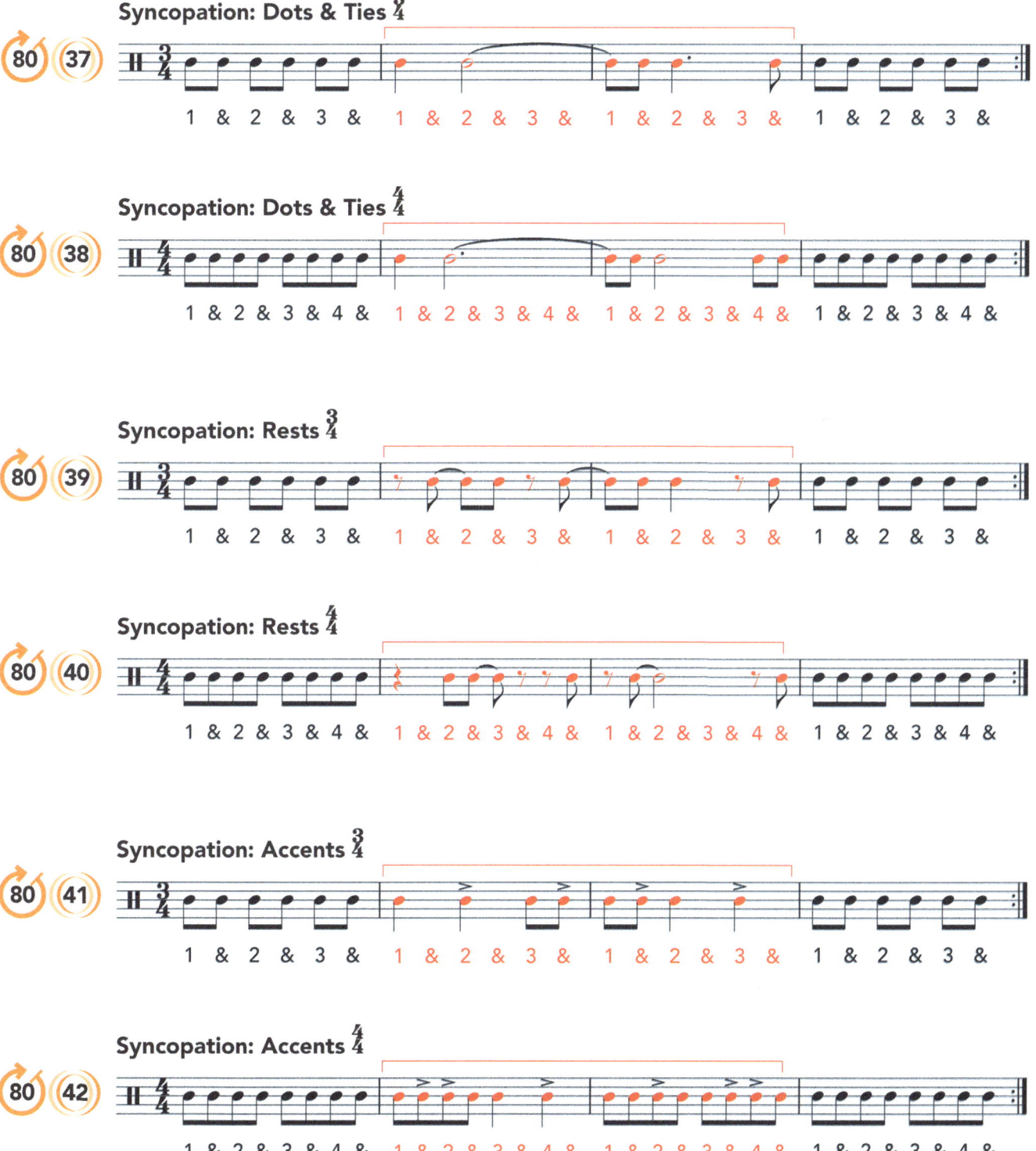

Syncopation: Compound Meter

Beat Unit Syncopation: Compound Meter

Attacks on strong beats are avoided by giving emphasis to weaker beats. Syncopation is red. The black notation gives you a foundation with which to compare the syncopation in mm. 2-3. Because the beat unit is already a dotted note, we will focus on ties and weaker beats and beat divisions. **Clap all examples.**

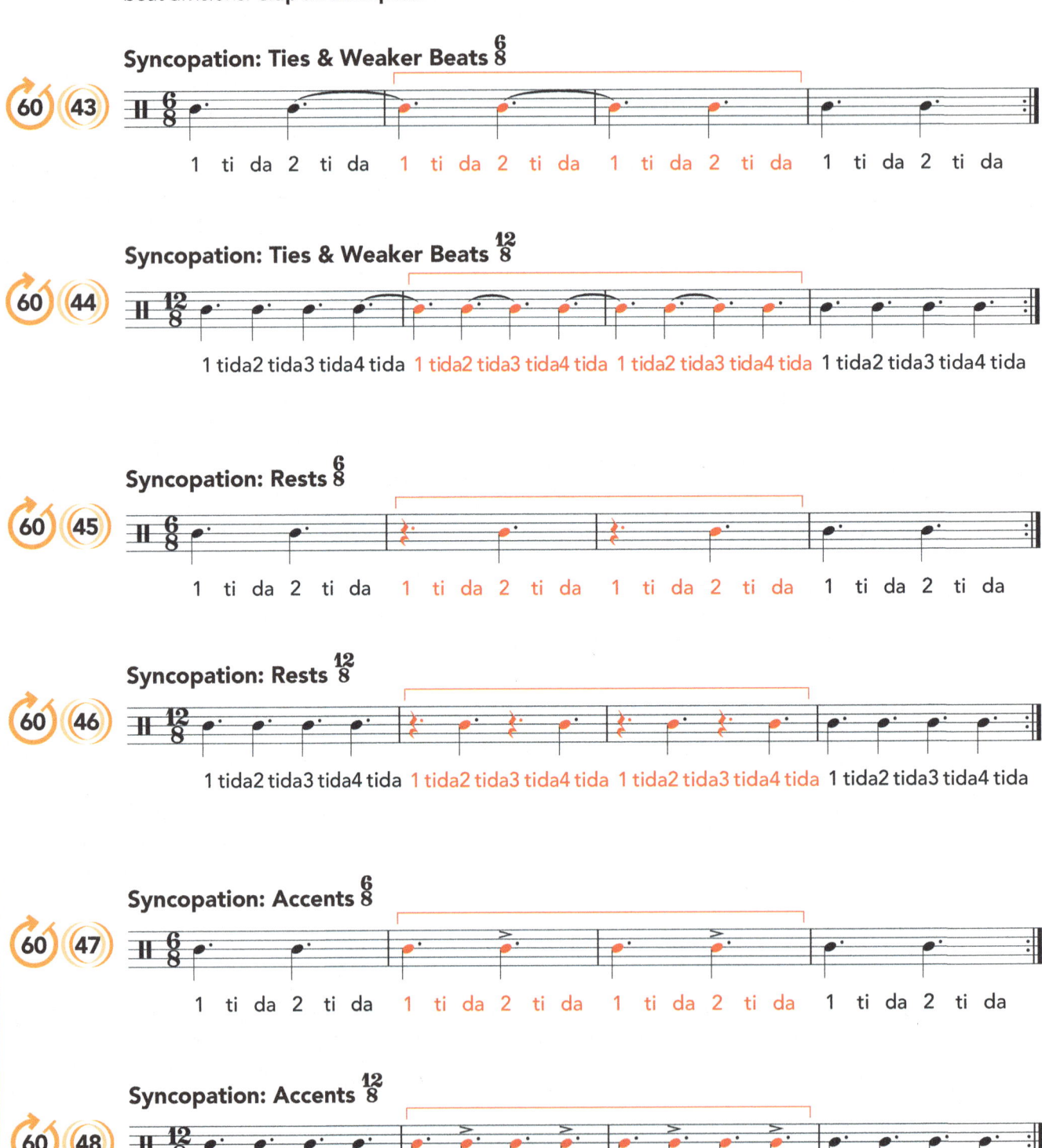

Beat Division Syncopation: Compound Meter

An interesting thing happens with beat divisions in compound meter. Each beat becomes a mini measure of 3/4 and the syncopation sounds like mini 3/4 syncopations. Attacks on strong beats are avoided by giving emphasis to weaker beats. Syncopation is red. The black notation gives you a foundation with which to compare the syncopation in mm. 2-3. Because the beat unit is already a dotted note, we will focus on ties and weaker beats and beat divisions. **Clap all examples.**

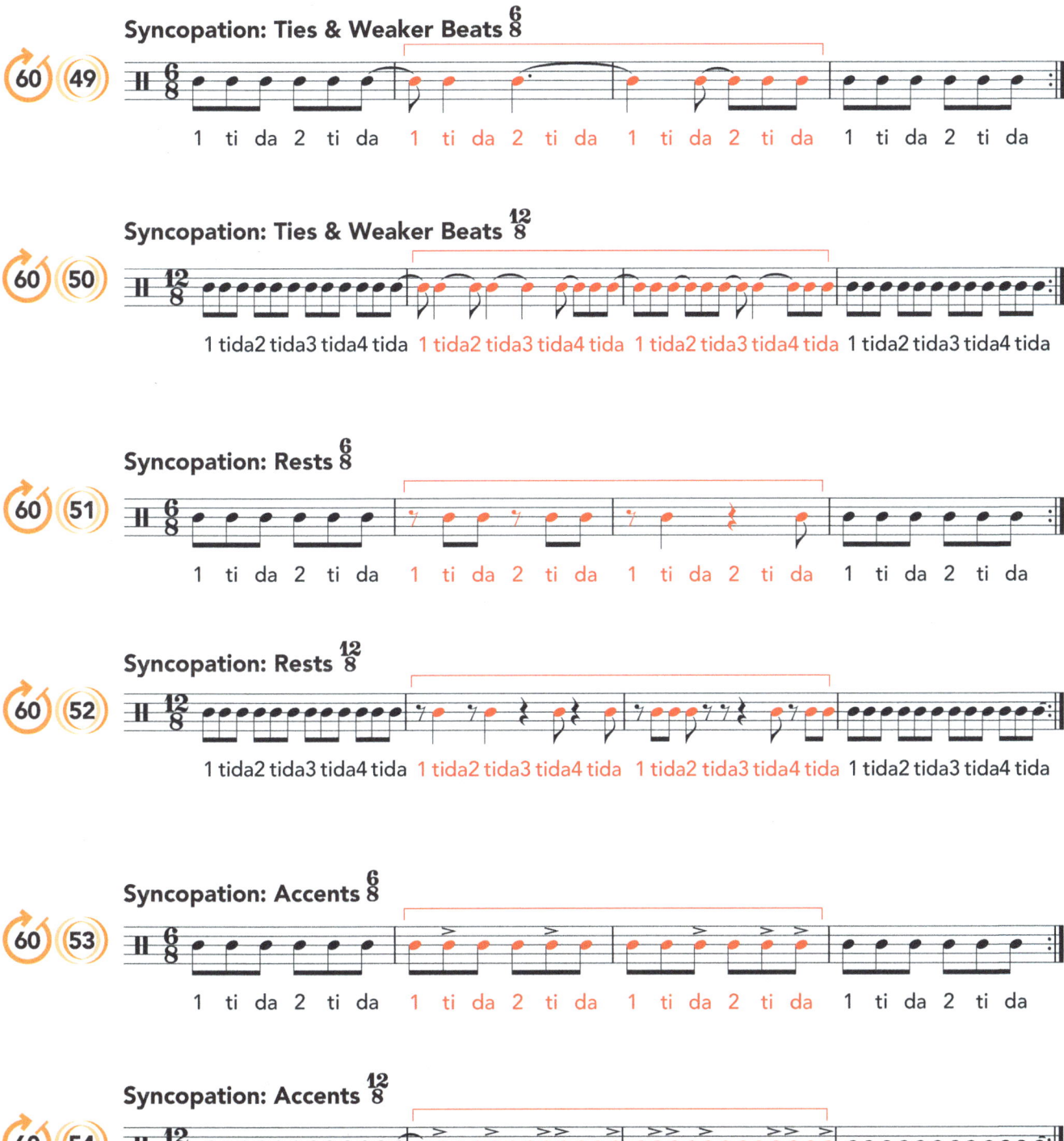

Beat Unit & Division Syncopation: Compound Meter

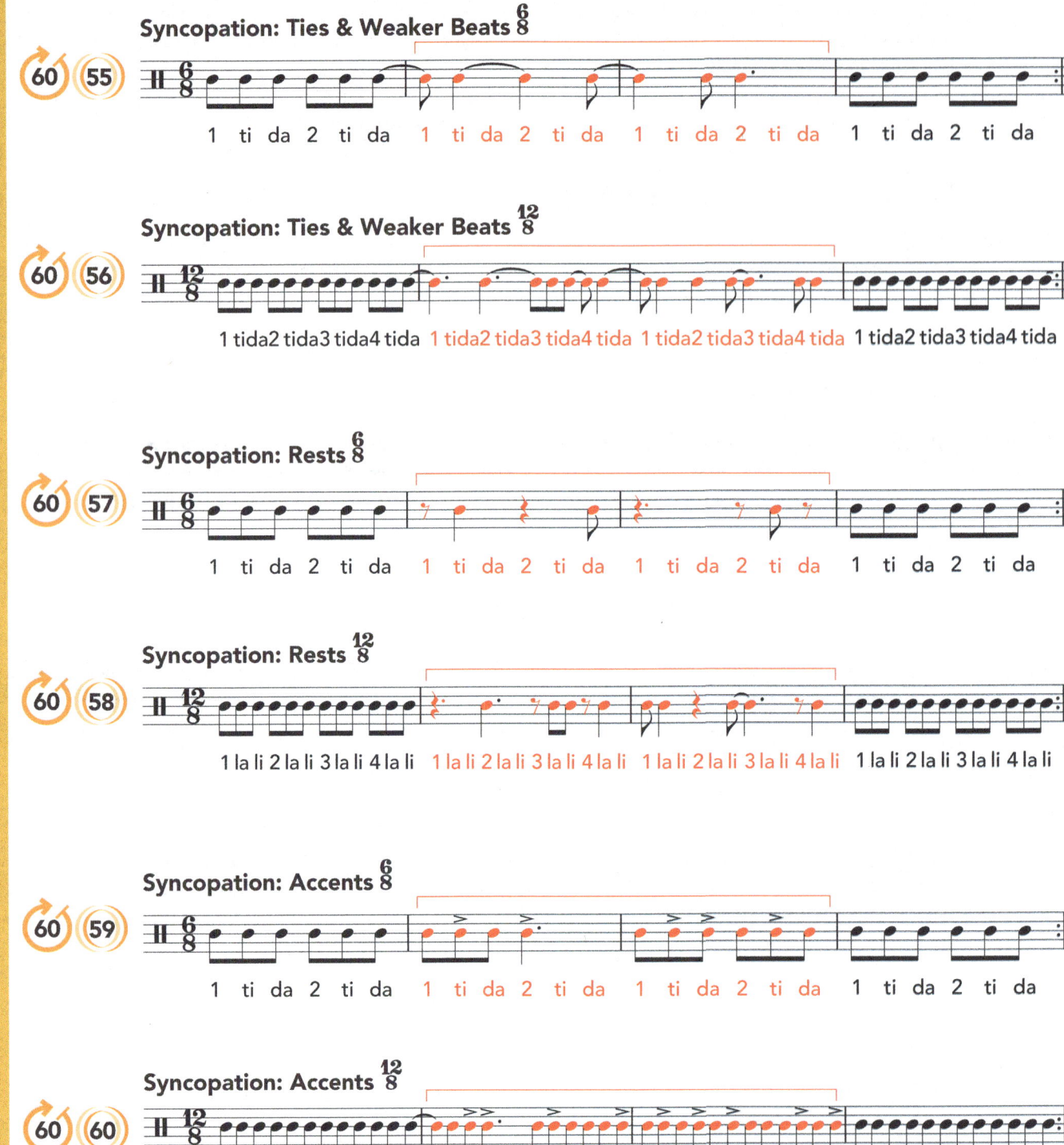

How to Write Syncopation

1. Move the emphasis away from strong beats and onto weaker beats and beat divisions.
2. Take inspiration from the examples in this chapter.
3. **Use dots, ties, rests, and articulation marks along with writing notes that start on weaker beats.**
4. **Use <u>any combination</u> of dots, ties, rests, and articulation marks along with writing notes that start on weaker beats.**
5. Syncopation will stand out more and have a greater effect if you first get the listener's ear used to hearing rhythms that are less syncopated or not syncopated at all.

Syncopation Example

Symphony No. 3 in E-flat Major, "Eroica," Op. 55, mm. 26-35   Ludwig van Beethoven

This syncopation is genius. The progression of syncopation builds from mm. 28-32. The slurred quarter notes in mm. 28-31 slide our ears into the syncopated quarter notes, tied from the weakest beat (3) to strongest (1). This interrupts the expected pattern of strongest, weak, weakest, because the weak and weakest beats are getting the attacks, and the strongest beat is not.

The staccati notes in mm. 33-34 amplify and call even greater attention to the tied quarter notes that are creating the weak beat syncopation. It is not the staccati alone that create this effect. It is the combination of the weak beat syncopation with ties and the dry emphasis of the staccato notes that achieve the effect.

Review

- Syncopation
    - Syncopation using dots and ties
    - Syncopation using weaker beats
    - Syncopation using rests
    - Syncopation using accents

- Simple meter syncopation
    - Beat unit syncopation
    - Beat division syncopation
    - Beat unit & division syncopation

- Compound meter syncopation
    - Beat unit syncopation
    - Beat division syncopation
    - Beat unit & division syncopation

- How to write syncopation

New Words You Should Know

1. Syncopation

Rhythm 16: Turnkey Triplets + Sassy Swing & Shuffle

Eighth notes can be used to create completely different rhythmic "feelings" in music like swing and shuffle!

Eighth Note Triplets

Eighth note triplets are the 3 equal divisions of the beat unit from compound meter... borrowed and used in simple meter. There are two styles of triplets that you will see in the real world. Style 1 has brackets and the number 3. Style 2 has only the number 3. You will see Style 2 when there are just eighth note triplets without any rests or quarter notes (see Eighth Note Triplets Part 2).

Eighth Note Triplets Style 1   **Eighth Note Triplets Style 2**

> **Clapping the change between double and triplet eighth notes in simple meter takes significant practice to do well. Clapping rhythms is a "performance" skill and not a "theory" skill. You can work on it if you want, but move forward in the book while you do. It is not required to master clapping these examples.**

Eighth Note Triplets Part 2

Just like in compound meter, you can mix and match quarter and eighth notes and rests within each triplet. In the cases where rests or quarter notes are present, use eighth note triplet Style 1.

How to Write Eighth Note Triplets

There are only a few rules for writing triplets. As you have already seen in this book, we are starting to bend and break rules and using the goal of making the music "easy to read" as our guide.

How to Write Eighth Note Triplets by Hand

1. If you are writing by hand, map out your measure or measures that will use eighth note triplets. Write the triple eighth notes and any rests or quarter notes you will use in the triplet. Use pencil first. Then use ink.
2. Write brackets and 3s above or below the triplets, whatever is easier to read.
3. Tilt brackets when a notehead, stem, or beam gets in the way of the brackets being straight and horizontal.
4. Do not be afraid to write your music out two or more times. The first is a rough draft, and the second is a final draft. You can make changes and improvements between the first and second draft if you want.
5. After you check your measure math, write the brackets with the number 3 for any triplet group that includes rests or quarter notes.

How to Write Eighth Note Triplets with Software

1. If you are writing music with software, after you select the option to create triplets, the computer will auto-generate everything.
2. You can check and manually adjust the way the triplets are written by your software if it makes them easier to read.

Eighth Note Triplets Example

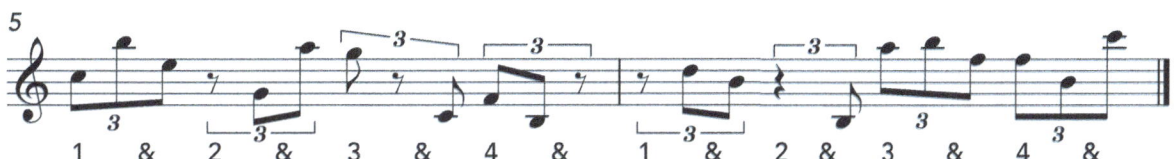

Swing Eighth Notes

- A swung eighth note is taken from an eighth note triplet (kinda).
- Swing is a spectrum of rhythms that **are close to, but different** than eighth note triplets. Computers have 4-10+ different "versions" or "levels" of how "swung" the music is.
- Swung eighth notes' "feeling" can change slightly from person to person and when people are playing together. It is a small change, but that small change is significant.
- The "feeling" is a musician playing a few microseconds early or late from where the mathematical division of time of the beat or beat division would normally land.
- Swung eighth notes can also be called "swing eighth notes."
- Swing is written in simple meter.

How to Recognize Swing Eighth Notes

The writing or metric modulation will be above the staff of the first line of music on the page and in the same line as the tempo mark. See below.

1. Metric Modulation (Don't Use This...But You Will See It)

This "tempo equation" tells you to perform swing eighth notes instead of "straight" eighth notes.

2. Writing

Tells you to perform swing eighth notes. Some ways that you might see it written are:

1. **Swing** (Use This!)
2. **Swing Eighths** (Don't Use This...But You May See It)

Straight Eighth Notes vs. Swing Eighth Notes

Straight and swing eighths are counted and look the same but sound very different. Here is why:

Straight
Two equal divisions of the quarter note.
Down and up beats are the same duration.

Swing
Move the up beats away from down beats
Down and up beats are different durations.

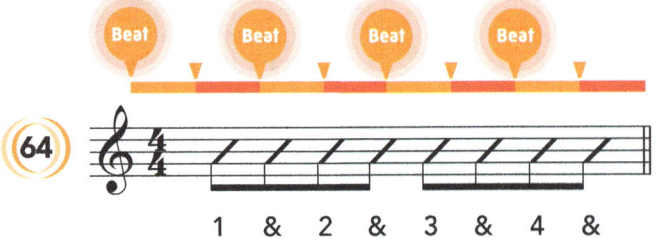
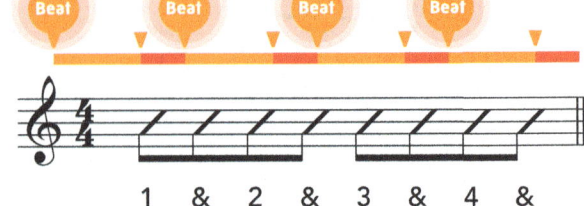

How to (kinda) Perform Swing Eighth Notes

1. Count and clap eighth note triplets as "one, two, three" aloud with each click.
2. Continue counting and clap your hands on the "three."
3. Continue counting and clap your hands on the "one" and "three."
4. Stop counting and continue clapping on the "one" and "three."
5. These are (kinda) swing eighth notes. Count them as "1 &, 2 &, 3 &, 4 &."

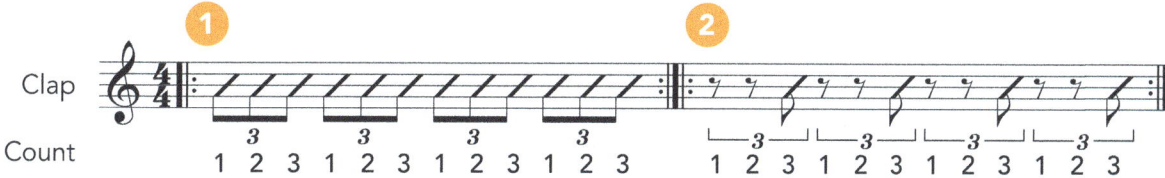

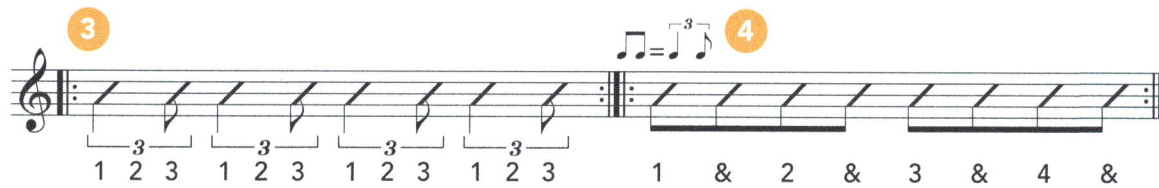

The best way to learn the true feeling of swing is to listen to great swing musicians, and to clap, sing, and play along with their recordings...and to play or sing swing music. Listen to: Wes Montgomery, Joe Pass, Miles Davis, Max Roach, Tony Williams, Elvin Jones, Art Blakey, Gene Krupa and Google "top 50 swing musicians of all time."

65 Compare Swing Examples

Listen to the different interpretations of swing that a computer can make. Imagine how many more variations exist with human players! Many people who play swing are specialists in these "feelings," especially jazz musicians.

How to Write Swing Music

How to Write Swing Music by Hand
1. Write **Swing *tempo mark*** as your tempo mark.   Swing ♩=150
2. Write your music in a simple meter time signature.

How to Write Swing Music with Software
1. Select the option to use swing eighths. You may be able to adjust how "swung" the eighth notes are. Some software has 10 or more different interpretations of swing.
2. Write **Swing *tempo mark***. You may need to use the tempo equation for the software.
3. Write your music in a simple meter.

Shuffle: Eighth Notes

- An eighth note shuffle is taken from an eighth note triplet (kinda).
- Eighth note shuffles are in $\frac{4}{4}$. You will also find them written in $\frac{12}{8}$.
- Not all songs in $\frac{12}{8}$ are eighth note shuffles.
- The drums emphasize the down beat and the "da," the third division of the dotted quarter note, which is what makes shuffle close to swing.
- Eighth note shuffles are different from swing. Shuffles are a "deeper," "more swung" version of swing. Shuffles also feature different ways of playing instruments that separate it from swing.
- Like swing (and all rhythms in all meters), there can be a unique "feeling" in eighth note shuffles as a musician plays a few microseconds early or late from where the mathematical division of time of the beat or beat division would normally land.

Shuffle vs. $\frac{12}{8}$

Shuffle In $\frac{4}{4}$

Shuffle ♩=120

Shuffle In $\frac{12}{8}$

Shuffle ♩=180

So if both of these eighth note shuffles sound almost the same...why write it in two different ways?

- Some musicians who are not familiar with the "feeling" of an eighth note shuffle will have a much easier time reading and performing the $\frac{12}{8}$ shuffle.
- Many musicians "think" of an eighth note shuffle as "being" in $\frac{12}{8}$.
- A lot of shuffle songs are in $\frac{12}{8}$ because the musicians play the "ti," the second division of the dotted quarter note.

Yeah...I Don't Hear It

If you are not hearing the difference between shuffle and swing...that is because the software in this book does not do justice to the difference between swing and shuffle. See a list of shuffle examples on the next page with full songs to get into the sound of shuffle. Then, compare it to the swing examples to hear and feel the difference.

How to Recognize Shuffle Eighth Notes

The writing will be above the staff of the first line of music on the page and in line with the tempo mark.

> **1. Writing**
>
> Tells you to perform the music with the "feeling" of shuffle eighth notes. Some ways that you might see it written are:
>
> **1. Shuffle** (Use This!)

Shuffle Examples

Sweet Little Angel	B.B. King
Higher Ground	Stevie Wonder
Wall of Denial	Stevie Ray Vaughan
Story of the Blues	Gary Moore
Old Brown Shoe	The Beatles
Pride and Joy	Stevie Ray Vaughan & Double Trouble

How to Write Shuffle Music

> **How to Write Shuffle Music by Hand**
>
> 1. Write **Shuffle *tempo mark*** as your tempo mark.
> 2. Write your music in a simple meter, or $\frac{12}{8}$.

> **How to Write Shuffle Music with Software**
>
> 1. Select the option to use shuffle eighths. You may be able to adjust how "shuffled" the eighth notes are.
> 2. Write **Shuffle *tempo mark*** as your tempo mark.
> 3. Write your music in a simple meter, or $\frac{12}{8}$.

Rhythm 16: Turnkey Triplets + Sassy Swing & Shuffle

Review

- Eighth note triplets
    - Style 1
    - Style 2

- How to write eighth note triplets
    - By hand
    - Using software

- Swing eighth notes
    - How to recognize swing eighth notes
    - Swing vs. straight eighth notes
    - How to write swing music

- Shuffle eighth notes
    - How to recognize shuffle eighth notes
    - How to write shuffle music

New Words You Should Know

1. Triplet
2. Swing
3. Shuffle

Rhythm 17: Multiple Endings

In this chapter you will learn about 3rd, 4th, and other multiple endings.

Multiple Endings

- There can be 3rd, 4th, 5th, even 6th endings.
- Only use multiple endings when it makes the music easier to read or understand.

Multiple Ending Rules

1. Different ending numbers can be in the same bracket to repeat the music in different orders.
2. **Only use multiple endings if it makes the music easier to read and understand.**
3. Example 3 is **not** easy to read or understand. **This is for demonstration purposes only**.

Multiple Endings 1

1. Read up to the first repeat sign in m. 3; the measure with the 1.2. above it is the 1st and 2nd ending.
2. Repeat back to m. 1.
3. Read up to the first repeat sign in m. 3; the measure with the 1.2. above it is the 1st and 2nd ending.
4. Repeat back to m. 1.
5. Read through the end of m. 2, then SKIP m. 3 with the 1.2. and go straight to m. 4; the 3rd ending with the 3. above it. Read to the end of the piece.

70 best music coach | the best music theory book for beginners 3

Multiple Endings 2
This Is Not Easy To Read, But It Is A Good Example Of How Multiple Endings Work

1. Read up to the first :|| repeat sign in m. 3.
2. Repeat back to m. 1.
3. Read up to the end of m. 2, then SKIP m. 3, and read up to the :|| in m. 4.
4. Repeat back to m. 1.
5. Read up to the first :|| repeat sign in m. 3.
6. Repeat back to m. 1.
7. Read up to the end of m. 2, then SKIP m. 3, and read up to the :|| in m. 4.
8. Repeat back to m. 1.
9. Read up to the end of m. 2, then SKIP mm. 3-4, and go straight to m.5. Read to the end of the music.

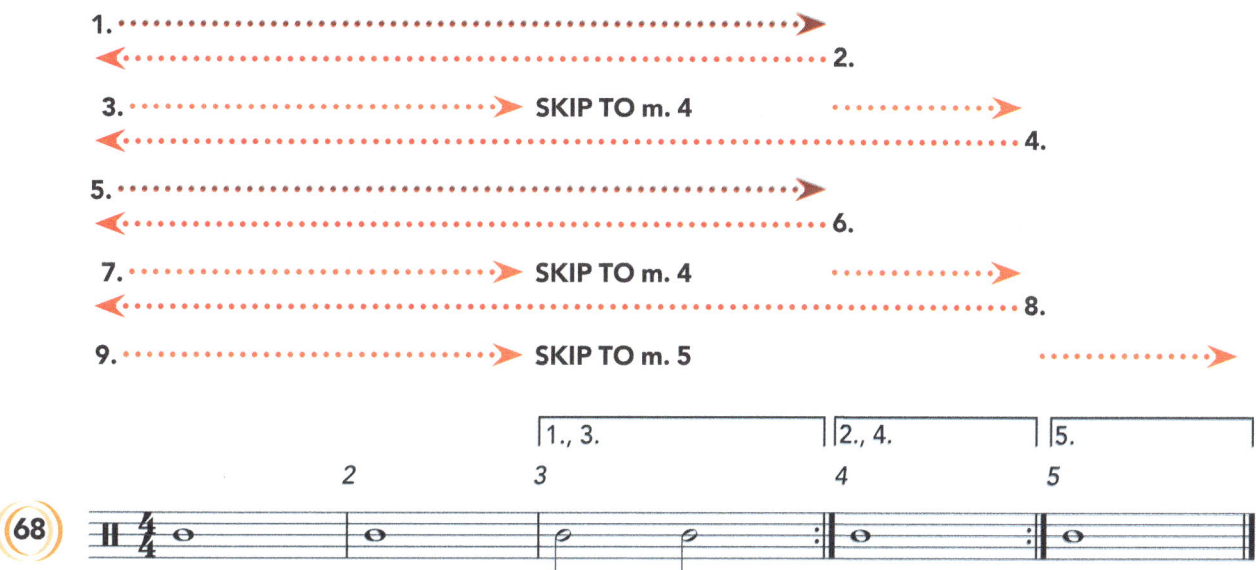

Now You Have Seen It...

Are multiple endings easier to read than writing out each repetition on a seperate line? I don't think so. It is more space efficient, but not as easily understood by a performer.

The truth is that I could not come up with an example of using more than 4 multiple endings that is objectively easier to read than writing out each repetition.

More than 4 multiple endings made sense when paper, ink, and the time of someone copying out the music was at stake. Now, we can use digital sheet music, copy and paste whole symphonies in seconds, and use Bluetooth foot pedals to turn pages.

A general rule: **Use multiple endings only when space or page turns are a consideration...or if it makes the music easier to read.**

Rhythm 17: Multiple Endings

How to Write Multiple Endings

Multiple Endings Rules:

1. The last ending bracket is open if there are two or more measures.
2. The last ending bracket is closed if it is the final measure of the piece of music, or the final measure of a section of music.
3. All closed brackets need a repeat sign. See all closed brackets in example 1 and 2 on this page.
4. Write multiple endings that count up without skipping numbers (1,2,3,4) as 1.2.3.4. See example 1 on this page.
5. Write multiple endings with numbers that are out of order (1,3,2,4) as 1., 3., 2., 4.,. Only use out-of-order multiple repeats if it truly makes the music easier to read and understand. See example 2 on this page (this is not easier to understand...**this is just an example**).

1.

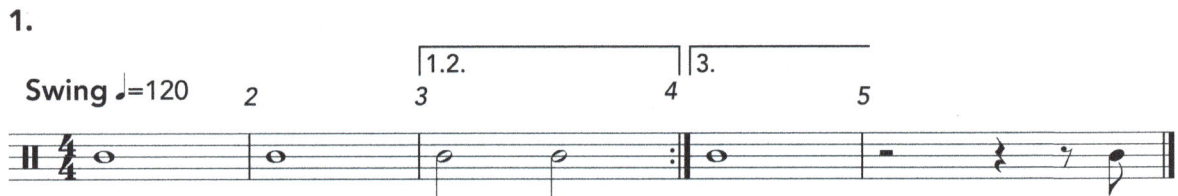

2.

Review

- Multiple endings
    - 2nd ending
    - 3rd ending
    - 4th ending
    - 5th ending
    - 6th ending

- How to write multiple endings

New Words You Should Know

1. Multiple endings
2. 3rd ending
3. 4th ending
4. 5th ending

Dynamic Marks 2, Performance Marks, & Tempo Marks

In this chapter you will learn how to read, write, and understand more dynamic marks and symbols as well as performance marks! Get ready to get very loud...or very quiet, and change speed!

Dynamics 2

Review: Dynamics are the way of describing variations in loudness. The variations in loudness can take place over a large duration of time, like a piece of music, or a short duration of time, from one note to the next. Musicians use dynamics to play music louder and quieter. Another word to describe dynamics is "volume."

Dynamic Marks

Terms and symbols used in musical notation to show different levels of loudness.

Loud
1. *ff* = fortissimo = very loud
2. *f* = forte = loud
3. *mf* = mezzo forte = sort of loud
4. *mp* = mezzo piano = sort of quiet
5. *p* = piano = quiet
6. *pp* = pianissimo = very quiet

Quiet

Dynamic Marks Rules:
1. A dynamic mark affects all notes that come after it.
2. The only thing that can change the volume set by a dynamic mark is another dynamic mark that is written after the first one.
3. There is no limit to the number of dynamic marks in a piece of music or song.

How to Write Dynamic Marks
1. Write dynamic marks below the staff.
2. Write dynamic marks with italics or slanted letters.
3. Write dynamic marks directly under or just before the first note that the mark applies to.

Rit., Rall., A tempo

Both ritardando (rit.) and rallentando (rall.) mean "to slow down." There are disagreements among musicians about the exact way to think about, write, and perform the two performance marks. We will set clear definitions here.

Rallentando (rall.)

From the Italian rallentare: "slow down, reduce speed, slacken, slow, die down, decelerate."
A rallentando is like your car coasting to a stop. It is an even decrease of speed that takes place during a set number of beats, measures, or lines of music. Many times, you will find rallentandi (more than one rallentando) at the end of pieces or before the change of a section of a song. A gentle, rolling stop.

Ritardando (rit.)

From the Italian ritardare: "be late, wait, lag, stay, lose, delay, set back, defer, put off."
A ritardando is like using your car's brakes to evenly come to a stop. It is also an even decrease of speed that takes place during a set number of beats, measures, or lines of music. You may see ritardandi (more than one ritardando) at the end of pieces of music and in the middle of a song or piece where the music slows down, then jumps back into the original tempo. A faster, sharp decrease in speed.

(70) Rall. vs. Rit.

Here is where things get spicy! Software and computers (well, mine at least) interpret rall. and rit. the same way. Listen to the example to hear and compare the two.

Return To Normal Speed (a tempo)

After a rallentando or ritardando, you can go back to the original speed of the music! This is called "a tempo" which means to return to the original speed shown in the tempo or metronome mark.

How to Write Rall., Rit., and A tempo

1. Tempo marks go above the staff.

2. Write small dashes after the "rit." or "rall." to show the duration of the "slowing down." Performers will calculate how much to evenly slow down based on their sense of the music combined with the duration of the rit. or rall.

3. In music that has more than one instrument, look for "groups" of instruments. The groups have a large "group bracket," different from the bracket for the grand staff. Write the rit., rall., or a tempo again on the staff for all instrument "groups." Music notation software will do this automatically.

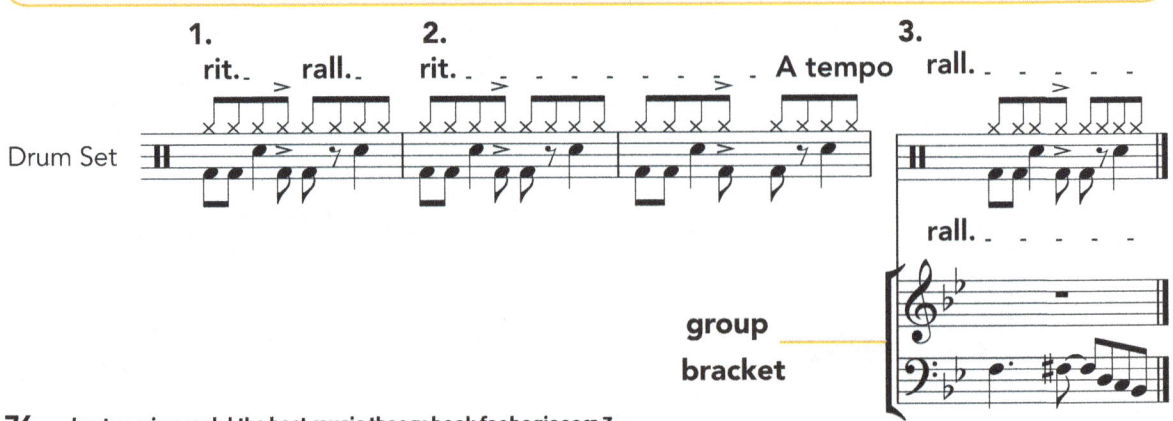

Tempo and Metronome Marks

In modern music, it is typical to see a metronome mark at the beginning of the music.

> 1. 99% of the time, metronome marks show the beat unit. This means that in compound meter, you will find and use a dotted note in the metronome mark.
> 2. There can be an "emotional" tempo mark before the metronome mark. This gives the performers an idea of how to approach the piece of music. This emotion tempo mark can change how performers interpret everything in the music, from articulations, to dynamics, to the overall "feeling" of the music.

1.

2.

Emotional Tempo Marks and Nuance

There is no right or wrong way to use emotional tempo marks. They translate the intention, and the overall idea of the music. The more experience and technical skill a performer has, the better they will translate the "feeling" of the music. Even though music is mathematically exact when it is written onto paper (or software), there are changes of milliseconds that an experienced performer will use to "push" or "pull" on the "feeling" of the music without losing the tempo.

An experienced performer will play a little louder on certain accents, more dry, on certain staccati, or give a different feeling when the time is right and it will serve the music. The same goes for any other part of music, from dynamics to rallentandi and ritardandi.

This is part of the magic of music and why it is so important to hear your music being played back, even if it is through an interface like Noteflight, Sibelius, Finale, or MuseScore to **FEEL** what your music is saying.

Dynamic Marks 2, Performance Marks, & Tempo Marks

Review

- Dynamic marks
    - $\boldsymbol{pp}$ = pianissimo = very quiet
    - $\boldsymbol{p}$ = piano = quiet
    - $\boldsymbol{mp}$ = mezzo piano = sort of quiet
    - $\boldsymbol{mf}$ = mezzo forte = sort of loud
    - $\boldsymbol{f}$ = forte = loud
    - $\boldsymbol{ff}$ = fortissimo = very loud
- Dynamic mark rules
- How to write dynamic marks
- Rallentando (rall.)
- Ritardando (rit.)
- A tempo
- How to write rall., rit., and a tempo
- Tempo and metronome marks
- Emotional tempo marks

New Words You Should Know

1. Pianissimo
2. Fortissimo
3. Rallentando
4. Ritardando
5. A tempo

Pitch and Notes 9: New Keys & Notes

Hacks and tips to read, write, and understand more keys and notes! See how many more scales are now available to you!

New Accidental Notes 3

Here are some new accidentals that allow you to write music, scales, intervals, and chords in more keys!

Sharp Notes

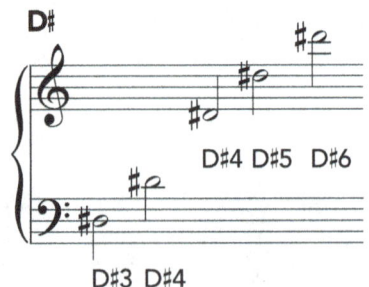
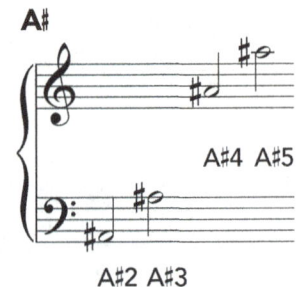

Flat Notes

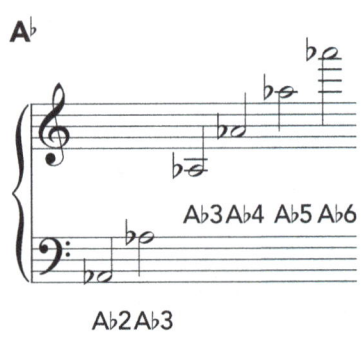
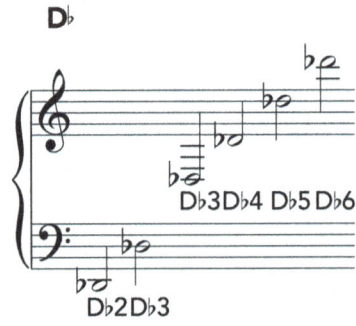

Key Signatures 3

How to Remember the Order of Accidentals

The sharps and flats in all key signatures follow a particular order. Memorize the mnemonics.

Father **C**harles **G**oes **D**own **A**nd **E**ats **B**reakfast

Breakfast **E**nds **A**nd **D**own **G**oes **C**harles's **F**ather

Sharps are the **opposite** order of flats!

FCGDAEB

New Sharp Key Signatures

> **Reminder: How to Identify Major Sharp Key Signatures: $\hat{7}$**
> The sharp that is the furthest to the right from the clef is on the line or space for the note that is $\hat{7}$.

> **Reminder: How to Identify Minor Sharp Key Signatures: $\hat{2}$**
> The sharp that is the furthest to the right from the clef is on the line or space for the note that is $\hat{2}$.

New Flat Key Signatures

> **Reminder: How to Identify Major Flat Key Signatures: $\hat{4}$**
> The furthest flat to the right from the clef is on the line or space for the note that is $\hat{4}$.

> **Reminder: How to Identify Minor Flat Key Signatures**
> The furthest flat to the right of the clef is on the line or space for the note that is $\flat\hat{6}$.

How to Remember the Number of Accidentals in a Key: 7

The quick trick for remembering how many accidentals are in a key is to use the number 7. Any letter of the basic musical alphabet (A, B, C, D, E, F, G) can have either sharps or flats in its key signature. With the exception of F major, all major key signatures with flats have a ♭ accidental after the letter name of the key. If these rules and "tricks" are more confusing than helpful, focus on memorizing key signatures.

This trick works for all keys. Below are two examples.

A Accidentals = 7

In an "A" major key signature (A major), there are 3 sharps. In an "A" major key signature with flats (A♭ major), there are 4 flats. Add the number of sharps to the number of flats (3 + 4), and you get 7.

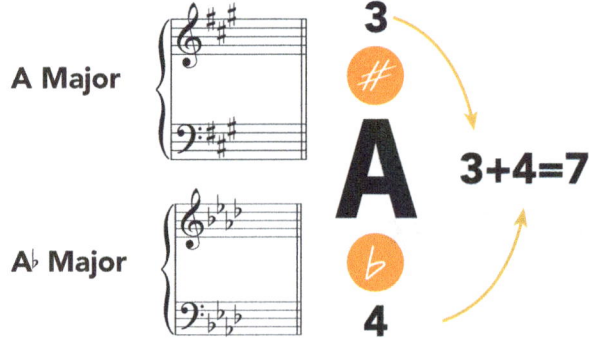

E Accidentals = 7

In an "E" major key signature (E major), there are 4 sharps. In an "E" major key signature with flats (E♭ major), there are 3 flats. Add the number of sharps to the number of flats (4 + 3), and you get 7.

Accidentals and Key Signatures: The Full Picture

The 7 Rule

As you saw on the previous page, the accidentals for every letter of the musical alphabet add up to 7 when you look at the key signatures for both sharp and flat keys. This rule applies to all keys. The reason C has 7 sharps and 7 flats is because the key of C major has 0 sharps and 0 flats. This means for both flat and sharp keys, all possible notes have an accidental (yes, that is one scary key signature).

C♯ Major    C♭ Major

The Add One Rule

Add One Rule: Sharps

The Add One Rule states that as you go forward through the order of sharps F, C, G, D, A, E, B, starting on G, you add one sharp to the key signature. G = 1, D = 2, A = 3, E = 4, B = 5, F = 6, C = 7

Add One Rule: Flats

The Add One Rule states that as you go backward through the order of flats B, E, A, D, G, C, F, starting on F, you add one flat to the key signature. F = 1, B = 2, E = 3, A = 4, D = 5, G = 6, C = 7

Parallel Keys and Scales

- Parallel keys are any major and minor key that have the same Tonic note.
- Parallel scales are any scales that have the same Tonic note.

Parallel Key Examples

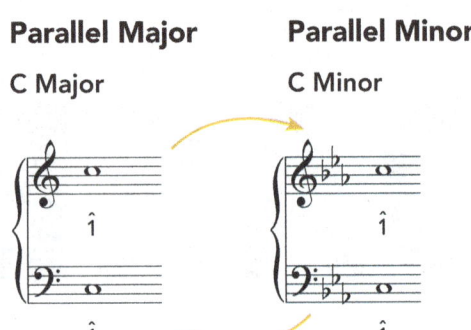
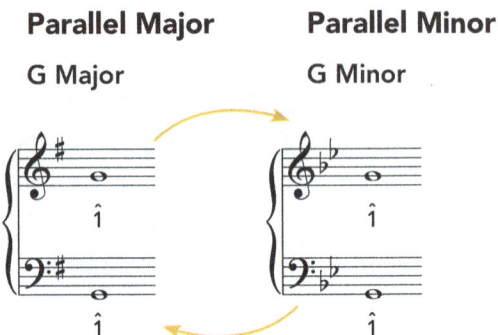
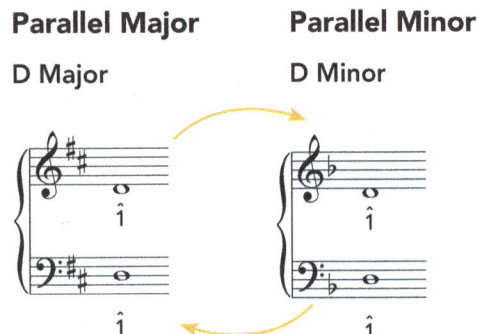
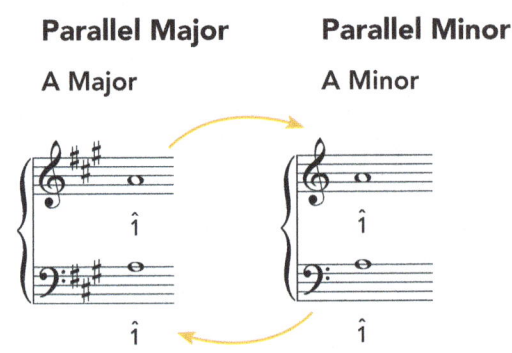
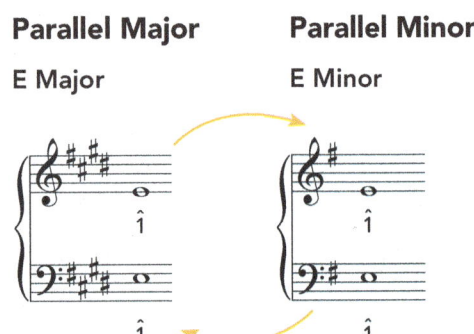
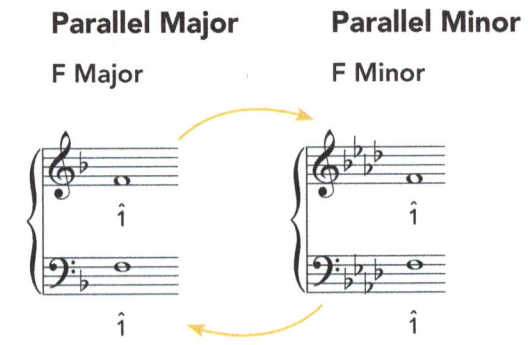

Circle of Fifths & Circle of Fourths

- Also called the "cycle" of fifths.
- Go to the right (ascending) around the circle, and it is the Circle of Fifths.
- Go to the left (descending) around the circle, and it is the Circle of Fourths.
- Classical music and much of modern music uses the Circle of 5ths for changing keys and more complex chord progressions.
- Modern music also uses the Circle of 4ths to change keys and to create more complex chord progressions.
- The inner circle is the relative minor keys that share the same key signature.

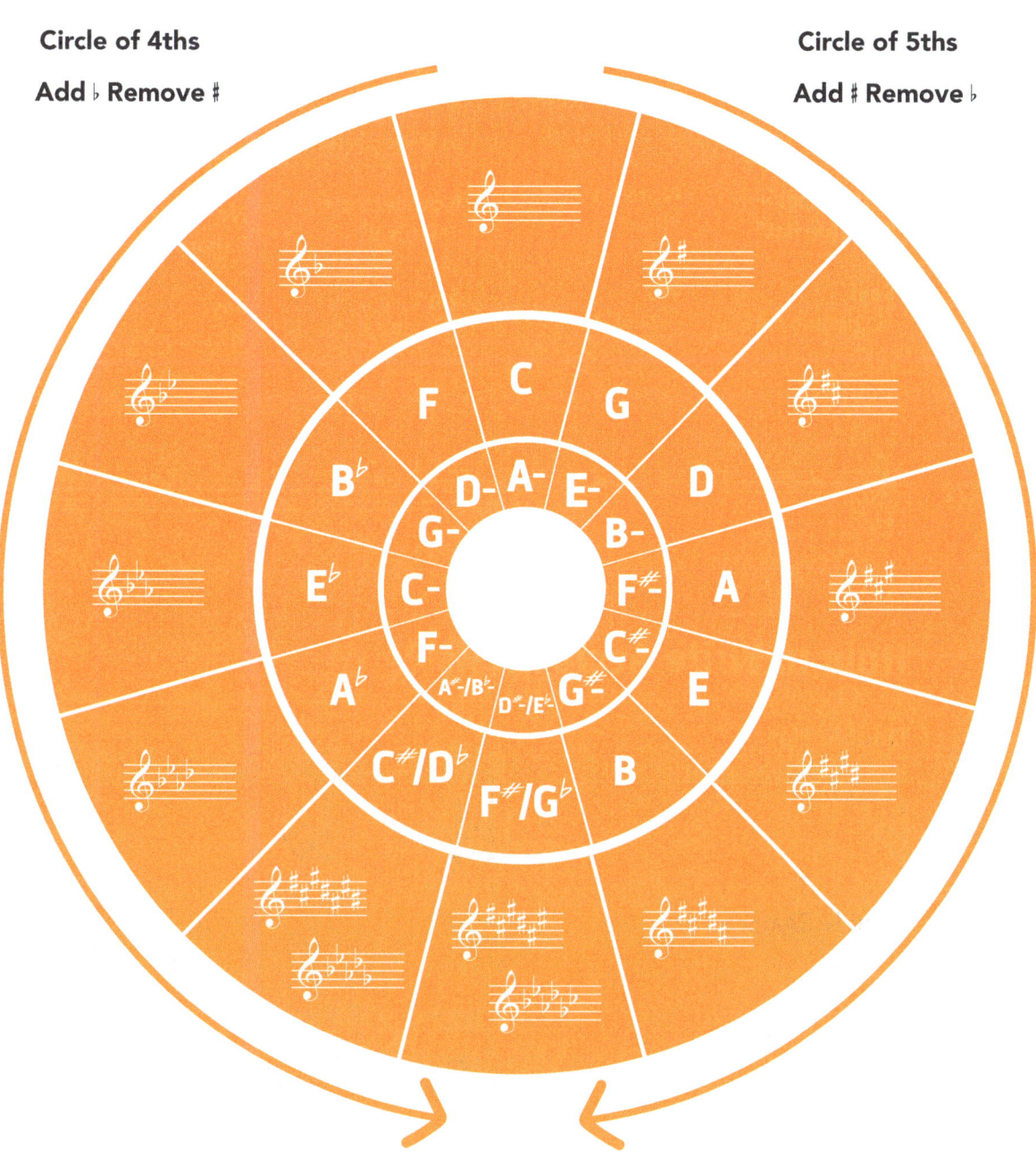

Circle of 4ths
Add ♭ Remove ♯

Circle of 5ths
Add ♯ Remove ♭

Accidentals 2

A musical symbol that raises or lowers a note or returns the raised or lowered note to its natural state.

- The note that is raised, lowered, or returned to its natural state can also be called an accidental.
- You will see accidentals in several forms in this and other Best Music Coach books. This is to prepare you for encountering accidentals in different fonts and handwritings in the real world!

Double Flat
Note is lowered one whole-step.

Note letter + "Double flat"

Say:
"D double flat"

Flat
Note is lowered one half-step.

Note letter + "Flat"

Say:
"D flat"

Natural
Note returns to original state.

Note letter + "Natural"

Say:
"D natural"

Sharp
Note is raised one half-step.

Note letter + "Sharp"

Say:
"D sharp"

Double Sharp
Note is raised one whole-step.

Note letter + "Double sharp"

Say:
"D double sharp"

How to Write Accidentals 2

Double Flat

1. Write a flat accidental.

2. Write another flat accidental.

Double Sharp

1. Write a letter x.

2. Write little squares or rectangles on the ends of the x.

How to Write Accidentals in Front of Notes

Accidentals are written in front (to the left) of the notehead, never behind it. This is because the accidental changes the note, and anyone reading or performing the music needs to know about the change to the note before they read or play it, not after.

1. Place the accidental to the left of the notehead, as close to the notehead as you can without touching the notehead.

2. **ACCIDENTALS ON A SPACE**
   Fill the space with the hole of the accidental.

3. **ACCIDENTALS ON A LINE**
   Align the hole of the accidental on the line.

How to Write Accidentals in a Measure

1. Accidentals only change the note for the measure the accidental is written in or until another accidental is written on the same note of the same pitch class and register. within that same measure. Think: accidentals only last one measure.

2. Accidentals only change the register of the pitch class on which they are written.

3. Accidentals that are tied to another measure or line remain in effect for the duration of the tie.

4. A natural accidental that comes after a double sharp, sharp, flat, or double flat cancels the sharp or flat accidental in the measure the sharp or flat is written.

Reminder: Courtesy Accidentals

Courtesy accidentals appear after another accidental to remind the performer which note to play. Courtesy accidentals are a way to be nice to anyone who is playing your music. It makes their job much easier and clearer, which will usually result in a better performance!

Pitch and Notes 9: New Keys & Notes

Review

- Accidentals
    - G♯
    - D♯
    - A♯
    - A♭
    - D♭
    - G♭

- How to remember the order of the accidentals
- New sharp key signatures
- New flat key signatures
- How to remember the number of accidentals in a key = 7
- Accidentals and key signatures: the full picture
    - The 7 rule
    - The add one rule
- Parallel keys and scales
- Circle of fifths
- Circle of fourths
- Accidentals
    - Double flat ♭♭
    - Flat ♭
    - Natural ♮
    - Sharp ♯
    - Double sharp 𝄪

> **New Words You Should Know**
>
> 1. Double sharp
> 2. Double flat

Pitch and Notes 10: Compound Intervals

What happens if a note is more than one octave away from another note?

Compound Intervals

- Compound intervals are any interval larger than one octave.
- Compound intervals exist so we can talk about notes, scales, intervals, and chords that have notes that are further away than one octave from the Root or Tonic.

(73) Melodic Compound Intervals

There are two types of melodic intervals:

Ascending Compound Intervals

Ascending intervals measure the distance from a low-sounding note to a high-sounding note.

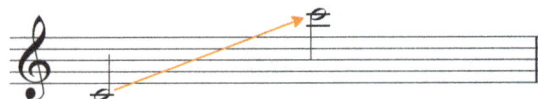

Descending Compound Intervals

Descending intervals measure the distance from a high-sounding note to a low-sounding note.

(74) Harmonic Compound Intervals

Harmonic intervals are not ascending or descending. They are different because two notes happen at the same time. Harmonic intervals are called "harmonic."

Compound Interval Numbers = 7

To find compound intervals, continue counting scale degrees after $\hat{7}$.

Simple Interval to Compound +7

Add 7 to a simple interval to get the compound interval number. For example, a 9th is really a 2nd up one octave. 2+7=9.

Compound Interval to Simple -7

Subtract 7 from a compound interval to get the simple interval number. For example, a 12th is really a 5th one octave up. 12-7=5.

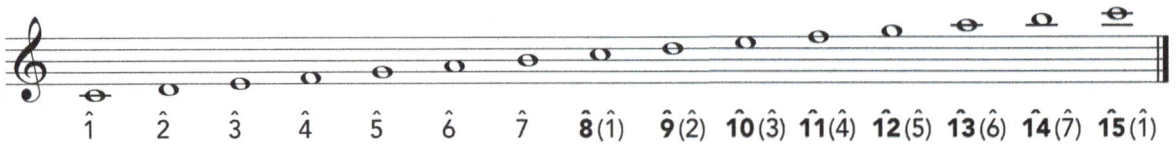

75. Interval Quality: Compound

Major Intervals = M

Major intervals align with $\hat{2}$, $\hat{3}$, $\hat{6}$, and $\hat{7}$ of the major scale.

	C to D	C to E		C to A	C to B
	M9	M10		M13	M14

Minor Intervals = m

Minor intervals are one half-step smaller than major intervals.

	C to D♭	C to E♭		C to A♭	C to B♭
	m9	m10		m13	m14

Perfect Intervals = P

Unisons, octaves, 4ths, and 5ths are perfect.

	C to F	C to G		C to C
	P11	P12		P15

Augmented Intervals = A

Perfect + major intervals raised by one half-step.

Diminished Intervals = d

Perfect + minor intervals lowered by one half-step.

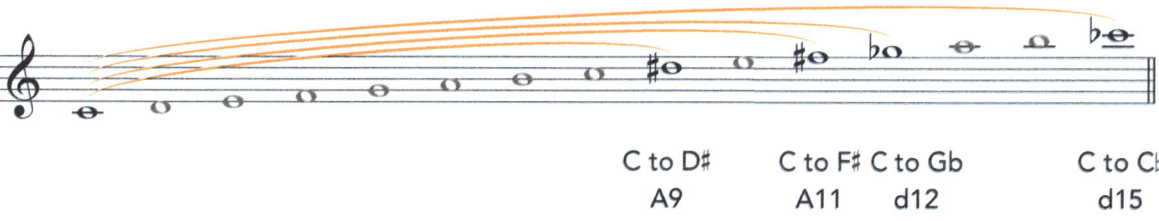

	C to D♯		C to F♯	C to G♭		C to C♭
	A9		A11	d12		d15

All intervals can be changed to become augmented or diminished.

How to Talk and Think about Compound Intervals

Scale Degree Name vs. Scale Degree

We are now adding a new way of thinking about scale degrees. For example, with scale degree **names**, the Supertonic is $\hat{2}$ in any octave register. Here, we will think of scale degrees in different ways depending on the distance (number of octaves) between the lowest and highest notes in the interval.

15 Is As Far As You Need To Go

Musicians generally do not correctly name intervals larger than a 15th. This is because it is easier to mentally calculate and speak "the major third two octaves up" than it is to say "a major 17th" and then waiting 30 seconds for everyone else to figure it out too.

Chord Tones and Chords

Generally, when we talk about chords, it does not matter what octave register the Root, Third, Fifth, and Seventh are in. We can call the chord tones "Root," "Third," "Fifth," and "Seventh" no matter the octave register the chord tones are in. We do not specify the chord tone's octave register.

C Major Chord with Compound Intervals + Chord Tones (Lowest to Highest)

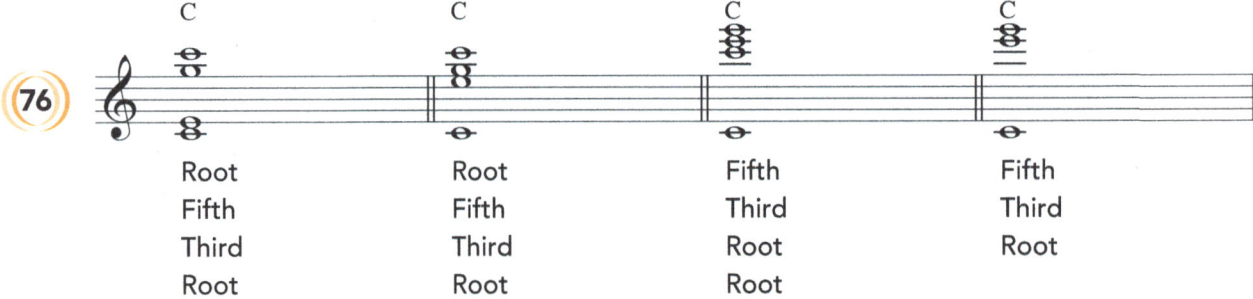

Each one of these C chords has compound intervals and different orders of notes. Even though the note order changes, and even though there are huge gaps between the lowest Root and the highest notes in each chord...they are all still regular ol' C major chords. Each chord has a different "voicing" or a different order of the notes. This does not matter for naming the chord. This does matter greatly for how the chord sounds and what emotion the chord will create in the listener.

> **"Voicing"**
> The order of the notes in any chord is the chord "voicing."

How to Write Compound Intervals

How to Write Compound Intervals: Melodic

> **How to Write Ascending and Descending Compound Intervals**
> 1. Write an ascending interval that is larger than 1 octave.
> 2. Write a descending interval that is larger than 1 octave.

1.

2.

How to Write Compound Intervals: Harmonic

> **Harmonic Interval Stem Rules:**
> 1. If the notehead closest to the open end of the stem is on one ledger line (above or below the staff), the stem length remains 4 staff lines long.
> 2. If the notehead closest to the open end of the stem is past one ledger line (above or below the staff), the stem reaches Line 3 of the staff.
> 3. If the notehead furthest away from Line 3 of the staff is above Line 3: stem down.
> 4. If the notehead furthest away from Line 3 of the staff is below Line 3: stem up.
> 5. If the noteheads are the same distance from Line 3 of the staff: stem down.

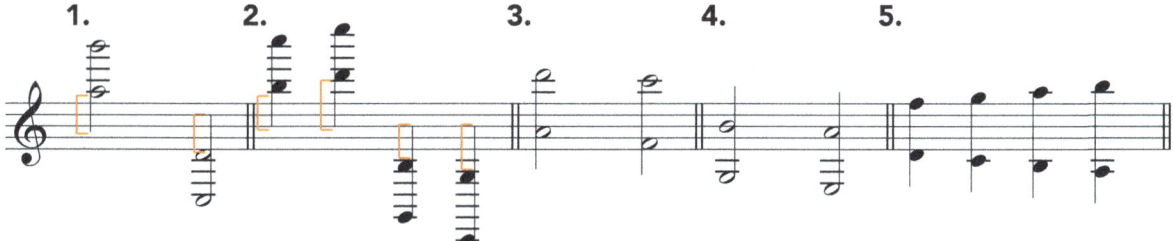

> **How to Write Harmonic Compound Intervals**
> 1. Write a harmonic interval that is larger than 1 octave.

1.
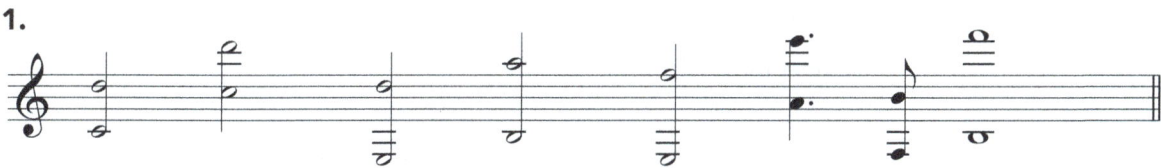

Augmented and Diminished Intervals: Anything Goes

- **Augmented Intervals Include**

    Any major interval that is raised by one half-step.
    Any perfect interval raised by one half-step.

- **Diminished Intervals Include**

    Any minor interval lowered by one half-step.
    Any perfect interval lowered by one half-step.

A7 and d2 are impractical but fun examples. A7 is enharmonic to a P8 and a d2 is enharmonic to a PU.

Augmented Intervals

M2 A2   M3 A3   P4 A4   P5 A5   M6 A6   M7 A7   M9 A9   P11 A11   M13 A13

Diminished Intervals

m2 d2   m3 d3   P4 d4   P5 d5   m6 d6   m7 d7   m9 d9   P11 d11   m13 d13

Review

- Compound intervals
    - Add 7 to the simple interval distance
    - Scale degree name vs. scale degrees
    - Chord tones and chords

- How to write compound intervals
    - Melodic compound intervals
    - Harmonic compound intervals

- Augmented and diminished intervals

New Words You Should Know

1. Compound intervals
2. Voicing

Harmony 5: Seventh Chords 2

A deep dive into seventh chords and a new way of thinking about Roman Numerals.

Seventh Chord Quality 2

Fully Diminished Seventh Chord
The quality of the chord is fully diminished seven.
Say chord names as "___ fully diminished."
Made from $\hat{1}$, $♭\hat{3}$, $♭\hat{5}$, and $♭♭\hat{7}$ of a natural minor scale.
Starts like a dim. triad: m3 from $\hat{1}$ to $♭\hat{3}$, m3 from $♭\hat{3}$ to $♭\hat{5}$.
There is an interval of a m3 from $♭\hat{5}$ to $♭♭\hat{7}$.
There is an interval of a d5 from $\hat{1}$ to $♭\hat{5}$.
There is an interval of a d7 from $\hat{1}$ to $♭♭\hat{7}$.

Chord symbol options: C°7

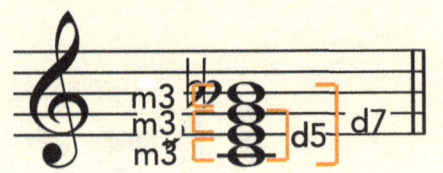

Augmented Seventh Chord
The quality of the chord is augmented seven.
Say chord names as "___ augmented seven."
Made from $\hat{1}$, $\hat{3}$, $♯\hat{5}$, and $♭\hat{7}$ of a major scale.
Starts like an augmented triad: M3 from $\hat{1}$ to $\hat{3}$, M3 from $\hat{3}$ to $♯\hat{5}$.
There is an interval of a d3 from $♯\hat{5}$ to $♭\hat{7}$.
There is an interval of an A5 from $\hat{1}$ to $♯\hat{5}$.
There is an interval of a m7 from $\hat{1}$ to $♭\hat{7}$.

Chord symbol options: C+7, C(♯5)7, C7(♯5)

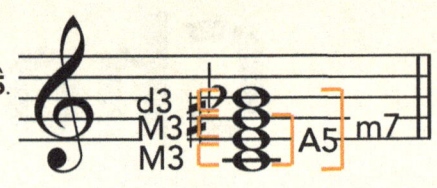

Augmented Major Seventh Chord
The quality of the chord is augmented major seven.
Say chord names as "___ augmented major seven."
Made from $\hat{1}$, $\hat{3}$, $♯\hat{5}$, and $\hat{7}$ of a major scale.
Starts like an augmented triad: M3 from $\hat{1}$ to $\hat{3}$, M3 from $\hat{3}$ to $♯\hat{5}$.
There is an interval of a m3 from $♯\hat{5}$ to $\hat{7}$.
There is an interval of an A5 from $\hat{1}$ to $♯\hat{5}$.
There is an interval of a M7 from $\hat{1}$ to $\hat{7}$.

Chord symbol options: C+Δ, C(♯5)Δ, CΔ(♯5)

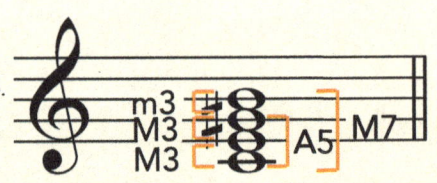

Minor Major Seventh Chord
The quality of the chord is minor major seven.
Say chord names as "___ minor major seven."
Made from $\hat{1}$, $♭\hat{3}$, $\hat{5}$, and $\hat{7}$ of a harmonic minor scale.
Starts like a minor triad: m3 from $\hat{1}$ to $♭\hat{3}$, M3 from $♭\hat{3}$ to $\hat{5}$.
There is an interval of a M3 from $\hat{5}$ to $\hat{7}$.
There is an interval of a P5 from $\hat{1}$ to $\hat{5}$.
There is an interval of a M7 from $\hat{1}$ to $\hat{7}$.

Chord symbol options: C-Δ, C-maj7

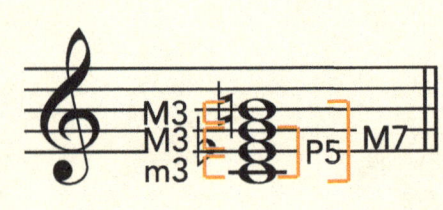

 Hear the sound of these seventh chords.

A New Look at Roman Numerals

In books 1 and 2 of this series, you analyzed harmonized scales and pieces of music using uppercase and lowercase Roman Numerals. You did this for several reasons.

> 1. More than 95% of music schools use the uppercase and lowercase system. This is not because the system works perfectly; it is because they have "always done it this way."
> 2. AP music theory, which gives college credit for 95% of music programs, uses this system.
> 3. 95% of learning content outside of Best Music Coach uses the upper and lower case system.
> 4. 95% of musicians use the uppercase and lowercase system to communicate with each other and analyze music.

You needed to understand how "most" people use Roman Numerals so you can be truly free to pursue your Dream Music Goal in any music arena.

Numeral Logic

There are a few reasons why the uppercase and lowercase Roman Numeral system does not work for modern music.

> 1. To label seventh chords, you must use redundant notations.
> 2. You cannot accurately label chords from harmonized harmonic and melodic minor scales.
> 3. You cannot accurately label chords outside common harmonized scales.
> 4. No direct connection exists between scale degrees and the Roman Numeral system.

1. $iv\text{-}^7$

2. $i\text{-}^\Delta$

3. $vii^{\varnothing 7}$

The problem with all examples above is that the Roman Numerals are lowercase. The lowercase Roman Numeral means that the Third of the triad is a m3 above the Root; it means the triad is minor.

1.

Lower case **iv** means that it is a minor triad built on $\hat{4}$. To communicate the quality of minor 7, a minus sign is used, which means we are saying the triad quality is minor...a second time. It is "minor, minor." In classical music analysis, it is assumed that the quality of a lowercase RN with a Seventh chord tone is minor seven. As we can see from example 2, this is not always the case.

2.

Again, we have a redundant minor minus symbol following the lower case RN **i**.

3.

The RN is technically telling you that the triad is minor...even though we know that the diminished degree symbol "o" is telling us that the Fifth is lowered by one half step as well as the Third.

Roman Numerals: Berklee Way

Berklee College of Music pioneered this logical use of Roman Numerals. Even though a small number of musicians use this system (mostly graduates of Berklee College of Music and their students) we must make this system the standard for Roman Numerals. All Roman Numerals from Level 3-7 in this series, all Best Music Coach courses, and live lessons from Level 3 up follow the Berklee system.

It is my hope that we can all move to this system together and one day I can go back and redo books 1 and 2 to ONLY use the Berklee system from the start.

> **The Berklee System Rules:**
> 1. All Roman Numerals are capitalized.
> 2. Roman Numerals only show the scale degree the chord is built on, not chord quality.
> 3. Because Roman Numerals show scale degrees, we will add ♭, ♮, and ♯ in front of the RNs to show the direct relation between scale degree and Roman Numeral. We compare all RNs to the major scale, like scale degrees. This works better for modern music where the parallel major and minor are often mixed together.
> 4. Show the quality of the chord like you would with a chord symbol after the RN.

C Major Scale Harmonized To The Fifth (Berklee System)

C Major Scale Harmonized To The Seventh (Berklee System)

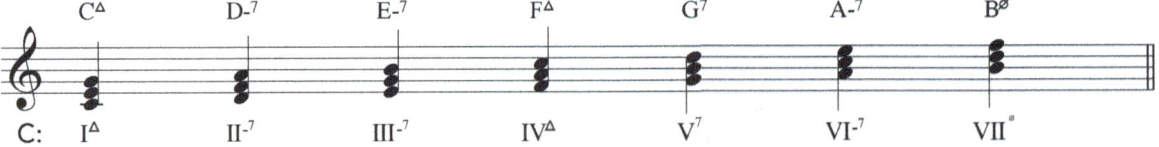

A Natural Minor Scale Harmonized To The Fifth (Berklee System)

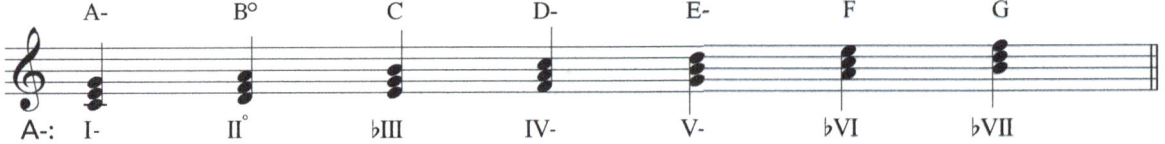

A Natural Minor Scale Harmonized To The Seventh (Berklee System)

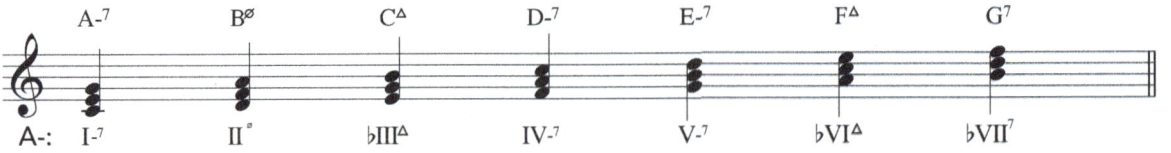

SD = RN

In this system, Roman Numerals match scale degrees perfectly. Everything is compared to the major scale. The tables below show each scale harmonized to the Fifth.

Major Scale

Scale Degree	$\hat{1}$	$\hat{2}$	$\hat{3}$	$\hat{4}$	$\hat{5}$	$\hat{6}$	$\hat{7}$	$\hat{1}(\hat{8})$
Roman Numeral	I	II-	III-	IV	V	VI-	VII°	I

Natural Minor Scale

Scale Degree	$\hat{1}$	$\hat{2}$	$\flat\hat{3}$	$\hat{4}$	$\hat{5}$	$\flat\hat{6}$	$\flat\hat{7}$	$\hat{1}(\hat{8})$
Roman Numeral	I-	II°	bIII	IV-	V-	bVI	bVII	I-

Harmonic Minor Scale

Scale Degree	$\hat{1}$	$\hat{2}$	$\flat\hat{3}$	$\hat{4}$	$\hat{5}$	$\flat\hat{6}$	$\hat{7}$	$\hat{1}(\hat{8})$
Roman Numeral	I-	II°	bIII	IV-	V	bVI	VII°	I-

Real Melodic Minor Scale

Scale Degree	$\hat{1}$	$\hat{2}$	$\flat\hat{3}$	$\hat{4}$	$\hat{5}$	$\hat{6}$	$\hat{7}$	$\hat{1}(\hat{8})$
Roman Numeral	I-	II-	bIII	IV	V	VI°	VII°	I-

More Roman Numerals for Seventh Chords

Major Seven
I^{Δ}

Minor Seven
$II\text{-}^{7}$

Dominant Seven
V^{7}

Half-Diminished
$VII^{\varnothing}$

Fully-Diminished Seven
$VII^{°7}$

Augmented Seven
$V+^{7}$

Augmented Major Seven
$V+^{\Delta}$

Minor Major Seven
$I\text{-}^{\Delta}$

Harmonic Minor Scale Harmonized to the Seventh

Harmonic Minor Harmonized to the Seventh Rules:

1. $\hat{7}$ changes the quality of four chords.
2. The quality of the chord on $\hat{1}$ is minor major seven. This is because the Seventh of the chord is $\hat{7}$, which is a M7 above the Root of the **I-** chord.
3. The triad on $\flat\hat{3}$ is augmented. This is because $\hat{7}$ is the Fifth of the chord. The Roman Numeral gets a "+" like a chord symbol. Because the Seventh is a M7 above the Root of the **III+** chord, the quality is augmented major seven.
4. The triad on $\hat{5}$ is major. This is because $\hat{7}$ is the Third of the chord. Because the Seventh of the chord is $\hat{4}$, a m7 above the Root of the **V** chord, the quality is dominant seven.
5. The triad on $\hat{7}$ is diminished. This is because $\hat{7}$ is the Root of the chord. Because the Seventh of the chord is $\flat\hat{6}$, a d7 above the Root of the **VII°** chord, the quality is fully diminished 7.

G Harmonic Minor Scale Harmonized to the Seventh + Chord Symbols

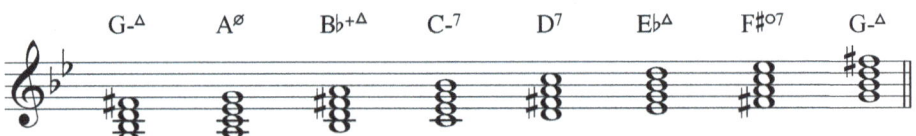

Scale Degree	$\hat{1}$	$\hat{2}$	$\flat\hat{3}$	$\hat{4}$	$\hat{5}$	$\flat\hat{6}$	$\hat{7}$	$\hat{1}(\hat{8})$
Triad Quality	Minor	Diminished	Augmented	Minor	Major	Major	Diminished	Minor
Triad RNs	I-	II°	♭III+	IV-	V	♭VI	VII°	I-
7th Quality	Minor Major 7	Half-Dim.	Aug. Major 7	Minor 7	Dominant 7	Major 7	Fully-Dim. 7	Minor Major 7
7th RNs	I-△	II⌀	♭III+△	IV-7	V7	♭VI△	VII°7	I-△
A harm. minor	A	B	C	D	E	F	G#	A
E harm. minor	E	F#	G	A	B	C	D#	E
B harm. minor	B	C#	D	E	F#	G	A#	B
F# harm. minor	F#	G#	A	B	C#	D	E#	F#
G♭ harm. minor	G♭	A♭	B♭♭	C♭	D♭	E♭♭	F	G♭
D♭ harm. minor	D♭	E♭	F♭	G♭	A♭	B♭♭	C	D♭
A♭ harm. minor	A♭	B♭	C♭	D♭	E♭	F♭	G	A♭
E♭ harm. minor	E♭	F	G♭	A♭	B♭	C♭	D	E♭
B♭ harm. minor	B♭	C	D♭	E♭	F	G♭	A	B♭
F harm. minor	F	G	A♭	B♭	C	D♭	E	F
C harm. minor	C	D	E♭	F	G	A♭	B	C
G harm. minor	G	A	B♭	C	D	E♭	F#	G
D harm. minor	D	E	F	G	A	B♭	C#	D

Real Melodic Minor Scale Harmonized to the Seventh

> **Real Melodic Minor Harmonized to the Seventh Rules:**
> 1. Every chord quality is different from a harmonized natural minor scale. There will not be a breakdown comparing the two.

G Real Melodic Minor Scale Harmonized to the Seventh + Chord Symbols

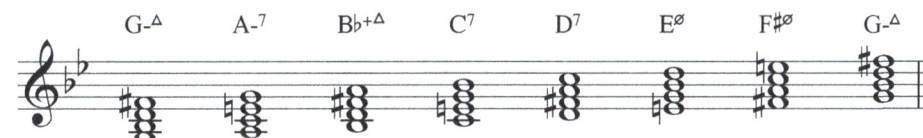

Scale Degree	$\hat{1}$	$\hat{2}$	$\flat\hat{3}$	$\hat{4}$	$\hat{5}$	$\hat{6}$	$\hat{7}$	$\hat{1}(\hat{8})$
Triad Quality	Minor	Minor	Augmented	Major	Major	Diminished	Diminished	Minor
Triad RNs	I-	II-	♭III+	IV	V	VI°	VII°	I-
7th Quality	Minor Major 7	Minor 7	Aug. Major 7	Dominant 7	Dominant 7	Half-Dim.	Half-Dim.	Minor Major 7
7th RNs	I-△	II-7	♭III+△	IV7	V7	VIø	VIIø	I-△
A r. mel. minor	A	B	C	D	E	F#	G#	A
E r. mel. minor	E	F#	G	A	B	C#	D#	E
B r. mel. minor	B	C#	D	E	F#	G#	A#	B
F# r. mel. minor	F#	G#	A	B	C#	D#	E#	F#
G♭ r. mel. minor	G♭	A♭	B♭♭	C♭	D♭	E♭	F	G♭
D♭ r. mel. minor	D♭	E♭	F♭	G♭	A♭	B♭	C	D♭
A♭ r. mel. minor	A♭	B♭	C♭	D♭	E♭	F	G	A♭
E♭ r. mel. minor	E♭	F	G♭	A♭	B♭	C	D	E♭
B♭ r. mel. minor	B♭	C	D♭	E♭	F	G	A	B♭
F r. mel. minor	F	G	A♭	B	C	D	E	F
C r. mel. minor	C	D	E♭	F	G	A	B	C
G r. mel. minor	G	A	B♭	C	D	E	F#	G
D r. mel. minor	D	E	F	G	A	B	C#	D

Inversions 2: Seventh Chords

Seventh Chord Inversion Rules:

1. Seventh chord inversions work the same way as interval inversions and triad inversions. The lowest note in the chord becomes the highest note in the chord.
2. In a seventh chord inversion, the lowest note is moved up one octave register higher at the same pitch class. This changes the lowest note into the highest note of the chord.
3. Root Position: when the Root is the lowest note in the seventh chord.
4. 1st Inversion: when the Third is the lowest note in the seventh chord.
5. 2nd Inversion: when the Fifth is the lowest note in the seventh chord.
6. 3rd Inversion: when the Seventh is the lowest note in the seventh chord.

Seventh Chord Inversions

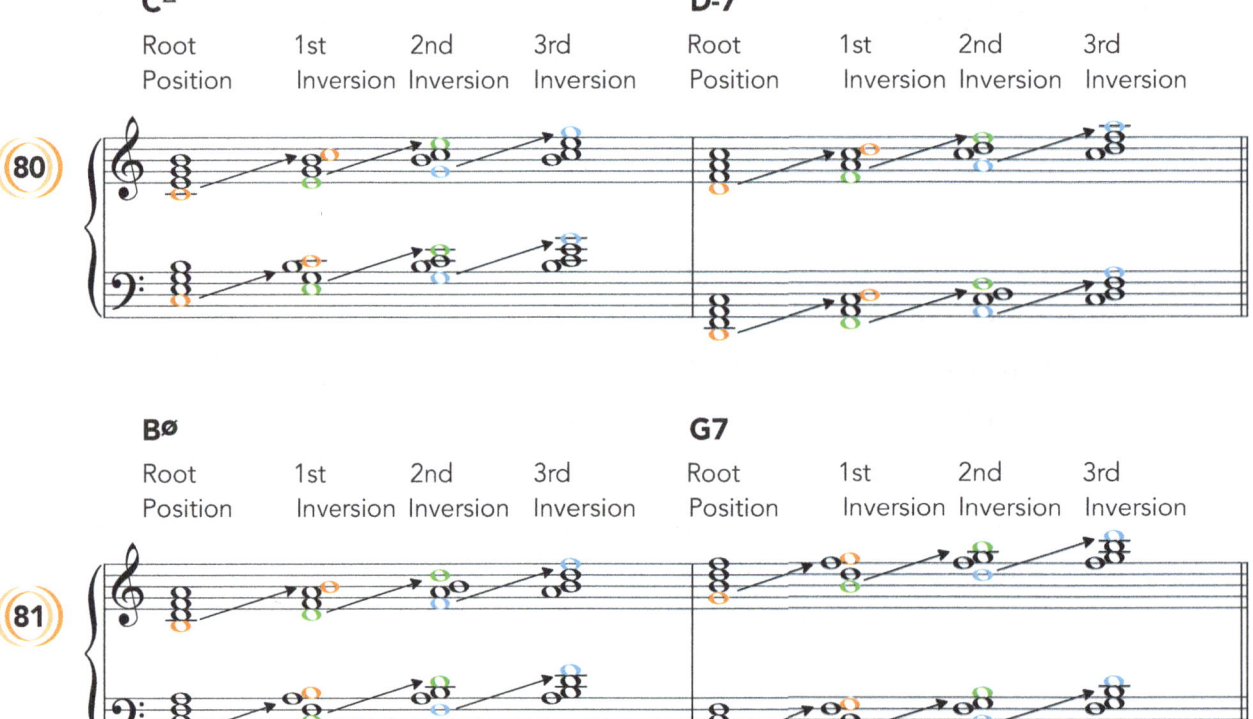

How to Identify Inverted Seventh Chords

Seventh Chord Inversion Rules: 2

1. Root position seventh chords are spelled using only thirds.
2. Any time a d2/m2/M2/A2 interval is in a seventh chord, the seventh chord is inverted.
3. 1st Inversion: d2/m2/M2/A2 between the two highest notes of the seventh chord.
4. 2nd Inversion: d2/m2/M2/A2 between the middle two notes of the seventh chord.
5. 3rd Inversion: d2/m2/M2/A2 between the lowest two notes of the seventh chord.

Seventh Chord Figured Bass

Just like triad figured bass, seventh chord figured bass shows the intervals of the notes compared to the lowest note for each inversion. Also like triad figured bass, only one or two of the interval numbers are used for each chord. We will explore a better solution for inversions in a few chapters.

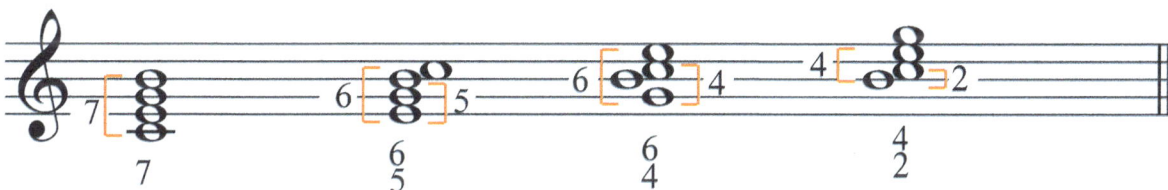

Seventh Chord Slash Chords

Just like triad slash chords, seventh slash chords show the chord symbol and the lowest note of the chord.

$$C^7/B\flat$$

Just like triads, the chord spelling does not matter as long as all notes for the chord are present.

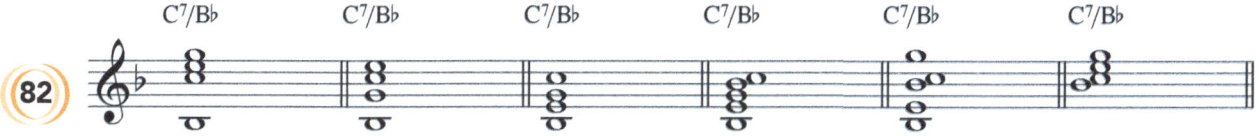

Review

- Seventh chord qualities
    - Fully diminished seven
    - Augmented seven
    - Augmented major seven
    - Minor major seven

- New Roman Numeral logic
    - Roman Numerals match scale degrees
    - Show the quality of the chord like a chord symbol

- Minor scales harmonized to the Seventh
    - Harmonic minor scale
    - Real melodic minor scale

- Seventh chord inversions
    - Root position
    - First inversion
    - Second inversion
    - Third inversion

- How to identify seventh chord inversions
- Seventh chord figured bass
- Seventh chord slash chords

New Words You Should Know

1. Fully diminished seven
2. Augmented seven
3. Augmented major seven
4. Minor major seven

Harmony 6: sus, ADD, Extended, Omit, and Advanced Inversions

SO MANY CHORDS! Let's get moving so you can see the wonderful, wild harmonies that are waiting for you.

More Chord Tones

- Any note can be added to a chord to create a new chord tone.
- Yes, any note.
- Write and speak these notes with the same system as Root, Third, Fifth, and Seventh.

Scale Degree	$\hat{1}$	$\hat{2}$	$\hat{3}$	$\hat{4}$	$\hat{5}$	$\hat{6}$	$\hat{7}$
Chord Tones	Root	Second	Third	Fourth	Fifth	Sixth	Seventh

♯ vs. +

The Correct Way

With chord symbols it is correct to label, write, and speak all chord tones with the same language as intervals.

> - Any Perfect interval is augmented when raised by one half-step. Use "+" to show augmented fifths and fourths in a chord.
> - The "+" should only be used for chords with a Fifth raised by one half-step, also known as an augmented chord.

C+7

The Common Way

> - It is also common to say "sharp five" or "sharp four" for notes that are technically augmented.
> - It is also common to see chord symbols with a ♯5 or ♯4 instead of +5 or +4.

C(♯5)7

> **You will see both ways of expressing augmented chord tones in the real world.**

ADD Chords

- Almost any note can be added to a triad or seventh chord.
- The note is "added" to the chord.

ADD or No add?

1. You will see "ADD" or "add" in the chord symbol.
2. It is common to see no "ADD" but only the number of the scale degree that is being added to the chord for Sixths and sometimes other chord tones.
3. You may also see numbers in parentheses that are being added to the chord. These are not technically add chords, because they function with tension instead of adding a diatonic (from the major scale) chord tone, but we will explore them here anyway.

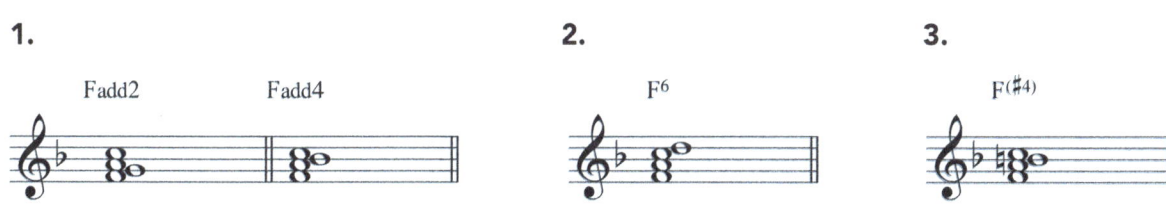

ADD Chords: Major

Major Add Chord Exceptions And Notes

- There is no add ♭4 because ♭4 is enharmonic to the M3 above the Root, which is the Third of the chord.
- There is no add ♭5 because ♭5 is enharmonic to ♯4. It would be confusing to have two different qualities of Fifth in the same chord. Using an augmented Fourth works better.
- The add ♭6 is like having an augmented Fifth and perfect Fifth in the same chord!
- There is no add ♯6 because ♯6 is enharmonic to ♭7, which would make the chord a dominant seventh chord.

ADD Chords: Minor

Minor Add Chord Exceptions And Notes

- There is no add #2 because #2 is enharmonic to the m3 above the Root, which is the Third of the chord.
- There is no add ♭5 because ♭5 is enharmonic to #4.
- The add ♭6 is basically like having an augmented Fifth and perfect Fifth in the same chord! Wild stuff...
- There is no add #6 because #6 is enharmonic to ♭7, which would make the chord "some kind of" seventh chord, depending on the notes in the triad.

ADD Chords: Seventh Chords

ADD Chords Major Seven

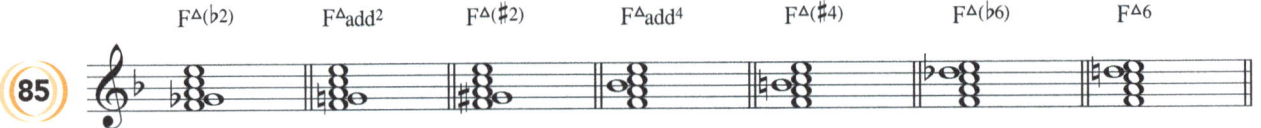

ADD Chords Minor Seven

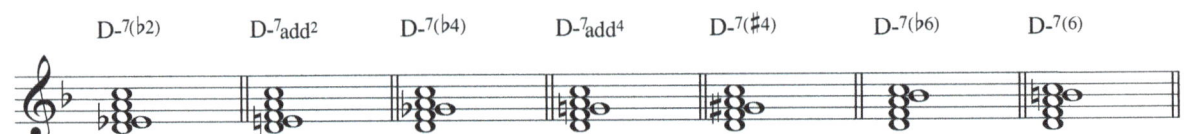

ADD Chords Dominant Seven

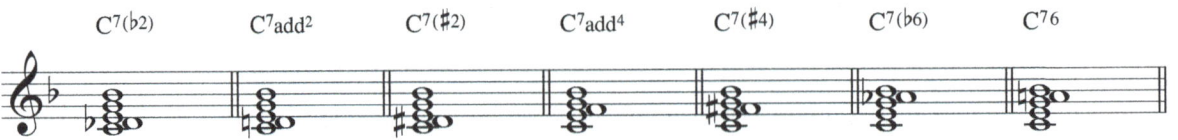

Extended Chords

- Extended chords use notes above the octave from the Root.
- Extended notes are taken from compound intervals.
- There are two types of notes that can be added to any extended chord. They are tensions and alterations.

Chord Tones Above The Octave

- Chord tones can go past an octave using compound intervals, but we will still say "Root," "Third," "Fifth," and "Seventh" no matter which octave register they are in.
- Label and speak other chord tones past an octave as Ninth, Eleventh, Thirteenth.
- Just like compound intervals, we never go above 15. The highest chord tone is 13.

Tensions

- Tensions are any chord tone from the major or natural minor scale above the octave besides Root, Third, Fifth, and Seventh.
- Tensions can be added to any triad or seventh chord.
- These are technically "add" notes that are added to the chord. Sometimes you will see "add," and sometimes just the number or the numbers in parentheses, like add chords. When you write these chords, use only the tension number. Do not use "add."

All Possible Tensions

1. 9 ($\hat{2}$ up an octave above the Root, like the compound interval)
2. 11 ($\hat{4}$ up an octave above the Root, like the compound interval)
3. 13 ($\hat{6}$ up an octave above the Root, like the compound interval)

1.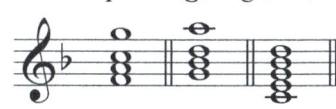

2.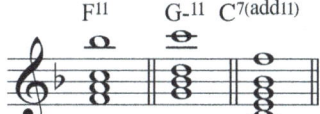

3.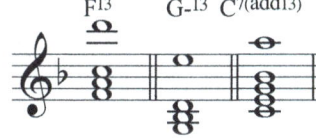

Tensions Combine

Combining tensions can be fun! You can do this with any chord quality. Add a comma between each tension when there is more than one tension in a chord.

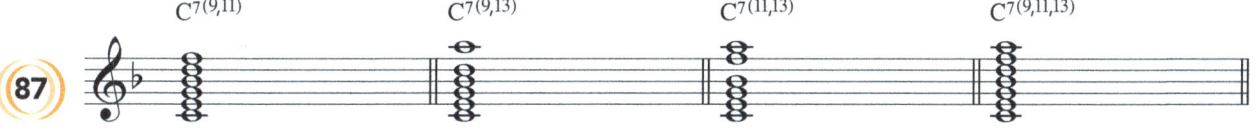

Alterations

- Alterations are any note above the octave that is "altered" from the major scale.
- When the Fifth or Fourth of a seventh chord is changed from a P5 or P4 to an A5, d5, or A4 above the Root, we can also call this an altered chord. This means that an augmented seven chord is an altered chord, and an augmented triad is an altered chord.
- Alterations are typically added to dominant seven chords.
- Alternations can also be added to any chord of any quality.
- Altered chords generally serve the purpose of increasing the tension of a **V** chord.

All Possible Alterations

1. ♭9
2. ♯9
3. ♯11
4. ♭5
5. ♯5
6. ♭13

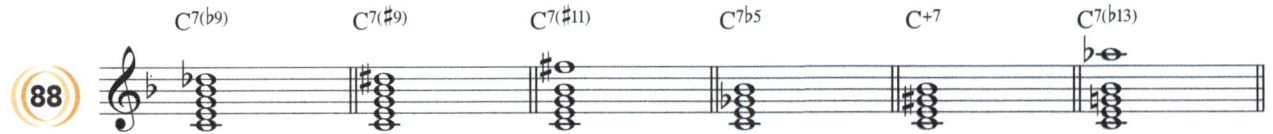

Alt.

Sometimes you will see "alt" in the chord symbol for dominant seven chords. This means the performer can pick and choose which altered notes to include in the chord.

$$C^7\text{alt.}$$

More Altered Chord Information

- The ♯9 in a dominant seven chord means you will have both a major Third and a minor Third chord tone...in the same chord, usually separated by a M7!
- The ♯9 dominant seven chord is also called the "Jimi Hendrix" chord because he used it a lot in songs like "Purple Haze" and "Foxy Lady."
- ♯5 and ♭13 are enharmonic. You will not find or use both in the same altered chord.
- ♭5 and ♯11 are enharmonic. You will not find or use both in the same altered chord.
- There are certain combinations of altered notes that are more common than others, but do not let that stop you from experimenting with these wonderful chords!

Alterations Combine

There are so many combinations of altered notes to create wild and wonderful sounds! These are a few examples and all examples are without inversion and in a linear voicing. This means that the order of the notes in the chord is Root, Third, Fifth, Seventh, Ninth, Eleventh, Thirteenth.

♯5 Alterantion Combinations

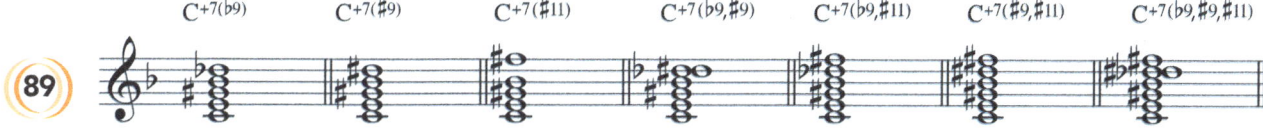

♭5 Alteration Combinations

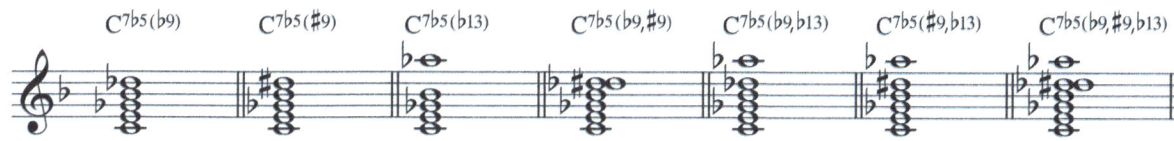

More Alteration Combinations

Altered Chords That Are Not Dominant

△(♯11)

The wild thing about this chord is that when it is used to harmonize $\hat{4}$ on **IV**, it is diatonic, because the ♯11 is $\hat{7}$ of the major scale. You will also find this chord on a harmonized $\hat{1}$ on **I**.

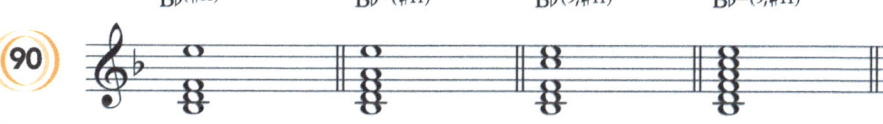

-7(♯5)

This chord shows up everywhere, in the James Bond theme, pop music, and video game music!

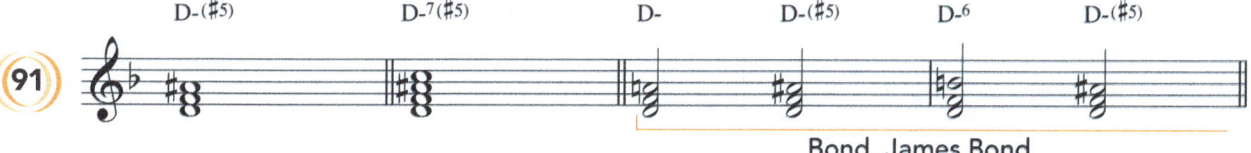

Bond, James Bond

The Octave Puzzle

If an instrument is supposed to play the Ninth of a chord but instead plays the Second of the chord (same note one octave lower), has the instrument played the Ninth or the Second?

Single Instrument

You Know The Voicing (Notation)

The only way to know the exact voicing of a chord is to write it out for a performer in notation.

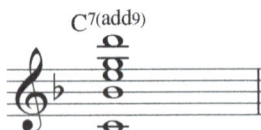

You Don't Know The Voicing (Lead Sheet)

Lead sheets leave the voicing of the chord up to the performer. Here are a few ways the same chord symbol might be interpreted. The notation shows different voicings of the same chord.

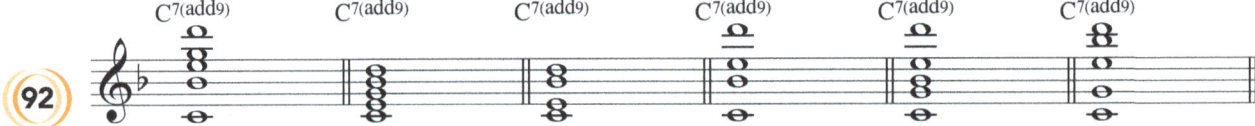

More Than One Instrument

You Know Which Instruments Are Playing (Notation)

A high-sounding instrument can play a Second relative to its Root, but because a lower-sounding instrument is playing a Root at a lower octave, that turns the Second into a Ninth.

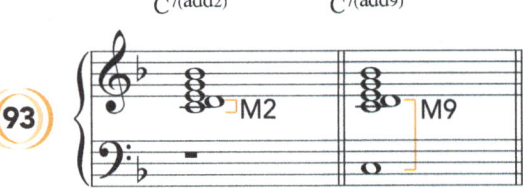

> The lowest note present in a chord (even if it is from a different instrument) defines the way we think of the octave of all notes above it.

You Don't Know Which Instruments Are Playing (Lead Sheet)

Lead sheet interpretation includes an instrument in the bass clef playing a "bass line" where chord tones and non-chord tones are played. Below are different ways that a piano player might interpret the same chord in a lead sheet song. A broken chord!

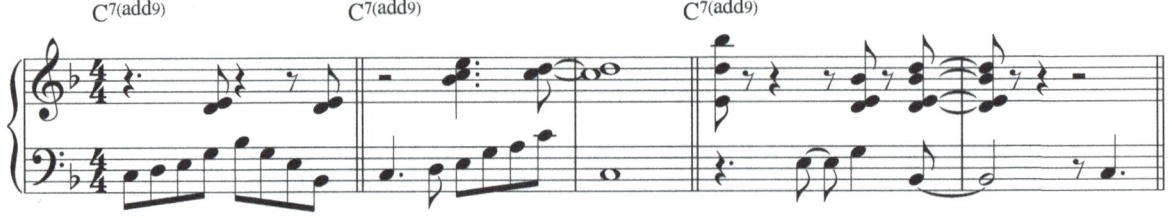

sus Chords

- sus is short for "suspended."
- sus chords have no Third; it is "suspended" up to the Fourth or down to the Second.
- The quality of the chord is "sus."
- sus chords are not minor or major because they have no Third.

sus2

sus2 chords have three chord tones but are not triads.

Root
The Root can be any note from the full musical alphabet. We can think of the Root as being related to $\hat{1}$.

Second
The Second is the same note as $\hat{2}$ from the major scale of the $\hat{1}$ note that is the Root.

Fifth
Just like triads the Fifth is the same note as $\hat{5}$ from the major scale of the $\hat{1}$ note that is the Root.

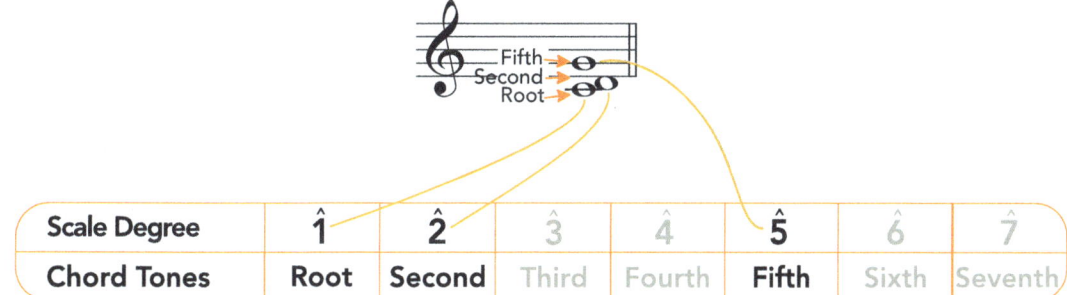

Scale Degree	$\hat{1}$	$\hat{2}$	$\hat{3}$	$\hat{4}$	$\hat{5}$	$\hat{6}$	$\hat{7}$
Chord Tones	Root	Second	Third	Fourth	Fifth	Sixth	Seventh

sus Chord Modern Uses

- Anything goes in modern music with sus2 and sus4 chords.
- You can transform or replace any triad with a sus chord for a new sound, including sus notes that are not from the scale. For example, if you use notes from a major scale, you will find sus♭2 chords, harmonizing $\hat{3}$, IIIsus♭2 because of the half-step between $\hat{3}$ and $\hat{4}$.
- You can find and write songs or sections of songs that use only sus chords.
- The suspended note can be at any octave register above the Root, as long as no Third is present in the chord.

sus4

sus4 chords have three chord tones but are not triads.

Root

The Root can be any note from the full musical alphabet; we can think of the Root as being related to $\hat{1}$.

Fourth

The Fourth is the same note as $\hat{4}$ from the major scale of the $\hat{1}$ note that is the Root.

Fifth

Just like triads the Fifth is the same note as $\hat{5}$ from the major scale of the $\hat{1}$ note that is the Root.

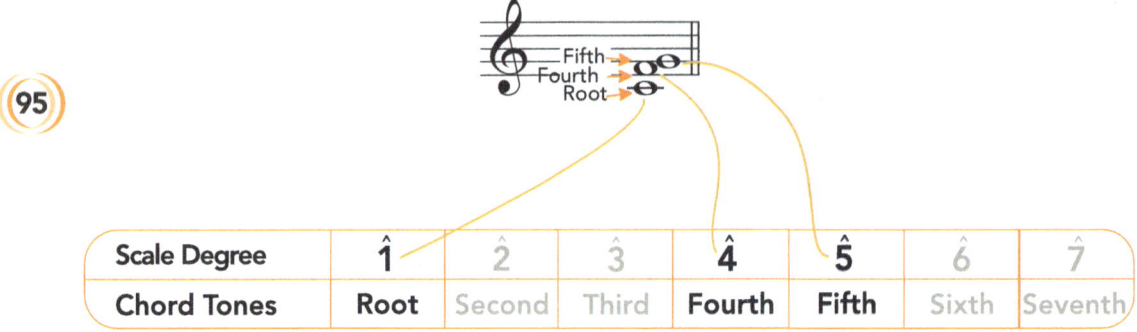

sus + Seventh Chords + ADD

You can find and write any chord as a sus chord. Below are some examples, and there are many, many more options.

- sus chord with any quality of Seventh
- sus with any extended chord (tensions and alterations)
- Any inversion of any chord (your only limit is your imagination)

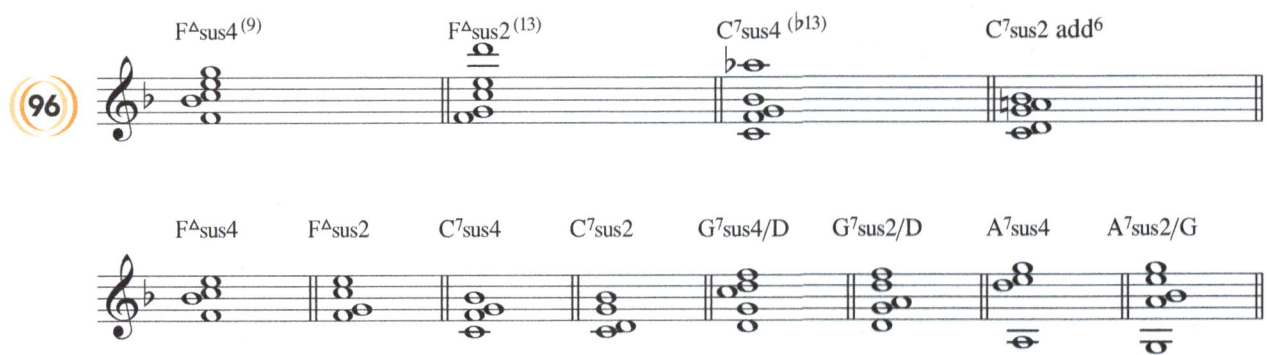

Omit Chords

- "Omit" means to skip or not include something.
- Omit chords are also called "no" chords.
- Omit chords remove a chord tone from a chord.
- Only use Omit chords when there is no other option for a chord symbol.

How Not To Use Omit Chords

Do not "omit" a note if you can find a clearer way of writing the chord symbol.

1. You cannot omit the Third from a major or minor triad. This makes a power chord.
2. You cannot omit the Seventh from a seven chord. This makes a triad.
3. You cannot omit an ADD note from a chord...you are left with the basic triad or seventh chord you started with.
4. You cannot omit the Second from a sus2 or the Fourth from a sus4. This makes a power chord.

How to Use Omit Chords

There are many different ways of using Omit chords. Here are a few ideas and examples.

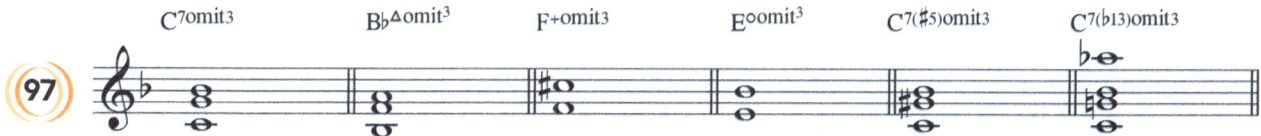

Advanced Slash Chords

Now that you understand ADD chords, inversions go to a new level. Now slash chord symbols and notation of ADD chord inversions can include notes that are not from the triad or seventh chord. These notes are called non-chord tones or "NCT."

Much of the time, the upper structure (the top part of the chord) remains the same and only the bass note changes. This means that the NCT in the "bass" (the lowest note) of the chord is not really "in" the chord. NCT in the bass of a chord does not mean the chord must be an ADD chord in inversion.

Sometimes this lowest note is like a secondary melody, being played in the lowest notes of the harmony. We can call this a "bass line" or "bass movement."

Advanced Slash Chord Examples

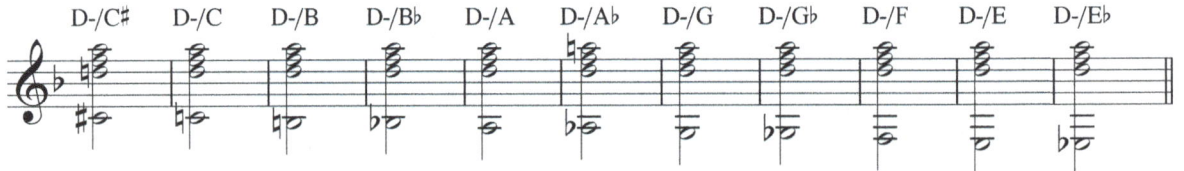

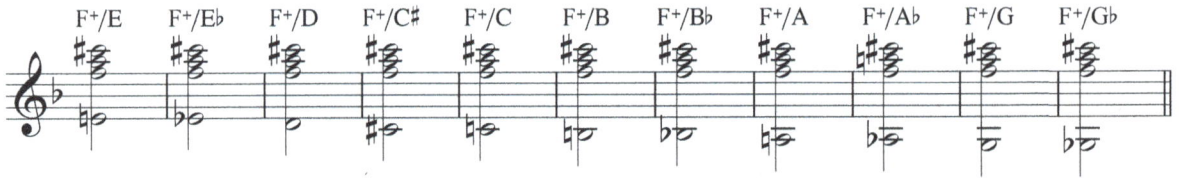

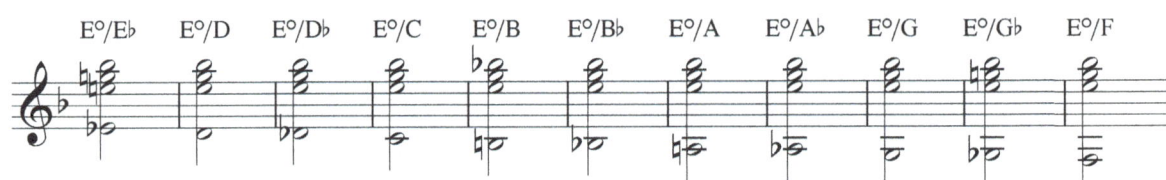

Pop/Rock Example

A New Look at Inversions

In books 1 and 2 of this series, you analyzed all inversions using figured bass. You did this for several reasons.

1. More than 95% of music schools use the figured bass system. This is not an endorsement of how well the system works; "this is the way they have always done it."
2. AP music theory, which gives college credit for 95% of music programs, uses the system.
3. 95% of the content outside of Best Music Coach uses the figured bass system.
4. 95% of musicians use the figured bass system to communicate with each other as well as analyze music.

You needed to understand how "most" people (as of 2023) use Figured Bass so you can be truly free to pursue your Dream Music Goals in any music arena.

Figured Bass Logic

There are a few reasons why the figured bass system does not work for modern music.

1. It does not work for non-chord tones as the lowest note of the chord.
2. You cannot accurately label chords outside common harmonized scales.

Inversions: The Modern Way

There is a much easier system for analyzing and labeling inversions.

1. Write the Roman Numeral of the chord along with any 7th, ADD, sus, extensions, and omit information.
2. Write a slash (like a slash chord!).
3. Write the scale degree number (no caret) that the note in the bass is in relation to the key of the music. Add accidentals when the note is different from the major scale, like scale degrees.

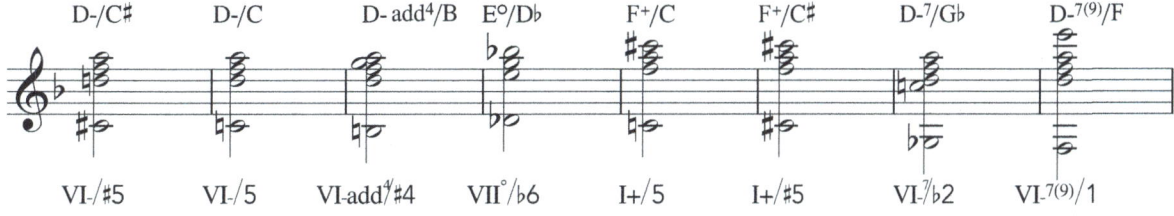

Review

- More chord tones
    - Root
    - Second
    - Third
    - Fourth
    - Fifth
    - Sixth
    - Seventh
    - Ninth
    - Eleventh
    - Thirteenth

- ADD chords
    - Major Add chords
    - Minor Add chords
    - Seventh Add chords

- Extended chords
    - Tensions
    - Alterations

- Tensions
    - 9
    - 11
    - 13

- Alterations
    - ♭9
    - ♯9
    - ♯11
    - ♭5
    - ♯5
    - ♭13

New Words You Should Know

1. ADD
2. Extensions
3. Tensions
4. Alterations
5. sus
6. Omit

- The octave puzzle
    - Single instrument
    - More than one instrument

- sus chords
    - sus2
    - sus4
    - suspended seventh chords
    - sus + ADD chords

- Omit chords

- Advanced slash chords

- Inversions
    - Inversions logic
    - Why figured bass is limited
    - Modern inversions

Harmony 7: Harmonized Scales Summary

A summary of all harmonized scales you have learned in all keys.

All Major Scales

Harmony 7: Harmonized Scales Summary

Scale Degree	$\hat{1}$	$\hat{2}$	$\hat{3}$	$\hat{4}$	$\hat{5}$	$\hat{6}$	$\hat{7}$	$\hat{1}(\hat{8})$
Triad Quality	Major	Minor	Minor	Major	Major	Minor	Diminished	Major
Triad RNs	I	II-	III-	IV	V	VI-	VII°	I-
7th Quality	Major 7	Minor 7	Minor 7	Major 7	Dominant 7	Minor 7	Half-Dim.	Major 7
7th RNs	I△	II-7	III-7	IV△	V7	VI-7	VIIø	I-△
C major	C	D	E	F	G	A	B	C
G major	G	A	B	C	D	E	F♯	G
D major	D	E	F♯	G	A	B	C♯	D
A major	A	B	C♯	D	E	F♯	G♯	A
E major	E	F♯	G♯	A	B	C♯	D♯	E
B major	B	C♯	D♯	E	F♯	G♯	A♯	B
F♯ major	F♯	G♯	A♯	B	C♯	D♯	E♯	F♯
G♭ major	G♭	A♭	B♭	C♭	D♭	E♭	F♯	G♭
C♯ major	C♯	D♯	E♯	F♯	G♯	A♯	B♯	C♯
D♭ major	D♭	E♭	F	G♭	A♭	B♭	C	D♭
A♭ major	A♭	B♭	C	D♭	E♭	F	G	A♭
E♭ major	E♭	G	G	A♭	B♭	C	D	E♭
B♭ major	B♭	C	D	E♭	F	G	A	B♭
F major	F	G	A	B♭	C	D	E	F

All Natural Minor Scales

Scale Degree	$\hat{1}$	$\hat{2}$	$\flat\hat{3}$	$\hat{4}$	$\hat{5}$	$\flat\hat{6}$	$\flat\hat{7}$	$\hat{1}(\hat{8})$
Triad Quality	Minor	Diminished	Major	Minor	Minor	Major	Major	Minor
Triad RNs	I-	II°	♭III	IV-	V-	♭VI	♭VII	I-
7th Quality	Minor 7	Half-Dim.	Major 7	Minor 7	Minor 7	Major 7	Dominant 7	Minor 7
7th RNs	I⁻⁷	II⌀	♭III△	IV⁻⁷	V⁻⁷	♭VI△	♭VII⁷	I⁻⁷
A nat. minor	A	B	C	D	E	F	G	A
E nat. minor	E	F♯	G	A	B	C	D	E
B nat. minor	B	C♯	D	E	F♯	G	A	B
F♯ nat. minor	F♯	G♯	A	B	C♯	D	E	F♯
G♭ nat. minor	G♭	A♭	B♭♭	C♭	D♭	E♭♭	F♭	G♭
D♭ nat. minor	D♭	E♭	F♭	G♭	A♭	B♭♭	C♭	D♭
A♭ nat. minor	A♭	B♭	C♭	D♭	E♭	F♭	G♭	A♭
E♭ nat. minor	E♭	F	G♭	A♭	B♭	C♭	D♭	E♭
B♭ nat. minor	B♭	C	D♭	E♭	F	G♭	A♭	B♭
F nat. minor	F	G	A♭	B♭	C	D♭	E♭	F
C nat. minor	C	D	E♭	F	G	A♭	B♭	C
G nat. minor	G	A	B♭	C	D	E♭	F	G
D nat. minor	D	E	F	G	A	B♭	C	D

Harmony 7: Harmonized Scales Summary

Harmony 7: Harmonized Scales Summary

All Major Pentatonic Scales

Scale Degree	$\hat{1}$	$\hat{2}$	$\hat{3}$	$\hat{5}$	$\hat{6}$	$\hat{1}(\hat{8})$
C major penta	C	D	E	G	A	C
G major penta	G	A	B	D	E	G
D major penta	D	E	F♯	A	B	D
A major penta	A	B	C♯	E	F♯	A
E major penta	E	F♯	G♯	B	C♯	E
B major penta	B	C♯	D♯	F♯	G♯	B
F♯ major penta	F♯	G♯	A♯	C♯	D♯	F♯
G♭ major penta	G♭	A♭	B♭	D♭	E♭	G♭
D♭ major penta	D♭	E♭	F	A♭	B♭	D♭
A♭ major penta	A♭	B♭	C	E♭	F	A♭
E♭ major penta	E♭	G	G	B♭	C	E♭
B♭ major penta	B♭	C	D	F	G	B♭
F major penta	F	G	A	C	D	F

All Minor Pentatonic Scales

Scale Degree	1	♭$\hat{3}$	$\hat{4}$	$\hat{5}$	♭$\hat{7}$	$\hat{1}(\hat{8})$
A minor penta	A	C	D	E	G	A
E minor penta	E	G	A	B	D	E
B minor penta	B	D	E	F♯	A	B
F♯ minor penta	F♯	A	B	C♯	E	F♯
G♭ minor penta	G♭	B♭♭	C♭	D♭	F♭	G♭
D♭ minor penta	D♭	F♭	G♭	A♭	C♭	D♭
A♭ minor penta	A♭	C♭	D♭	E♭	G♭	A♭
E♭ minor penta	E♭	G♭	A♭	B♭	D♭	E♭
B♭ minor penta	B♭	D♭	E♭	F	A♭	B♭
F minor penta	F	A♭	B♭	C	E♭	F
C minor penta	C	E♭	F	G	B♭	C
G minor penta	G	B♭	C	D	F	G
D minor penta	D	F	G	A	C	D

All Harmonic Minor Scales

Scale Degree	1	$\hat{2}$	$\flat\hat{3}$	$\hat{4}$	$\hat{5}$	$\flat\hat{6}$	$\hat{7}$	$\hat{1}(\hat{8})$
Triad Quality	Minor	Diminished	Augmented	Minor	Major	Major	Diminished	Minor
Triad RNs	I-	II°	$\flat$III+	IV-	V	$\flat$VI	VII°	I-
7th Quality	Minor Major 7	Half-Dim.	Aug. Major 7	Minor 7	Dominant 7	Major 7	Fully-Dim. 7	Minor Major 7
7th RNs	I-$^\Delta$	II$^\varnothing$	$\flat$III+$^\Delta$	IV-^{7}	V^7	$\flat$VI$^\Delta$	VII$^{°7}$	I-$^\Delta$
A harm. minor	A	B	C	D	E	F	G$\sharp$	A
E harm. minor	E	F$\sharp$	G	A	B	C	D$\sharp$	E
B harm. minor	B	C$\sharp$	D	E	F$\sharp$	G	A$\sharp$	B
F$\sharp$ harm. minor	F$\sharp$	G$\sharp$	A	B	C$\sharp$	D	E$\sharp$	F$\sharp$
G$\flat$ harm. minor	G$\flat$	A$\flat$	B$\flat\flat$	C$\flat$	D$\flat$	E$\flat\flat$	F	G$\flat$
D$\flat$ harm. minor	D$\flat$	E$\flat$	F$\flat$	G$\flat$	A$\flat$	B$\flat\flat$	C	D$\flat$
A$\flat$ harm. minor	A$\flat$	B$\flat$	C$\flat$	D$\flat$	E$\flat$	F$\flat$	G	A$\flat$
E$\flat$ harm. minor	E$\flat$	F	G$\flat$	A$\flat$	B$\flat$	C$\flat$	D	E$\flat$
B$\flat$ harm. minor	B$\flat$	C	D$\flat$	E$\flat$	F	G$\flat$	A	B$\flat$
F harm. minor	F	G	A$\flat$	B$\flat$	C	D$\flat$	E	F
C harm. minor	C	D	E$\flat$	F	G	A$\flat$	B	C
G harm. minor	G	A	B$\flat$	C	D	E$\flat$	F$\sharp$	G
D harm. minor	D	E	F	G	A	B$\flat$	C$\sharp$	D

Harmony 7: Harmonized Scales Summary

All Real Melodic Minor Scales

Harmony 7: Harmonized Scales Summary

Scale Degree	$\hat{1}$	$\hat{2}$	$\flat\hat{3}$	$\hat{4}$	$\hat{5}$	$\hat{6}$	$\hat{7}$	$\hat{1}(\hat{8})$
Triad Quality	Minor	Minor	Augmented	Major	Major	Diminished	Diminished	Minor
Triad RNs	I-	II-	♭III	IV	V	VI°	VII°	I-
7th Quality	Minor Major 7	Minor 7	Aug. Major 7	Dominant 7	Dominant 7	Half-Dim.	Half-Dim.	Minor Major 7
7th RNs	I-$^\Delta$	II-^{7}	♭III+$^\Delta$	IV^7	V^7	VI°	VII°	I-$^\Delta$
A r. mel. minor	A	B	C	D	E	F♯	G♯	A
E r. mel. minor	E	F♯	G	A	B	C♯	D♯	E
B r. mel. minor	B	C♯	D	E	F♯	G♯	A♯	B
F♯ r. mel. minor	F♯	G♯	A	B	C♯	D♯	E♯	F♯
G♭ r. mel. minor	G♭	A♭	B♭♭	C♭	D♭	E♭	F	G♭
D♭ r. mel. minor	D♭	E♭	F♭	G♭	A♭	B♭	C	D♭
A♭ r. mel. minor	A♭	B♭	C♭	D♭	E♭	F	G	A♭
E♭ r. mel. minor	E♭	F	G♭	A♭	B♭	C	D	E♭
B♭ r. mel. minor	B♭	C	D♭	E♭	F	G	A	B♭
F r. mel. minor	F	G	A♭	B	C	D	E	F
C r. mel. minor	C	D	E♭	F	G	A	B	C
G r. mel. minor	G	A	B♭	C	D	E	F♯	G
D r. mel. minor	D	E	F	G	A	B	C♯	D

Analysis 5: Harmonic Function 1

In this chapter you will discover the function (the job) of different chords so you can write and understand music faster and more effectively.

Harmonic Function

The harmony of a lot of music is broken down into three areas. Each area is created with chords and chord progressions.

> 1. Tonic Area. This is home. This is Resolution or a starting point.
> 2. Subdominant Area. This is the journey.
> 3. Dominant Area. The drama, the tension, the trials.

Harmonic function is the idea that all chords and notes relate to a "tonal center."

Tonal Center

Many music cultures share the idea of tonal centers. Tonal centers have evolved and continue to evolve as our ears and our minds search for new and different ways to give the listener a sense of "home" in music.

We compare everything in notes and harmony to the tonal center.

At a basic level, a tonal center is resolution, or a feeling of home, and everything else is some kind of tension. The different degrees or amount of tension between different notes and chords is what gives music interest and movement. It tells the story of the music even if there are no lyrics.

The tonal center of a scale is $\hat{1}$. We compare every other note in the scale to this starting place. When writing or playing scales, much of the time, we start and end on $\hat{1}$. We start and end in the tonal center.

When we harmonize scales and create chords, it is the same idea. The **I** or **I-** chord built from $\hat{1}$ is home. Many chord progressions start or end in this tonal center.

Many songs start and end on the **I** or **I-** chord. This is so we have a starting sound with which we will compare everything else in the music that follows. This establishes a reference, like non-syncopated rhythms establishing a reference so we can appreciate and have fun with syncopation.

 Tonal Center Example

The name for the area that defines and establishes the tonal center for music is called the Tonic Area.

Tonic Area (T)

- The Tonic Area is different from the Tonic of a scale.
- The Tonic Area functions to create a sense of home.
- We will compare all other Areas to the Tonic Area.

Chords That Create A Tonic Area

The chords that create Tonic Areas are the relative major and minor "home base" **I** and **VI-** chords for major keys and **I-** and **♭III** in minor keys. Both of these chords create a Tonic Area because they are only 1 or 2 notes different from each other. The chords sound different, but they serve the same purpose overall, which is to create a feeling of home.

Major Key Tonic Area Notes In Common: I or I△ or III- or III-7 or VI- or VI-7

VI- is one note away from **I**. **VI-7** contains the chord tones for the triad of **I**. Any of these chords by themselves in root position, inversion, or in combination with each other can be used to create a Tonic Area in major keys. One reason these chords feel like home is that none of them have the tension of $\hat{4}$.

1. I + VI-
2. I + VI-7
3. I△ + VI-
4. I△ + VI-7
5. I + III-
6. I + III-7
7. I△ + III-
8. I△ + III-7

1.
2.
3.
4.
5.
6.
7.
8.

Minor Key Tonic Area Notes In Common: I- or I-7 or ♭III or ♭III△

I- is one note away from ♭III. I-7 contains the chord tones for the triad of ♭III. Any of these chords by themselves in root position, inversion, or in combination with each other can be used to create a Tonic Area in minor keys.

1. I- + ♭III
2. I- + ♭III△
3. I-7 + ♭III
4. I-7 + ♭III△

Why Not V- In Minor Keys?

The **III-** chord in a major key is the same as the **V-** chord in the relative minor. The reason we use **III-** in major keys but we do not use **V-** in minor keys as a Tonic Area chord is because the **V-** and **V** chord is different in its function. The **V** chord functions in the Dominant Area. The **V-** chord does not have the same relationship of tension to the **I** chord as we discussed in *The Best Music Theory Book for Beginners 2*, Analysis 4: Dominant to Tonic Tension (the second to last chapter).

Dominant Area (D)

- This is an area of high tension that either resolves to the Tonic Area or remains unresolved to emphasize tension or larger cycles of tension and resolution.

Chords That Create A Dominant Area

These chords sound different, but they serve the same purpose overall, which is to create a feeling of tension.

Dominant Chords That Are Not Built On $\hat{5}$

Because the whole point of the Dominant Area is the harmonic "function," there are chords that are other qualities than dominant. These chords are not dominant by themselves, but in certain situations they "act like" or "function" as dominant chords, which means they work in the Dominant Area.

Major Key Dominant Area Chords: V or V7 or VII° or VIIø or VII°7

V is one note away from **VII°**. **VII°** has a tritone like **V7** that creates a big resolution, moving to imperfect or perfect consonance in the Tonic Area. Any of these chords by themselves in root position, inversion, or in combination with each other can be used to create a Dominant Area in major keys.

Major Key Dominant Area Notes In Common: V or V7 or VII° or VIIø or VII°7

> 1. **V + VII°**
> 2. **V + VIIø**
> 3. **V7 + VII°**
> 4. **V7 + VIIø**
> 5. **V + VII°7**
> 6. **V7 + VII°7**

1.

G: V   VII°

2.

V   VII°

3.

V7   VII°

4.

V   VII°

5.

G: V   VII°7

6.

V7   VII°7

Analysis 5: Harmonic Function 1

Minor Key Dominant Area Chords: V or V7 or VII° or VII°7

The big moments of Dominant Area tension in minor keys come from **V** and **V7** borrowed from the parallel major and **VII°7** (fully diminished seventh). Any of these chords by themselves in root position, inversion, or in combination with each other can be used to create a Dominant Area in minor keys.

Minor Key Dominant Area Notes In Common: V or V7 or VII° or VII°7

1. V + VII°
2. V + VII°7
3. V7 + VII°
4. V7 + VII°7

1.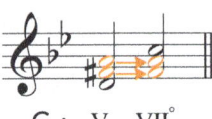
G-: V   VII°

2.
V   VII°7

3.
V7   VII°

4.
V   VII°7

Dominant Chords That Are Not Built On $\hat{5}$

VII°

The diminished chord built on $\hat{7}$ works for both major and minor keys. In minor keys we are "borrowing" the triad from a harmonized major key, but we will not add a ♮ or ♯ accidental in front of the Roman Numeral, even though it is built on $\hat{7}$ instead of ♭$\hat{7}$. Reminder: We will only add accidentals to Roman Numerals when the chord is changed from the scale degrees of the major scale. **VII°** functions as a Dominant chord because of the number of notes that are similar between it and **V** and **V7**.

VIIø

The half-diminished seven chord built on $\hat{7}$ works for both major and minor keys, but is usually found in major keys. **VIIø** functions as a dominant chord because of the number of common notes between it and **V** and **V7**. We can also think about **VIIø** as being a **V7**(9) chord in 1st inversion without the Root.

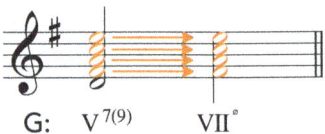
G: V7(9)   VIIø

VII°7

The fully-diminished seven chord built on $\hat{7}$ works for both major and minor keys. **VII°7** functions as a dominant chord because of the number of common notes between it and **V** and **V7**. We can also think about **VII°7** as being a **V7(♭9)** chord in 1st inversion without the Root.

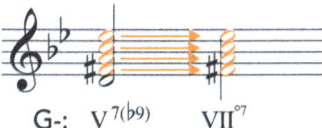

What Do You Think?

Please take 40 seconds and help someone else experience the fun and joy of making music by leaving a rating for this book!

1. Scan the QR code for your country, and if you feel this book has earned it, leave a 5-star rating.

United States

United Kingdom

Canada

T - D - T

- T - D - T stands for "Tonic - Dominant - Tonic."
- The most basic music that "makes sense" to our ears follows the pattern of a Tonic Area that moves to a Dominant Area which resolves to another Tonic Area.
- Songs that follow this pattern generally sound harmonically simple like children's and folk songs.
- A lot of classical music follows this pattern. This is an old-fashioned way of structuring music, but it still sounds great.

T - D - T Possible Chords: Major Keys

Any combination of these chords in any inversion works together to create a T - D - T harmonic pattern. Generally a **I** or **I△** is the first chord to establish a Tonic Area in a major key, because if **VI-** comes first, it can be unclear if the key is major or minor. This depends on the chord progression and is a general rule.

T	D	T	T	D	T
I	**V**	I	I	V	I
I△	V7	I△	I△	V7	I△
VI-	VII°	VI-	VI-	VII°	VI-
VI-7	VIIø	VI-7	**VI-7**	**VIIø**	VI-7
III-	VII°7	III-	III-	VII°7	III-
III-7		III-7	III-7		III-7

T	D	T	T	D	T
I	V	I	I	V	I
I△	**V7**	I△	I△	V7	I△
VI-	VII°	VI-	VI-	VII°	VI-
VI-7	VIIø	VI-7	VI-7	VIIø	VI-7
III-	VII°7	III-	**III-**	**VII°7**	III-
III-7		III-7	III-7		III-7

T	D	T	T	D	T
I	V	I	I	V	I
I△	V7	I△	I△	V7	I△
VI-	**VII°**	VI-	VI-	VII°	VI-
VI-7	VIIø	VI-7	VI-7	VIIø	VI-7
III-	VII°7	III-	III-	VII°7	III-
III-7		III-7	**III-7**		III-7

T - D - T Possible Chords: Minor Keys

Any combination of these chords in any inversions works together to create a T - D - T harmonic pattern. Generally a **I-** or **I-7** is the first chord to establish a Tonic Area in a minor key, because if ♭**III** comes first, it can be unclear if the key is major or minor. This is a general rule and depends on the chord progression.

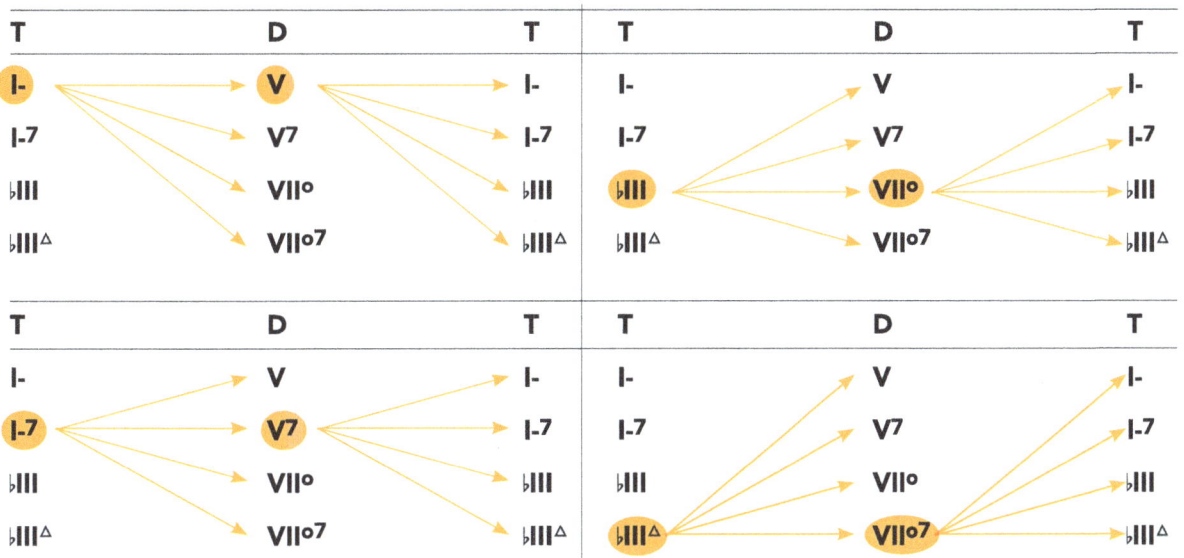

T - D - T Possible Chords: Major Keys

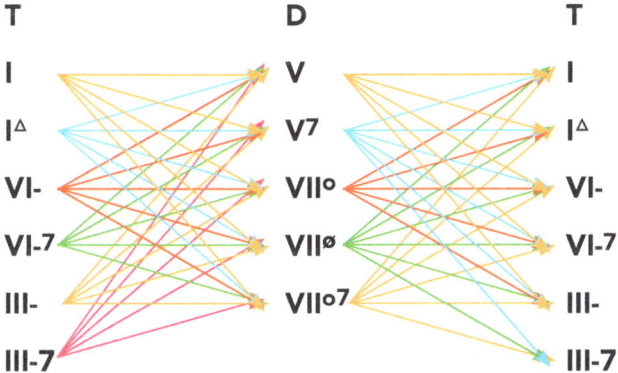

T - D - T Possible Chords: Minor Keys

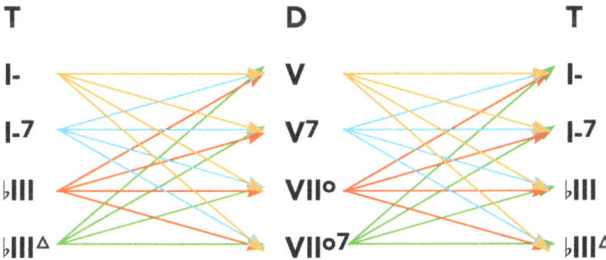

How Tension Resolves Moving D-T: Major Keys

V to I

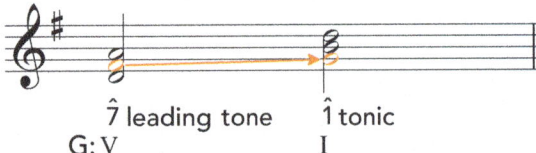
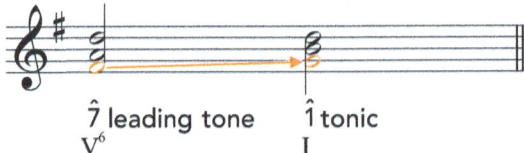

V7 to I

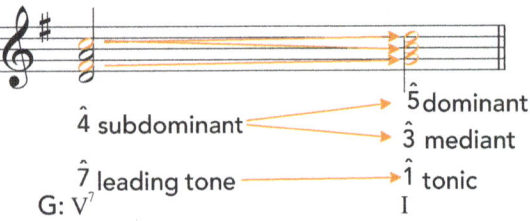
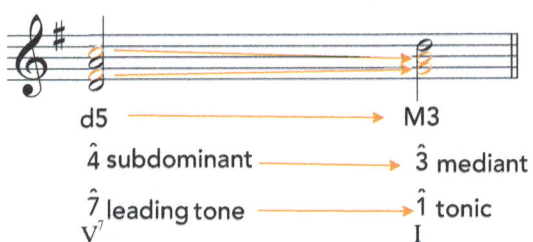

VII° to I

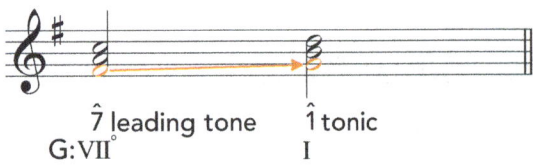
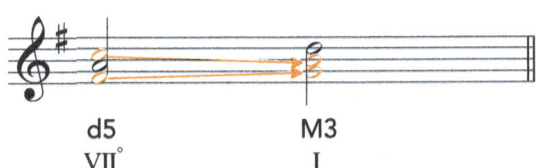

VII° to I

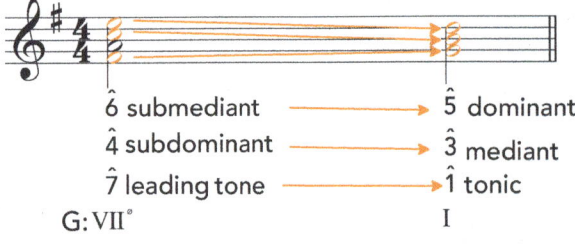
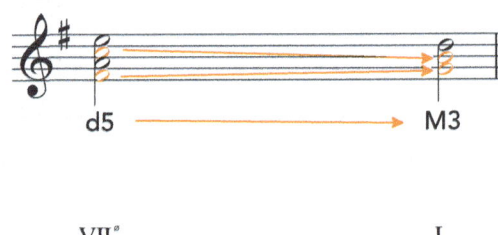

VII°7 to I

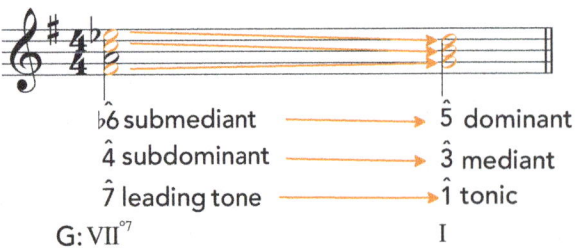
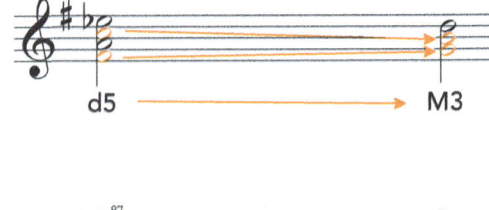

How Tension Resolves Moving D–T: Minor Keys

V to I-

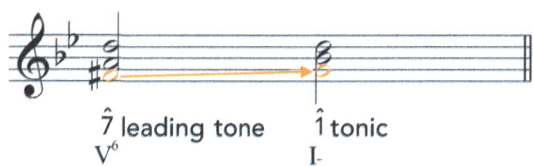

V7 to I-

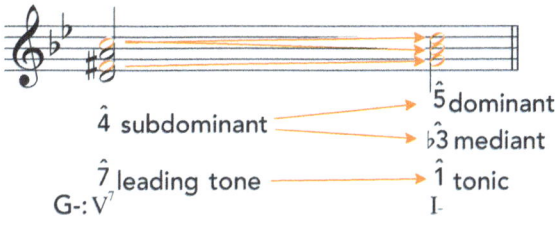

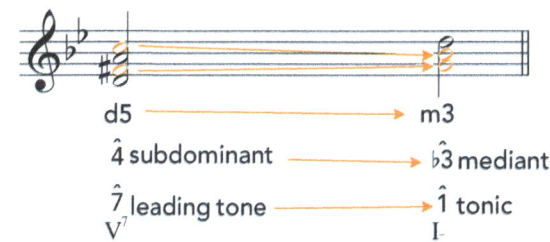

VII° to I-

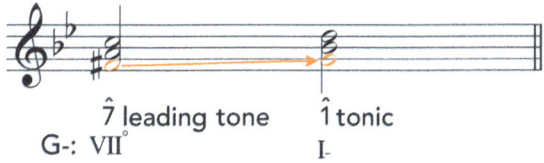

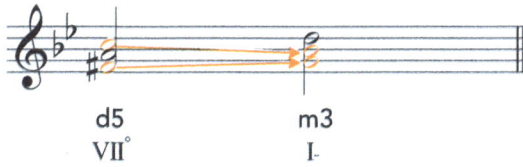

VII°7 to I-

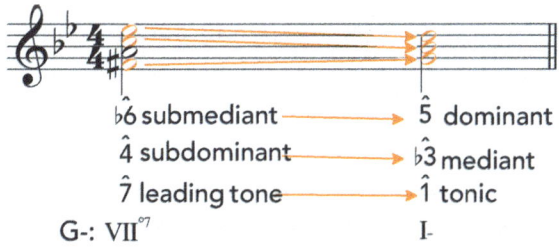

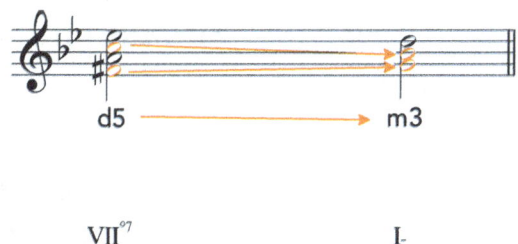

Dominant Area Resolutions: Major

1. V ⟶ I
2. V7 ⟶ I
3. VII° ⤏ I
4. VIIø ⤏ I
5. VII°7 ⤏ I

Dominant to Tonic Area resolutions that move up by one half-step get a dotted arrow. More on this later.

1.
G: V ⟶ I

2.
V7 ⟶ I

3.
VII° ⤏ I

4.
VIIø ⤏ I

5.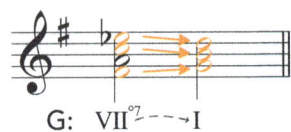
G: VII°7 ⤏ I

Dominant Area Resolutions: Minor

1. V ⟶ I-
2. V7 ⟶ I-
3. VII° ⤏ I-
4. VII°7 ⤏ I-

1.
G-: V ⟶ I-

2.
V7 ⟶ I-

3.
VII° ⤏ I-

4.
VII°7 ⤏ I-

All chords in the T - D - T can be in ANY inversion. The chords can be triads, seventh chords, broken chords...anything goes!

Dominant to Tonic Area resolutions that move up by one half-step get a dotted arrow. More on this later.

Subdominant Area (SD)

> - The Subdominant Area is also called the "Predominant Area" or SD.
> - This is an area of moderate tension that either resolves to the Dominant Area or back to the Tonic Area.

Chords That Create a Subdominant Area

Just like the Tonic Area, there are two chords that create a Subdominant Area. Just like the Tonic Area, the chords are only 1 or 2 notes different from each other. The chords sound different but they serve the same purpose overall, which is to create a feeling of moderate tension that will either build to a Dominant Area or resolve to a Tonic Area.

Major Key Subdominant Area - Notes In Common: II- or II-7 or IV or IV△

II- is one note away from **IV**. **II-7** contains the chord tones of the triad of **IV**. Any of these chords by themselves in root position, inversion, or in combination with each other can be used to create a Subdominant Area in major keys.

> 1. II- +IV
> 2. II- + IV △
> 3. II-7 +IV
> 4. II-7 + IV△

1.

G: II-   IV

2.

II-   IV△

3.

II-7   IV

4.

II-7   IV△

Analysis 5: Harmonic Function 1

Major Key Subdominant Area Chords: IV, or IV△, or IV7, or IV- or IV-7

Major keys can have a **IV** chord with the qualities of major, major seven, and dominant. Major keys can also borrow **IV-** from the parallel minor. In major keys, borrowing chords that have ♭$\hat{3}$ are something our ears are used to hearing (**IV7, IV-, IV-7** all have ♭$\hat{3}$ as a chord tone). This comes from The Blues (a genre of music), where notes and chords can alternate between major and minor in an artful way. More on The Blues later!

1. IV
2. IV△
3. IV7
4. IV-
5. IV-7

G: IV   IV△   IV⁷   IV-   IV-⁷

Minor Key Subdominant Area - Notes In Common: II° or IIø or IV- or IV-7

II° is one note away from **IV-**. **IIø** contains the chord tones for the triad of **IV-**. Any of these chords by themselves in root position, inversion, or in combination with each other can be used to create a Subdominant Area in minor keys.

1. II° + IV-
2. II° + IV-7
3. IIø + IV-
4. IIø + IV-7

   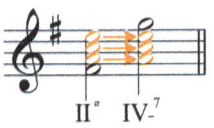

E-: II° IV-   II° IV-⁷   IIø IV-   IIø IV-⁷

Minor Key Subdominant Area Chords: IV- or IV-7 or IV or IV7 or VI or VI △

Minor keys can borrow **IV** chords with the qualities of major and dominant and can also use **VI**.

> 1. IV-
> 2. IV-7
> 3. IV
> 4. IV7
> 5. VI
> 6. VI △

1. 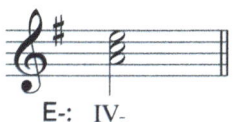 E-: IV-

2. 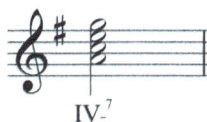 IV-7

3.  IV

4. 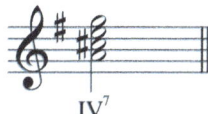 IV7

5. 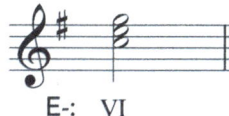 E-: VI

6.  VI △

The IV△ Clash In Minor

The Seventh of **IV△** is the $\hat{3}$ of the parallel major scale. It is not commonly used in modern music because the $\hat{3}$ in the chord tones of the Seventh clashes with the "minor" sound from ♭$\hat{3}$ in minor keys.

E-: IV△   i

T-SD-D-T

- T - SD - D - T stands for "Tonic - Subdominant - Dominant - Tonic."
- This way of building music creates many more possibilities.

Possible Chords: Major Keys

Any combination of these chords in any inversion works together to create a T - SD - D - T harmonic pattern. Generally a **I** or **I△** establishes a Tonic Area in a major key, because if **VI-** comes first, it can be unclear if the key is major or minor.

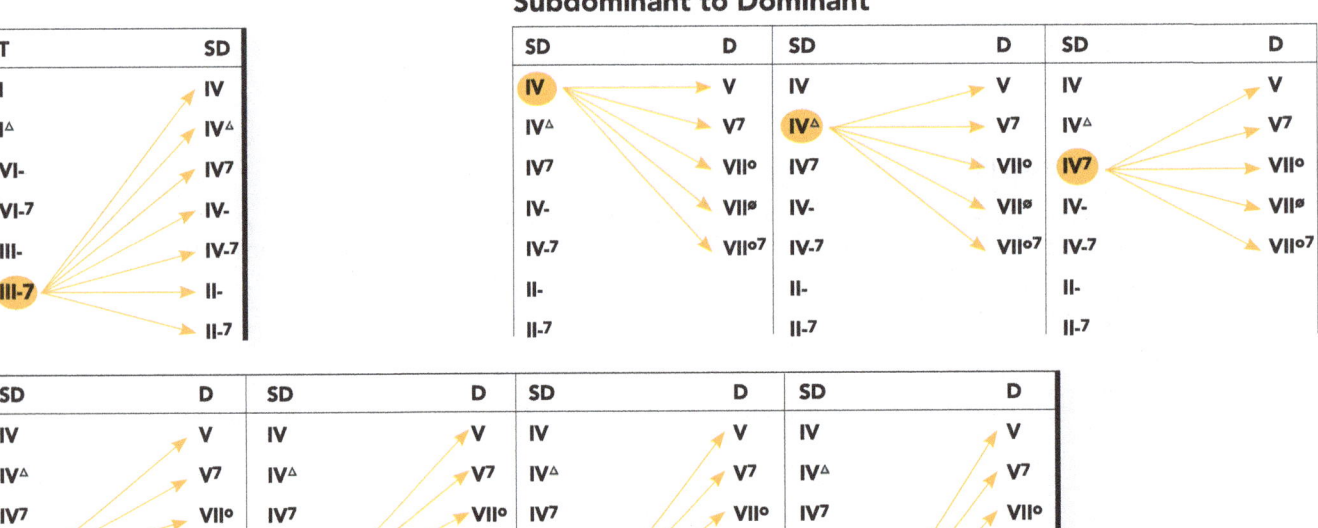

Possible Chords: Minor Keys

Any combination of these chords in any inversions works together to create a T - SD - D - T harmonic pattern. Generally a **I-** or **I-7** is the first chord to establish a Tonic Area in a minor key, because if ♭III comes first, it can be unclear if the key is major or minor.

Tonic to Subdominant

Subdominant to Dominant

Dominant to Tonic

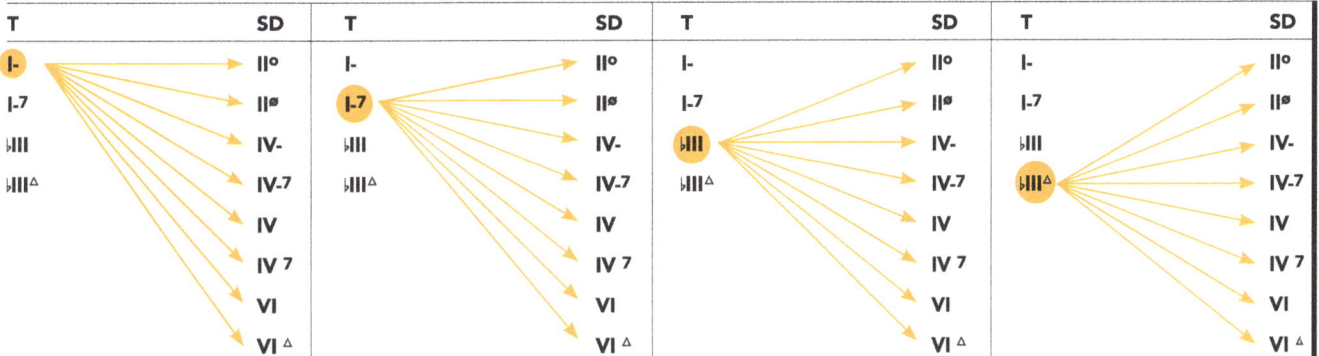

T – SD – D – T Possible Chords: Major Keys

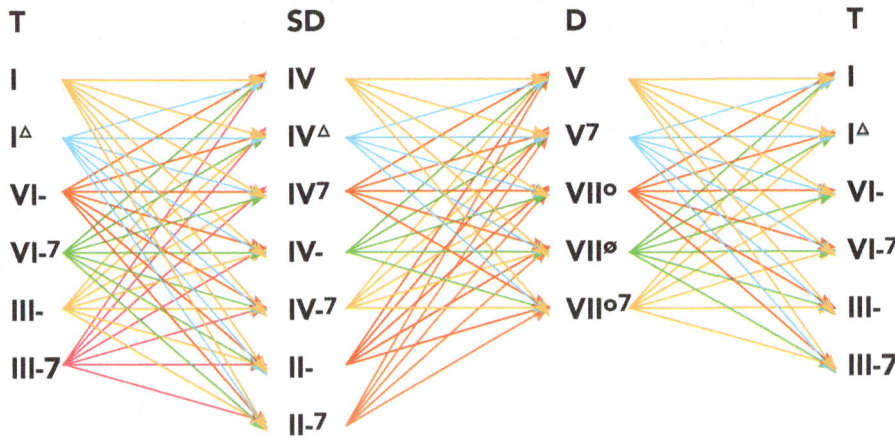

T – SD – D – T Possible Chords: Minor Keys

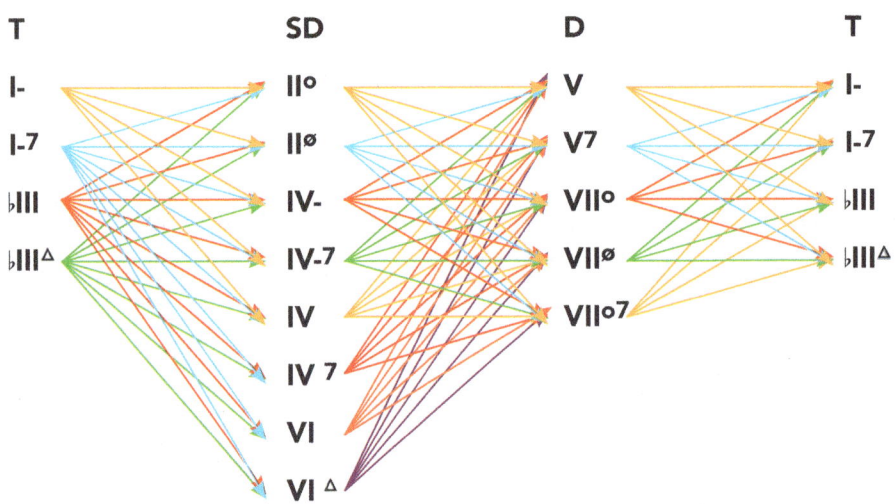

T – SD – D – T Examples

In each example, the harmonic function of each Area is written below the staff, under the Roman Numerals. By looking at common chord progressions, we can see the flow of tension and resolution.

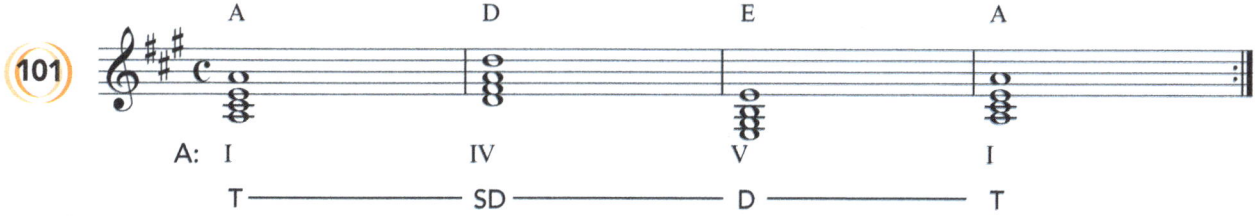

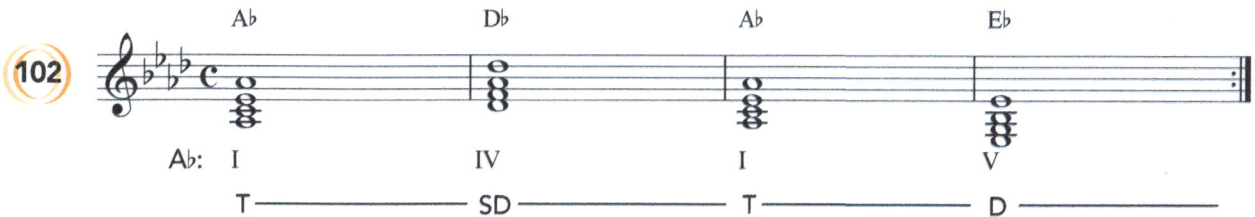

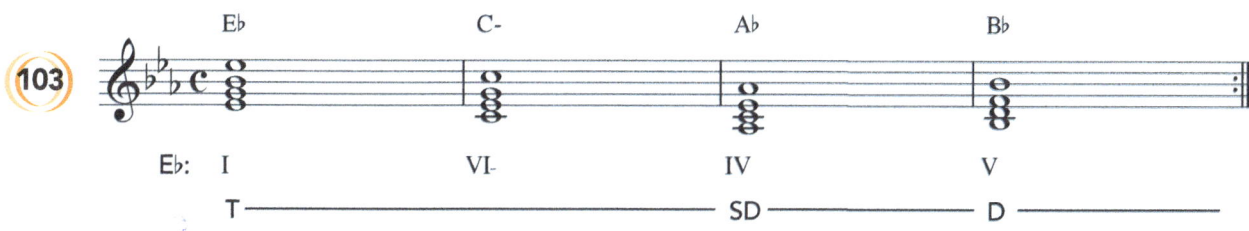

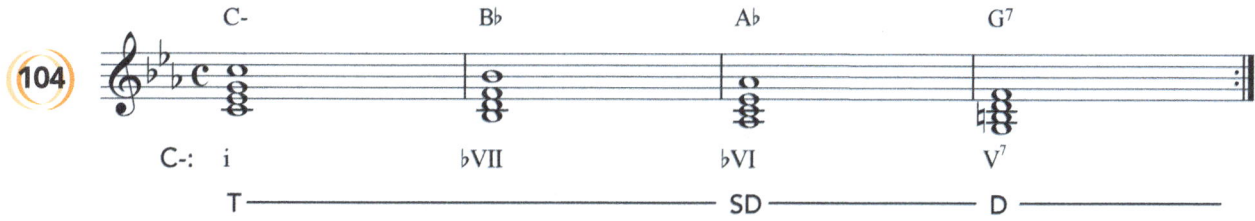

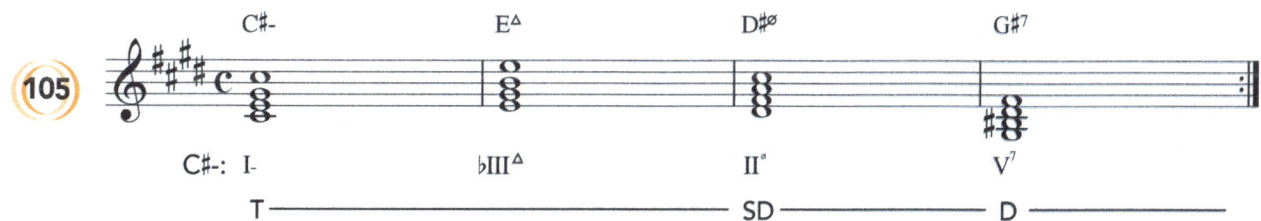

Analysis 5: Harmonic Function 1

Review

- Harmonic function
- Tonal center
- Tonic Area (T)
- Chords that create a Tonic Area in major keys
    - I
    - I△
    - III-
    - III-7
    - VI-
    - VI-7
- Chords that create a Tonic Area in minor keys
    - I-
    - I-7
    - ♭III
    - ♭III△
- Dominant Area (D)
- Chords that create a Dominant Area in major keys
    - V
    - V7
    - VII°
    - VII⌀
    - VII°7
- Chords that create a Dominant Area in minor keys
    - V
    - V7
    - VII°
    - VII°7
- T - D - T (Tonic Dominant Tonic)
- How tension resolves moving from Dominant Area to Tonic Area
    - In major keys
    - In minor keys
- Subdominant Area (SD)
- T - SD - D - T (Tonic Subdominant Dominant Tonic)
- Chords that create a Subdominant Area in major keys
    - II-
    - II-7
    - IV
    - IV△
    - IV7
    - IV-
    - IV-7
- Chords that create a Subdominant Area in minor keys
    - II°
    - II⌀
    - IV
    - IV7
    - IV-
    - IV-7

New Words You Should Know

1. Harmonic function
2. Tonal center
3. Tonic Area
4. Dominant Area
5. Subdominant Area

Pitch and Notes 11: Melody

Finally! In this chapter you will discover how melodies get made and how you can be creative with melodies even if you are "not feeling creative" or "not a creative person."

Melody

A melody is a series of sequential pitches that takes place over time. Many songwriters and composers try to make "pleasing" melodies. What you find pleasing may be different from what someone else thinks of as pleasing. Melody is subjective, which means that everyone can feel differently about a melody, and no one is right or wrong. They have their opinions.

- Often, pleasing melodies have some pattern that implies that the pitches belong together. This is a subjective statement, but much of the time, your pattern-recognizing brain will find and enjoy the patterns of some melodies more than others.

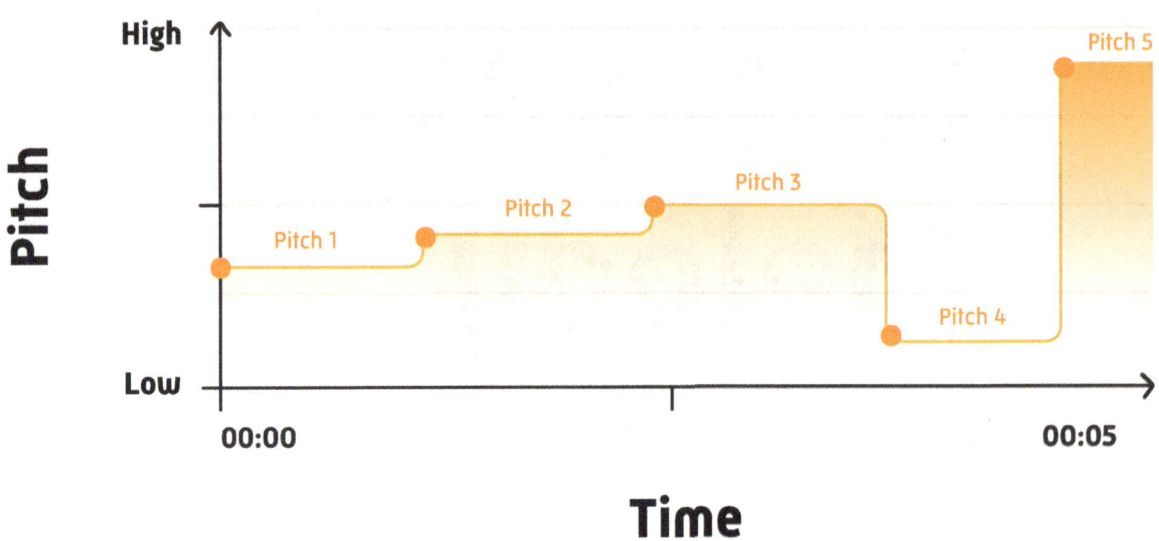

(106) **Melody Example 1**

(107) **Melody Example 2**

What Makes a "Good" Melody?

There are three things every pleasing melody needs.

1. Rhythm
2. Notes
3. Phrases

The stronger each one of these parts is, the "better" a melody will be. Strong does not mean complex. Strong means that the melody is using the right rhythm, notes, and phrasing to make it all come together to translate the emotion or feeling of the music.

This is where we will start to blur the lines between music theory and art.

Motif

- A motif (moh-teef) (also spelled motive) is the smallest recognizable musical idea, also the smallest recognizable part of a melody.
- Motifs are repeated often enough in one song or piece to the point that they are recognizable as belonging to that song or piece.
- A motif can be a rhythmic pattern, also called a rhythmic figure.
- A motif can be a pattern of notes.

Rhythmic Motif

- A rhythmic motif is a rhythmic figure (a specific rhythmic pattern).
- Notes can be in any order. What counts here is the rhythm only.

Beethoven's Fifth Symphony has a recognizable rhythmic motif.

Rhythmic Motif

This is a genius example of taking one simple rhythmic idea and then creating emotionally impactful music. Each time the rhythmic motif is repeated, it is circled in orange. In the second line of music starting at m.6, the 2 violin parts start playing ping-pong with the rhythmic motif.

Fifth Symphony mm. 1-12 Ludwig van Beethoven

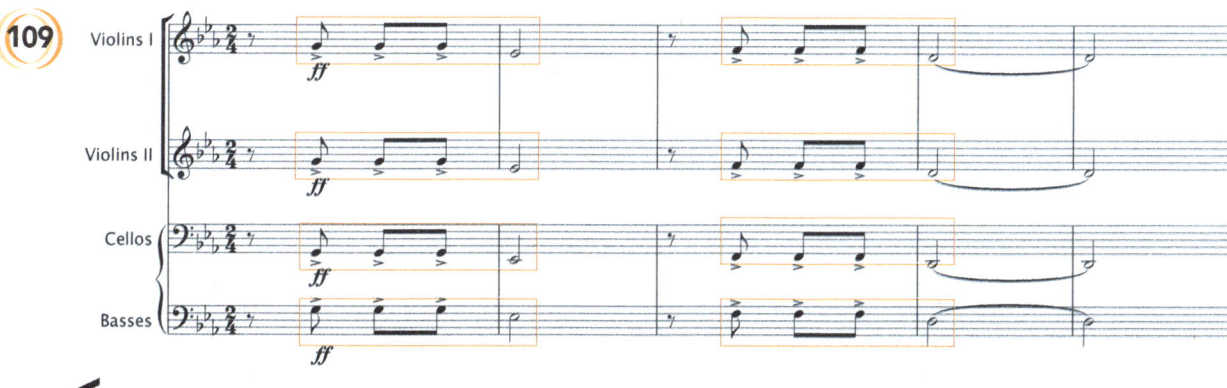

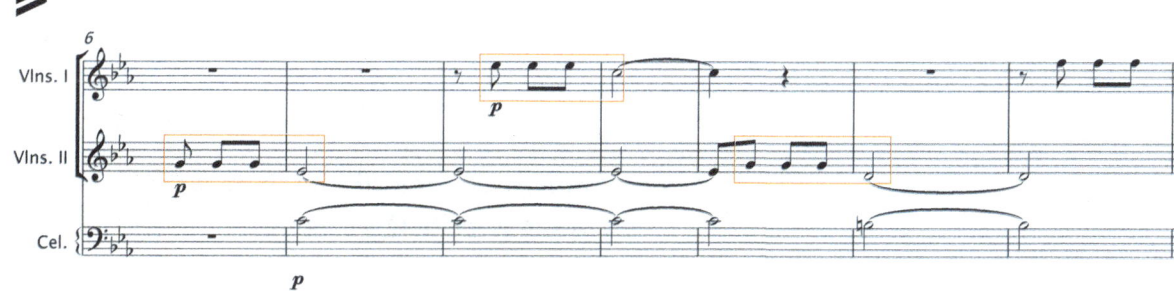

> ⸗ This symbol shows a separation between groups of staves.

Pitch and Notes 11: Melody

Contour Motif (Notes)

- The "contour" is the shape of the melody on the staff. If you played "connect the dots" with the noteheads of the melody, you would see a line going up, down, and flat. That line is the contour—the "shape" made by the intervals between noteheads.
- A contour motif is a short pattern of repeated notes and/or intervals.
- The short pattern that makes up a contour motif could also be called a "melodic fragment" or "melodic idea."

Beethoven's Fifth Symphony has a recognizable contour motif.

Contour Motif   **Contour of the Motif**

(110)

The contour is three repeated notes of the same pitch class and octave register followed by a descending interval of a M3. Each time the contour motif is repeated, it is circled in orange. In some cases, the motif descends by a m3 or P4. In both cases, it is still the same "idea" with some changes.

Fifth Symphony mm. 1-12   Ludwig van Beethoven

(111)

> It is common to call a motif (the rhythm and notes together) an "idea."

148 best music coach | the best music theory book for beginners 3

Motivic Development

There are 13 ways to take a motif (an idea) and develop it. If you write songs or compositions and hit writer's block, these are some of the ways you can take a single idea and turn it into a song!

1. Repetition

> 1. Repetition is the restatement of a motif with the same pitch classes in the same octave register. Repetition can be immediate (right after) or delayed (stuff bweeen repetitions).
> 2. Repetition includes altering pitches with accidentals to change between the parallel major and minor.

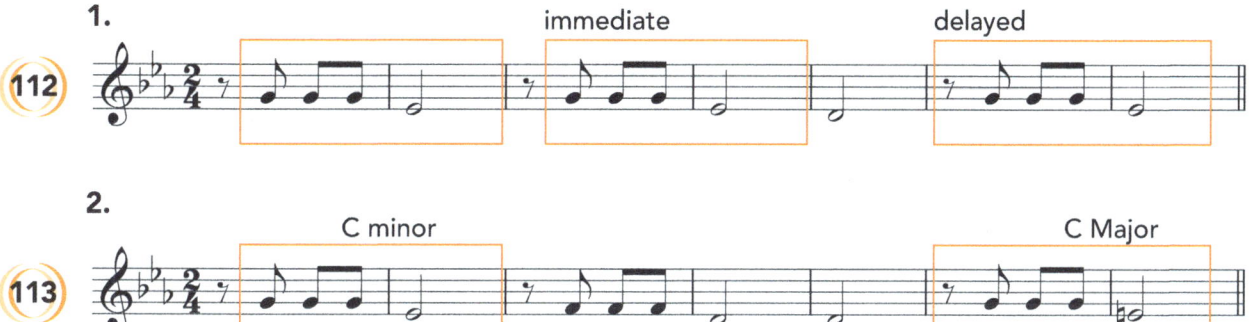

2. Transposition

Transposition is when a note or group of notes is moved up or down by a constant interval. Contour motif transposition makes all the notes sound higher or lower while keeping the same interval relationships between all notes. When you see the word transposition think "changing notes or key."

1. Chromatic Transposition (Exact Interval Quality + Distance)

In chromatic transposition all intervals in a contour motif stay the same quality and distance.

2. Tonal Transposition (Only Using Notes from the Scale of the Key)

Intervals stay the same distance. Intervals are only taken from the scale of the key, which means that the quality of the intervals can change to keep all notes in the key.

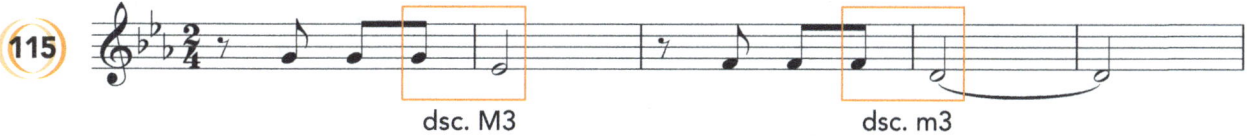

3. Sequence

A sequence is multiple repetitions of the same motif in a row, either ascending or descending in pitch by the same interval distance each time the motif is repeated. Repetitions can be chromatic or diatonic.

1. Diatonic Sequence: Ascending By Thirds

This sequence only uses notes from the scale associated with the key signature (C minor), and each time the motif is repeated, it is a diatonic third higher. Depending on the scale, sometimes the third distance is a m3, and sometimes it is a M3.

2. Chromatic Sequence: Descending By Half-Step (m2)

This sequence is chromatic, so it repeats down by a m2, even if it means notes will no longer be from the scale or in the key.

> Sequences can repeat by any ascnding or descending interval distance.

4. Variation

Variation is making a motif more complex by adding notes or making it simpler by removing notes.

1. Elaboration

The "idea" or "gesture" of the motif stays recognizable. Notes are added to create variation.

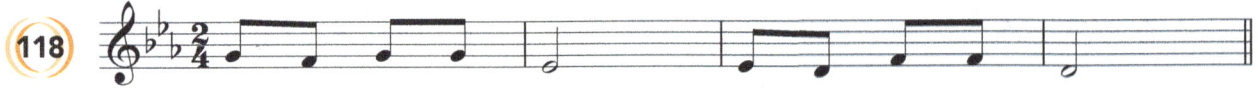

2. Simplification

The "idea" or "gesture" of the motif stays recognizable. Notes are removed to create variation.

5. Fragmentation

Taking a small part of a motif (fragment) and creating one or many new ideas with that fragment.

1. Fragmentation

Presenting only a fragment of the motif. This is fragmentation combined with simplification. This is also a form of Truncation (more on Truncation in a minute).

2. Fragmentation

This is an example from mm. 32-35 of the Violin II part from Beethoven's Fifth symphony. In this example he has taken a fragment of the motif, which is two repeated notes on the same pitch followed by a descending m3, and created a new idea...in which you can still kinda-sorta hear the original motif.

6. Interval Alteration

Interval alteration (also called intervallic alteration) means increasing or decreasing one or more intervals in a motif. Between mm. 9 and 10 of Beethoven's Fifth symphony interval alteration is used to change the descending interval of the motif to a P4 instead of a M3.

Interval Alteration of a Single Interval

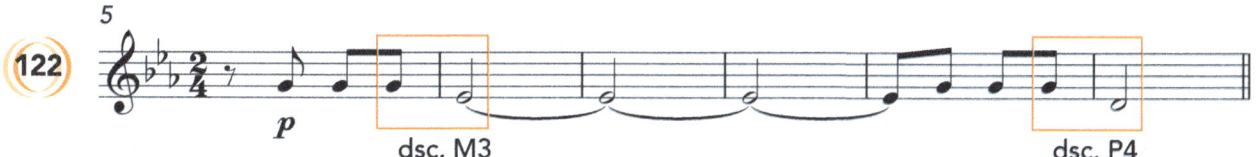

Interval Alteration of More Than One Interval

7. Rhythm Alteration

Rhythm alteration (also called rhythmic alteration) means increasing or decreasing one or more rhythmic values in the motif.

8. Inversion (Horizontal Mirror)

When motifs are inverted, the direction of every inverval after the first note changes: asc. becomes dsc., dsc. becomes asc. Unison invervals remain unison because they do not ascend or descend.
Chromatic inversions = same quality and distance + change asc. to dsc. or dsc. to asc.
Tonal inversions = quality from the scale, same distance + change asc. to dsc. or dsc. to asc.

Tonal Inversion (Only Using Notes from the Scale of the Key)

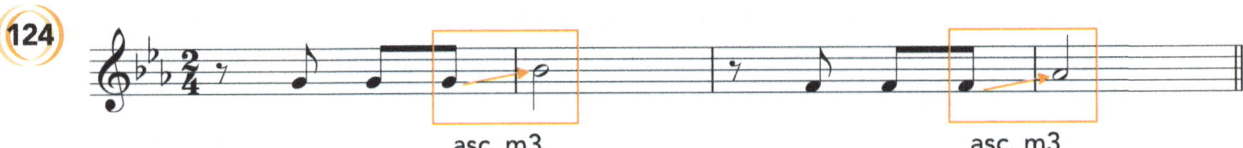

Chromatic Inversion (Same Interval Quality + Distance)

9. Retrograde (Vertical Mirror)

Retrograde is a fancy word for "backward." Flip a motif around backward, keeping the same notes and rhythms, and you have created a retrograde motif! This is like holding a vertical mirror next to the motif.

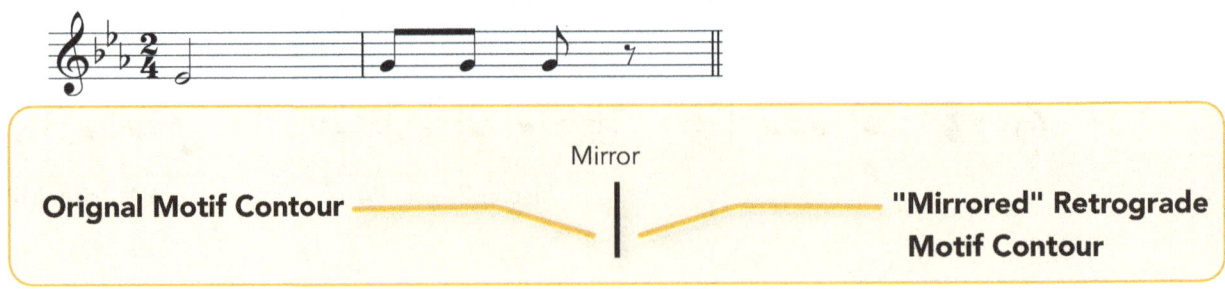

10. Augmentation

Augmentation means that the intervals of the motif remain the same, but the note values increase proportionally. The basic types of augmentation are 2X and 4X the rhythmic value of the note. Below is an example of augmentation in simple meter. You can also use augmentation in compound meter.

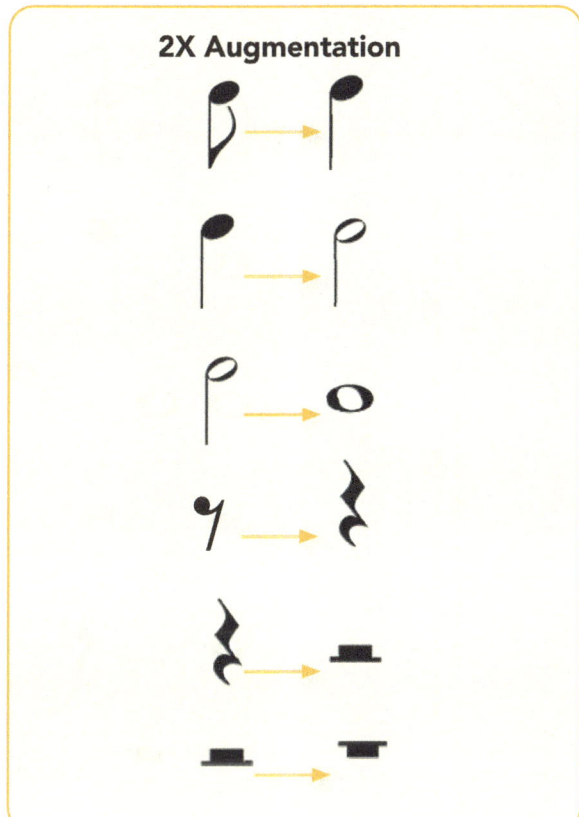

1. Original

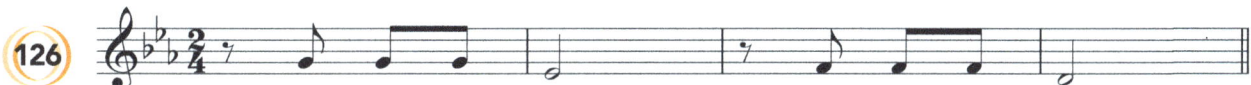

2. 2X Augmentation

3. 4X Augmentation

11. Diminution

Diminution means that the intervals of the motif remain the same, but the note values decrease proportionally. The basic types of diminution are 2÷ and 4÷ the rhythmic value of the note. Below is an example of diminution in simple meter. You can also use diminution in compound meter.

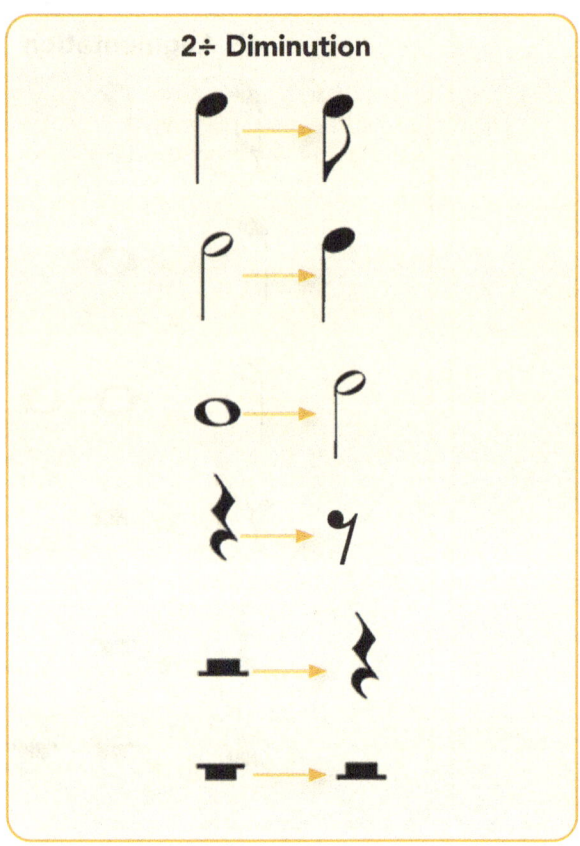
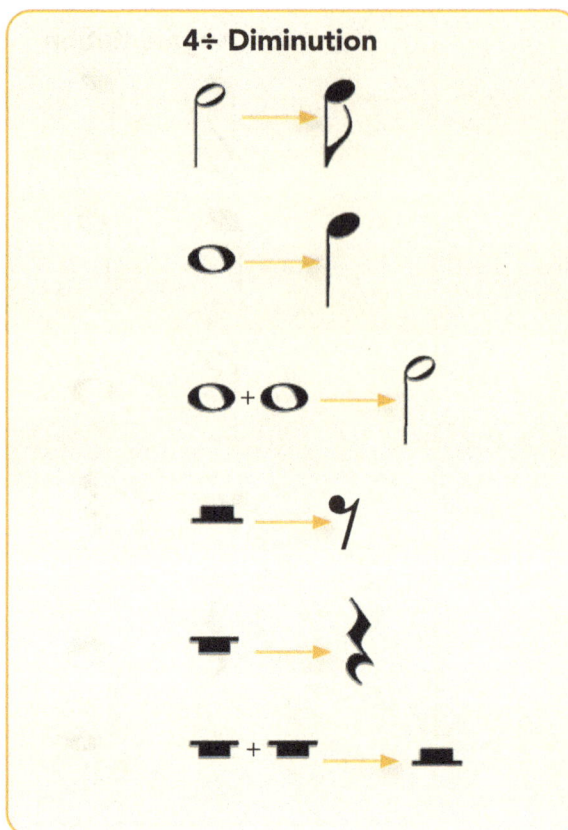

1. 4X Augmentation

2. 2÷ Diminution

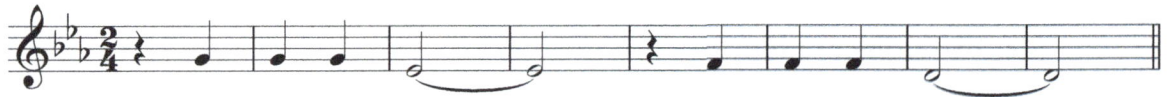

3. Original (4÷ Diminution)

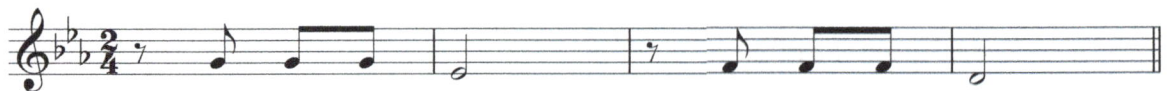

12. Extension

Extension means to take any part of the motif and repeat it to make the duration of the motif longer. You can repeat any number of notes as many or as few times as you want. Repeat some part of it to make it longer.

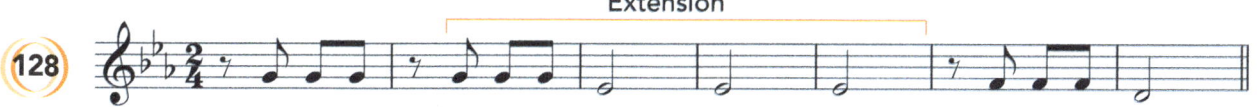

13. Truncation

Truncation means to take any part of the motif and make the duration of the motif shorter. Reduce the motif by any number of notes. Delete some part or parts to make it shorter.

Motif Madness

Combine any of the 13 ways of developing a motif for near-limitless ideas and possibilities. Here are a few ideas.

- Retrograde inversion (backward and upside down!)
- Augmentation truncation (increase note values, but shorten the overall motif)
- Rhythm alteration sequence (change the rhythm as you go through a sequence)
- Create any combination of 2, 3, or more ways of changing a motif!
- By combining the 13 ways, you can create thousands of variations!

Pitch and Notes 11: Melody

Phrase

- A phrase is a substantial musical idea that often ends with tension to resolution.
- The notes in phrases are made up of motifs and developed motifs.
- Phrases are created in music through an interaction of rhythm, notes, and harmony.
- Harmony is not required for a phrase to exist. Harmony serves to highlight the phrasing of the melody and create layers of texture, tension, and resolution that work with and against the melody.
- Sometimes you can quickly spot phrases because they are slurred together.

Basic Phrase

Phrases can be different. Some are more complex than others. We will start with basic phrases.

1. The most basic type of phrase is an 8- or 16-measure **question** and **answer**.
2. The notes of **the question** will end on the dominant or another scale degree. This leaves a sense of tension, which is a sense that something is incomplete.
3. The notes of **the answer** will end on the Tonic, Mediant, or Dominant. This creates a sense of resolution, of arriving home. The end of a story.
4. Basic phrases are made from motifs (ideas) or motifs that have been developed in one or more of the 13 ways you can develop a motif.

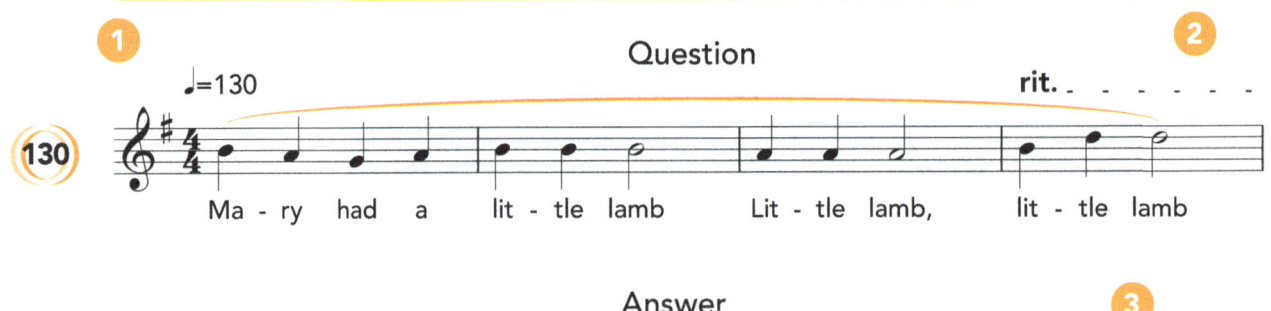

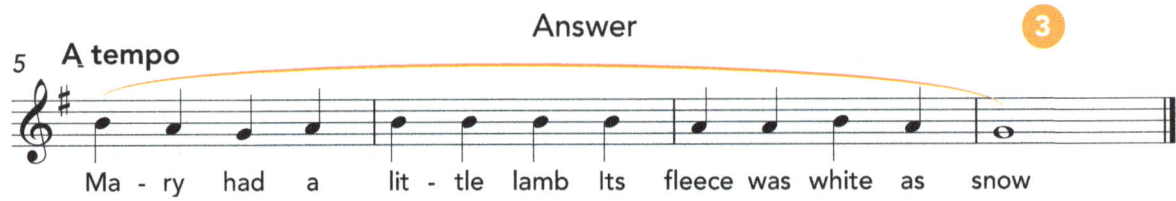

Antecedent and Consequent

- An **antecedent** is the "**question**" part of a phrase.
- A **consequent** is the "**answer**" part of a phrase.
- The question of the antecedent is tension which is resolved by the answer of the consequent.
- Motifs are used and developed to create antecedent and consequent phrases.

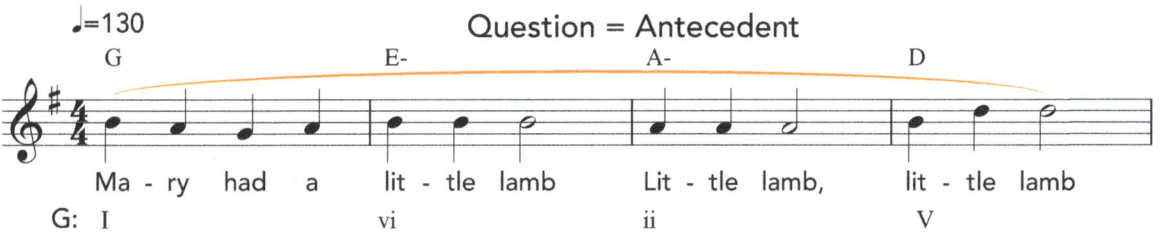

Subphrase

- A subphrase is a part of a phrase, a short, incomplete idea. This is a flexible term.
- In basic phrases, a subphrase will be 2 or 4 measures long.
- The line between subphrase and motif can be unclear. Generally, a motif is a smaller idea than the subphrase. This does not always line up perfectly, since motifs can extend to the length of a subphrase through motivic development.
- A subphrase could also be the antecedent and the consequent.
- In the first line of this example, the antecedent is the subphrase, and in the second line, ideas larger than a motif are the subphrase. Both are correct.

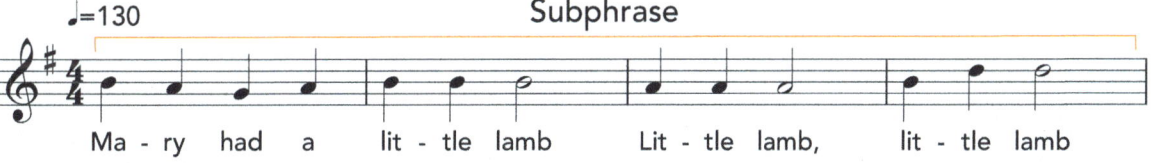

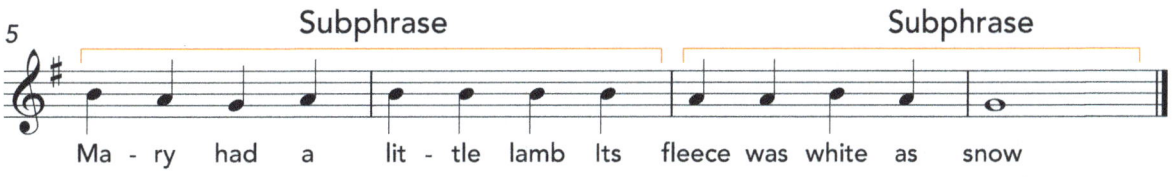

best music coach | the best music theory book for beginners 3

Pitch and Notes 11: Melody

Review

- What makes a melody "good"?
  - Rhythm
  - Notes
  - Phrases

- Motif
- Rhythmic motif
- Contour motif (notes)
- Motivic development
  - Repetition
  - Transposition
  - Sequence
  - Variation
  - Fragmentation
  - Interval alteration
  - Rhythm alteration
  - Inversion
  - Retrograde
  - Augmentation
  - Diminution
  - Extension
  - Truncation

- Phrase
- Basic phrase
  - Question = antecedent
  - Answer = consequent

- Subphrase

New Words You Should Know

1. Motif
2. Rhythm motif
3. Contour motif
4. Motivic development
5. Repetition
6. Transposition
7. Sequence
8. Variation
9. Fragmentation
10. Interval alteration
11. Rhythm alteration
12. Inversion
13. Retrograde
14. Phrase
15. Antecedent
16. Consequent
17. Subphrase
18. Augmentation
19. Diminution
20. Extension
21. Truncation

Analysis 6: Cadences 1

In this chapter you will discover the harmonic part of phrases.

Cadences

- Cadences are chords that move us from one harmonic function Area to another.
- Cadences highlight the notes of the melody (phrases) by creating layers of tension and resolution in the harmony.
- There are 7 common cadence types.

Music in Two Ways: Cadences

Cadences come from classical music. These cadences are also in modern music.

1. Some types of cadences do not apply to lead sheet analysis or writing songs.
2. All cadences apply for writing music that is not a lead sheet, where all chords and all parts of all instruments are written with music notation.

We will use this chapter in two ways.

1. A simple version of this information for understanding lead sheets and writing songs. Lead sheets leave the performer room for interpretation. They do not need to play every note exactly as the composer intended. The performer can bring their own ideas, flare, and style to the music.
2. A more nuanced version that we will use for understanding written music and for writing music that is more than a melody and chord symbols (composing). When it is important for a performer to follow the composer's exact vision, every single note is written down, and includes dynamics, articulations, notes, chords, and rhythms.

Both ways of creating or playing music are different. Neither one is better or worse than the other. Cadences that are important for notation-specific music and lead sheet cadences are mentioned in the cadence rules on each page.

All the cadence examples you are about to see and hear use major and minor triads and seventh chords. There are so many more options you can create using ADD, extensions, and tensions in all chords in all cadences.

Perfect Authentic Cadence: V

An authentic cadence is any time **V** and **I** chords move from the Dominant Area to the Tonic Area with a few rules. This is the most "traditionally" stable cadence.

Perfect Authentic Cadence: Notation

Perfect Authentic Cadence Rules
1. A perfect authentic cadence is a **NOTATION** cadence.
2. The chords must be root position **V** or **V7** to **I** or **I-**.
3. Leading Tone $\hat{7}$ of the scale related to the key must be the highest note of the **V** chord. $\hat{7}$ is the Third of the **V** or **V7** chord.
4. Tonic $\hat{1}$ of the scale related to the key must be the highest note of the **I** or **I-** chord.
5. "Perfect" cadences cannot include major or minor seven chords in the Tonic Area.
6. Tension to resolution arrows are included between Roman Numerals.
7. Labeled as P.A.C. below the staff and under any Roman Numerals.

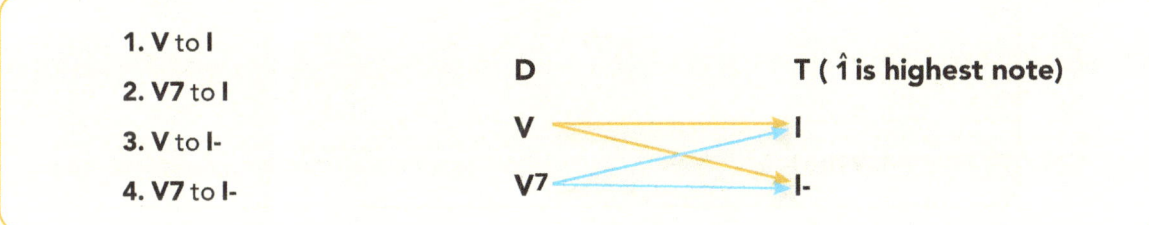

1. **V** to **I**
2. **V7** to **I**
3. **V** to **I-**
4. **V7** to **I-**

D   T ($\hat{1}$ is highest note)
V → I
V7 → I-

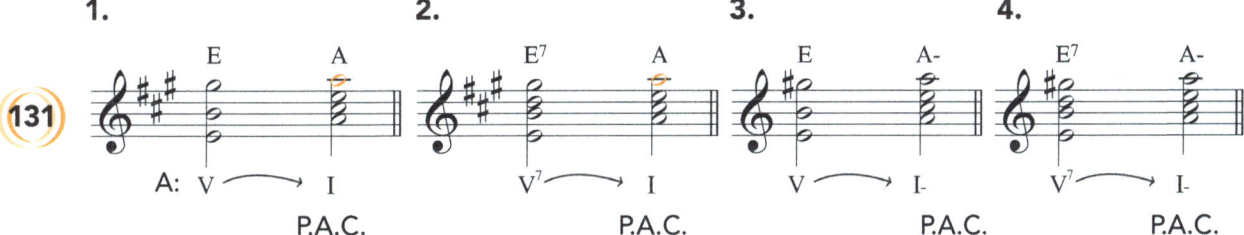

Perfect Authentic Cadence: Lead Sheet

Perfect Authentic Cadence Rules: Lead Sheets
1. You cannot know if a **V** or **V7** to **I** or **I-** cadence in a lead sheet is a P.A.C. because you cannot see the notes that make up the chord. So we generalize and call it an "authentic cadence."
2. Do not write P.A.C. on lead sheets...because we don't know if it is a P.A.C. because we can't see the notes of the chord. Just write the arrow.

Imperfect Authentic Cadence: V

An imperfect authentic cadence is any time chords move from the Dominant Area to the Tonic Area following a few rules. This is "traditionally" less stable and more common in all genres of music than the perfect authentic cadence.

> **Imperfect Authentic Cadence Rules: Notation**
> 1. An imperfect authentic cadence is a **NOTATION** cadence.
> 2. The chords can be root position or any inversion of **V** or **V7** to most qualities of **I** or **I-**.
> 3. The chords can be spelled in any way, including seventh chords in the Tonic Area.
> 4. It does not matter what note is highest in any chord.
> 5. Tension to resolution arrows are included between Roman Numerals.
> 6. Labeled as I.A.C. below the staff and under any Roman Numerals.

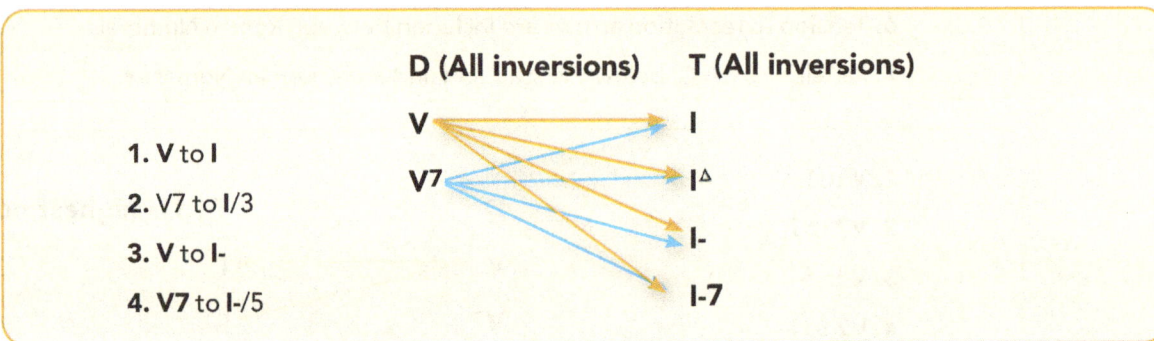

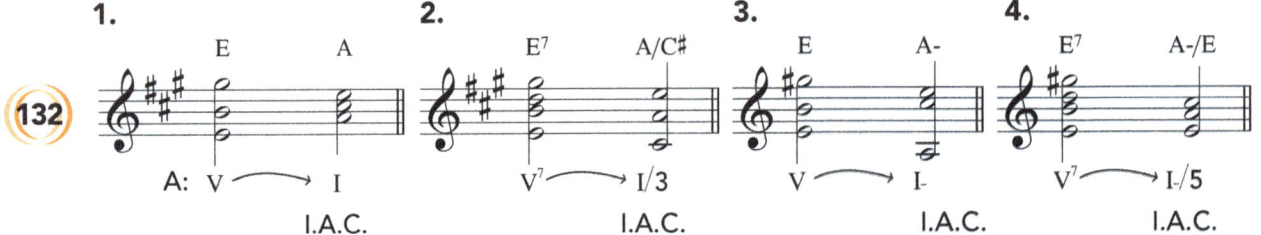

Imperfect Authentic Cadence: Lead Sheet

> **Imperfect Authentic Cadence Rules: Lead Sheets**
> 1. You cannot know if a **V** or **V7** to **I** or **I-** cadence in a lead sheet is an I.A.C. because you cannot see the notes that make up the chord. So we generalize and call it an "authentic cadence."
> 2. All I.A.C.s get a tension resolution arrow between Roman Numerals, like P.A.C.s.
> 3. Do not write I.A.C. on lead sheets...because we don't know if it is an I.A.C. because we can't see the notes of the chord. Just write the arrow.
> 4. There is no difference between a P.A.C. and I.A.C. in lead sheet analysis.

Theory and Art Meet

There are 49 major and 49 minor I.A.C.s that exist. But there are even more than these 98 options. You can find and write these I.A.C.s with different voicings and spellings to create a nearly infinite number of possible I.A.C.s. Once you include ADD chords, extensions, or tensions to all the chords, the number of possible I.A.C.s expands tremendously.

Below is a taste of the possibilities available to you for writing music...and what to look for when you analyze other people's music.

> There are 49 major and 49 minor I.A.C.s if you count all inversions of V, V7, I, I△, I-, I-7.

Your Voice: Your Move

If you want to write your own music, this should be the most exciting news ever. There are so many different ways to navigate the movement from Dominant Area to Tonic Area. This is TWO chords. Imagine the number of possibilities with 3, 4, or 20 chords. You don't need to use all these cadences, but you have a real opportunity to put your stamp on music and say something no one else has said before. It has not "all been done before." We await your music with excitement.

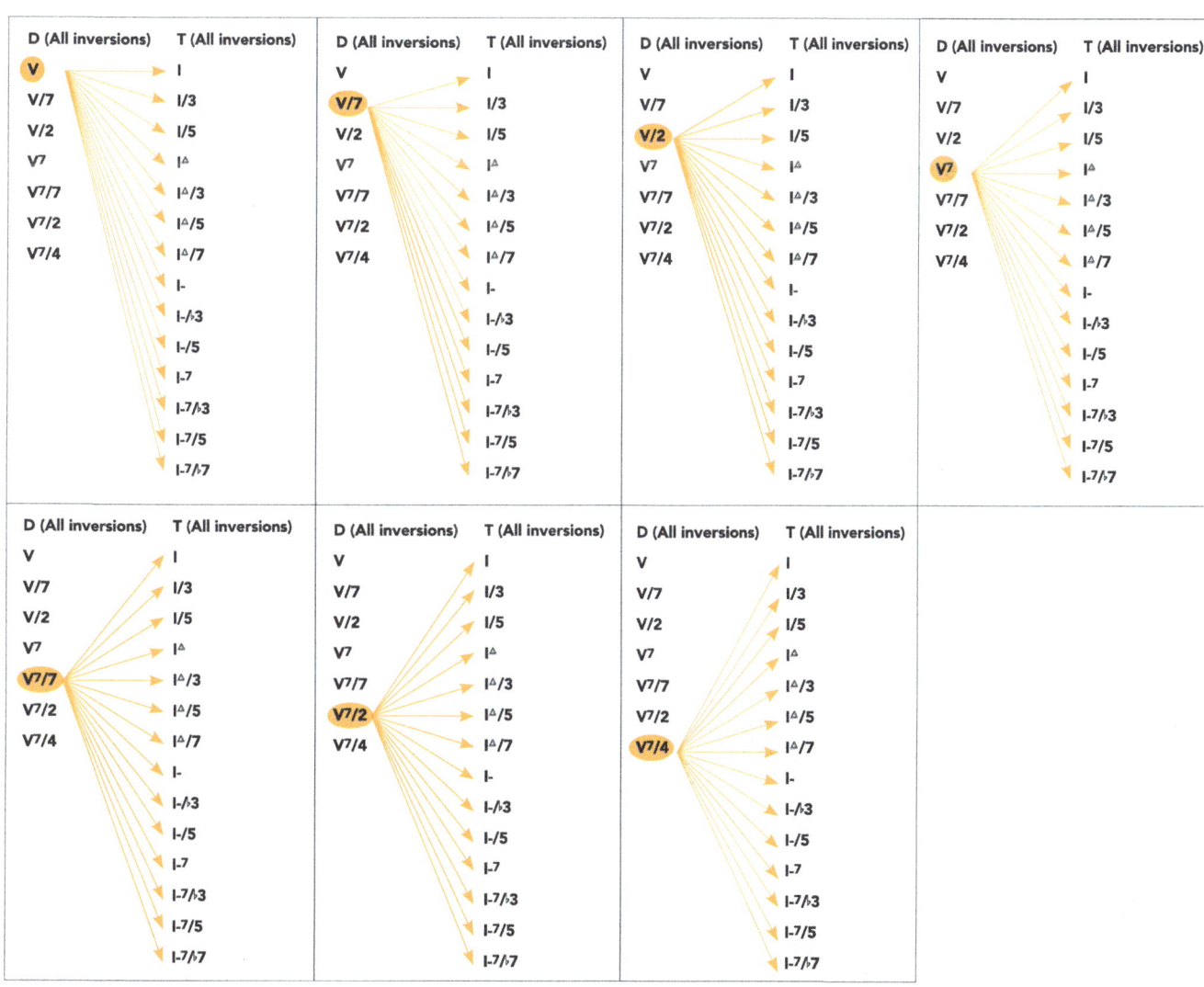

Leading Tone Imperfect Authentic Cadence: VII°

Leading Tone Imperfect Authentic Cadence Rules: Notation

1. A leading tone imperfect authentic cadence is a **NOTATION** cadence.
2. Chords can be root position or inversions of **VII°** or **VIIø** or **VII°7** to most qualities of Tonic Area **I** chords.
3. The chords can be spelled in any way, including seventh chords in the Tonic Area.
4. It does not matter what note is highest in any chord.
5. The dotted tension to resolution arrow shows that the chords' **Root notes** resolve up by 1 half-step. **V/7** (a **V** chord in first inversion) resolves to **I** or **I-** by 1 half-step, but not by Root movement. The half-step is created through an inversion, so no dotted arrow.
6. Labeled as L.T.I.A.C. below the staff and under any Roman Numerals.

1. VII° to I
2. VII° to I△
3. VIIø to I
4. VIIø to I△
5. VII°7 to I
6. VII°7 to I△

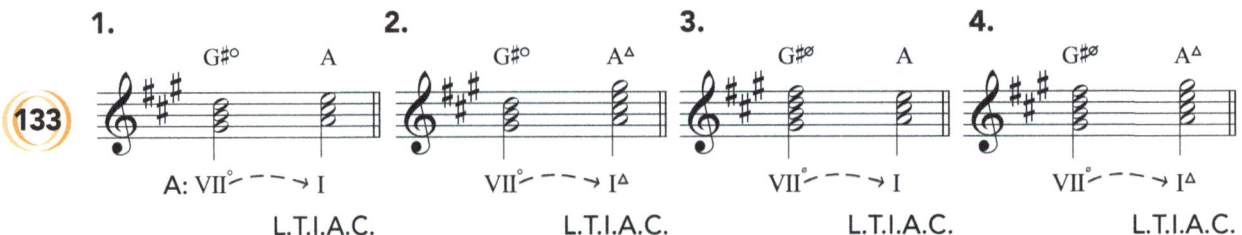

164 best music coach | the best music theory book for beginners 3

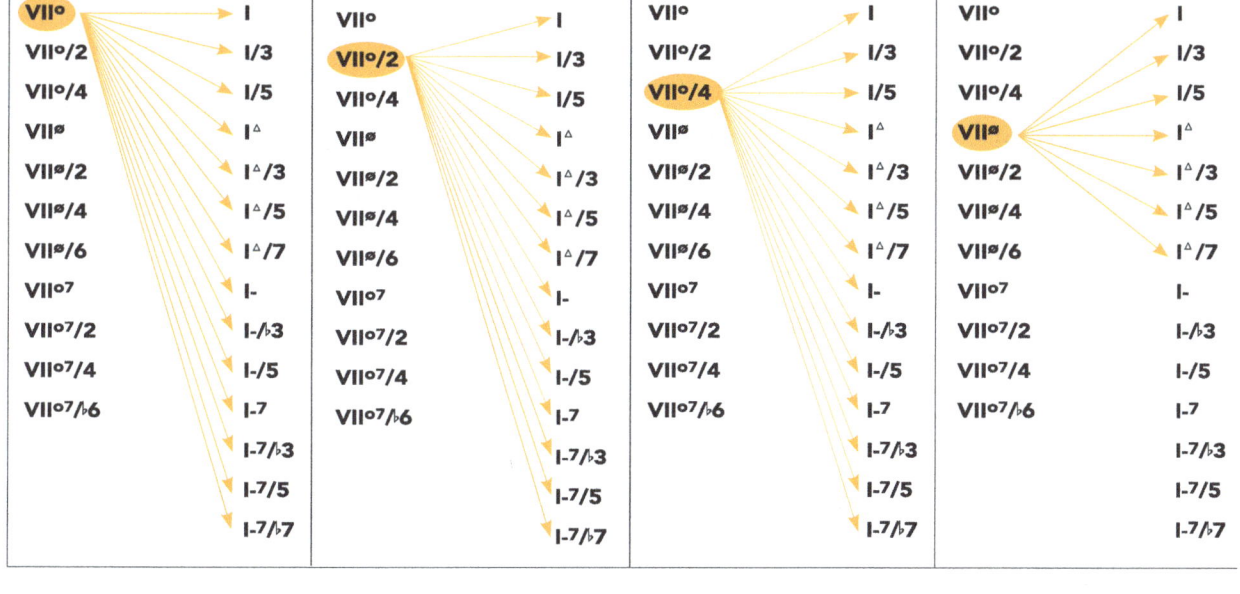

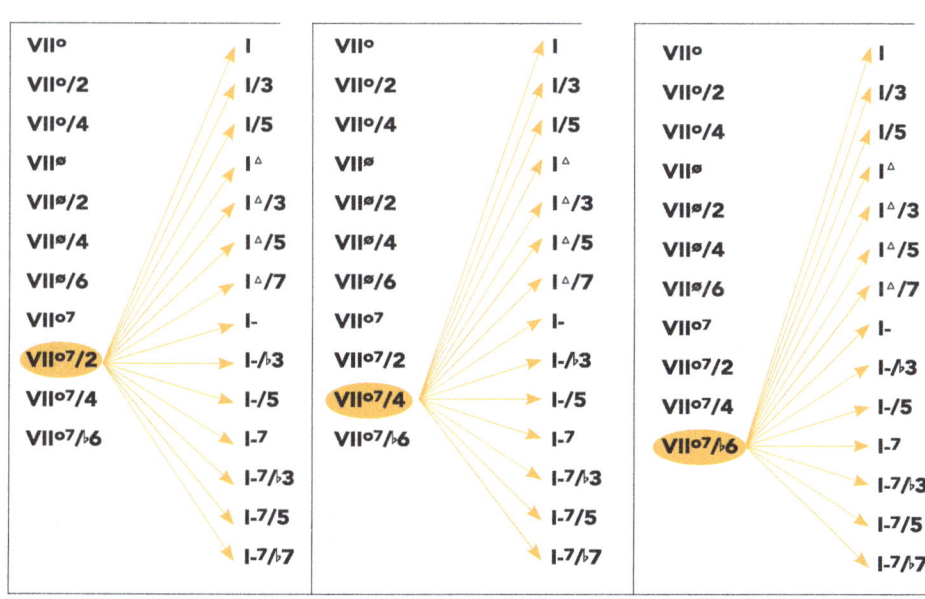

Analysis 6: Cadences 1

best music coach | the best music theory book for beginners 3   165

Analysis 6: Cadences 1

> 7. VII° to I-
> 8. VII° to I-7
> 9. VII°7 to I-
> 10. VII°7 to I-7

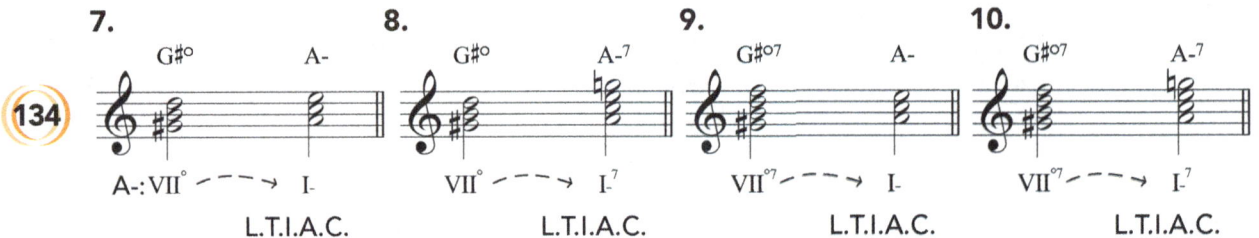

Leading Tone Imperfect Authentic Cadence: Lead Sheet

Leading Tone Imperfect Authentic Cadence Rules: Lead Sheets

1. Any chord that is diminished, half diminished, or fully diminished and resolves up to a chord that is 1 half-step higher gets a dotted tension to resolution arrow.
2. Do not write L.T.I.A.C. on lead sheets, use the dotted arrow.

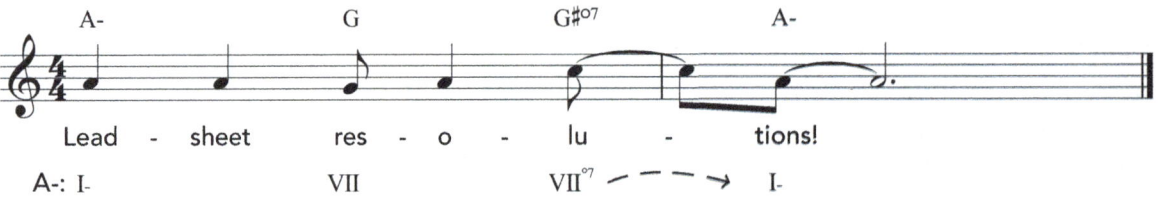

166   best music coach | the best music theory book for beginners 3

Plagal Cadence

A plagal cadence is a phrase ending with a movement of gentle resolution from the Subdominant Area **IV** chord to the Tonic area **I** or **I-** chord. Plagal cadences can sound more "modern" than authentic cadences.

> **Plagal Cadence Rules: Notation + Lead Sheet**
> 1. A plagal cadence in major keys includes a **IV** chord with the qualities of major, major seven, minor, minor seven, minor add 6, and dominant.
> 2. Minor keys can borrow **IV** chords with the qualities of major and dominant. The Seventh of **IV**△ is the $\hat{3}$ of the parallel major scale. You can try using it, but it is not commonly found in modern music because the $\hat{3}$ clashes with $\flat\hat{3}$ in the key.
> 3. The notes in the melody do not matter, just the chords and chord symbols.
> 4. Labeled as P.C. below the staff and below any Roman Numerals.

Major Plagal Cadences

> 1. **IV** to **I**
> 2. **IV** to **I**△
> 3. **IV**△ to **I**
> 4. **IV**△ to **I**△
> 5. **IV7** to **I**
> 6. **IV7** to **I**△
> 7. **IV-** to **I**
> 8. **IV-** to **I**△
> 9. **IV-7** to **I**
> 10. **IV-7** to **I**△

Minor Plagal Cadences

11. IV to I-
12. IV to I-7
13. IV7 to I-
14. IV7 to I-7
15. IV- to I-
16. IV- to I-7
17. IV-7 to I-
18. IV-7 to I-7

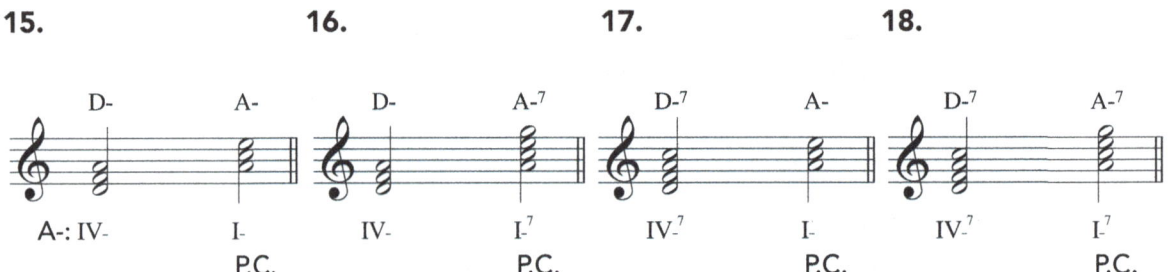

The Major Seven Clash

It is rare to find a **IV∆** in a minor key because the Seventh of the **IV∆** is $\hat{3}$, which can be dissonant against the $\flat\hat{3}$ that is found in the scale and key.

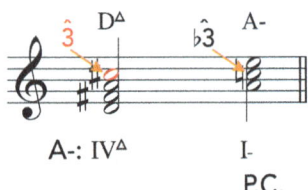

> There are so many more cadence options once you start using inversions, ADD, extensions, and tensions in chords! My personal favorite is iv-ADD6 to I.

Half Cadence

A half cadence is any time a phrase ends on a **V** chord in a Dominant Area without resolving to a Tonic Area. This creates a feeling of unresolved tension. Half cadences can be easy to spot when they are at the end of a line of staff. They also appear at the ends of subphrases in the middle of lines of measures.

> **Half Cadence Rules: Notation + Lead Sheet**
> 1. The notes in the melody do not matter. Look only at the chords and/or chord symbols.
> 2. Labeled as H.C. below the staff and under any Roman Numerals.

> 1. Major key phrase ending on **V**
> 2. Major key phrase ending on **V7**
> 3. Minor key phrase ending on **V**
> 4. Minor key phrase ending on **V7**

1.

2.

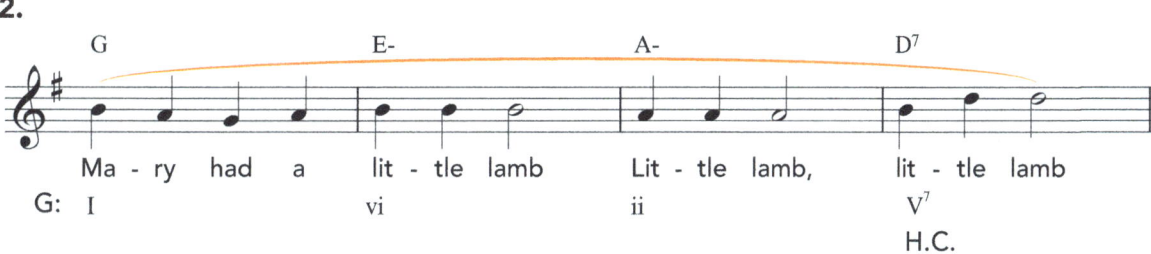

3.

4.

best music coach | the best music theory book for beginners 3

Deceptive Cadence

A deceptive cadence is when a phrase ends by moving from the Dominant Area to a chord that is not built from $\hat{1}$, the tonic (**I** or **I-**). A deceptive cadence makes your ears expect the phrase to resolve with certain chords and at the last moment, changes the direction of where you thought the chords were going.

> **Deceptive Cadence Rules: Notation + Lead Sheet**
> 1. A deceptive cadence starts on **V** and ends on a chord that is not built from $\hat{1}$ (**I** or **I-**).
> 2. The notes in the melody do not matter. Look at the chords and chord symbols.
> 3. Labeled as D.C. below the staff and under any Roman Numerals. Not to be confused with D.C. al Fine or D.C. al Coda.

> 1. Major key phrase ending with a deceptive cadence on **IV** instead of **I**.
> 2. Minor key phrase ending with deceptive cadence on ♭**II**^Δ instead of **I-**. This cadence works well because the G is the Seventh of the A♭^Δ chord
>   (Yes, ♭II^Δ is a real thing...more on this later).

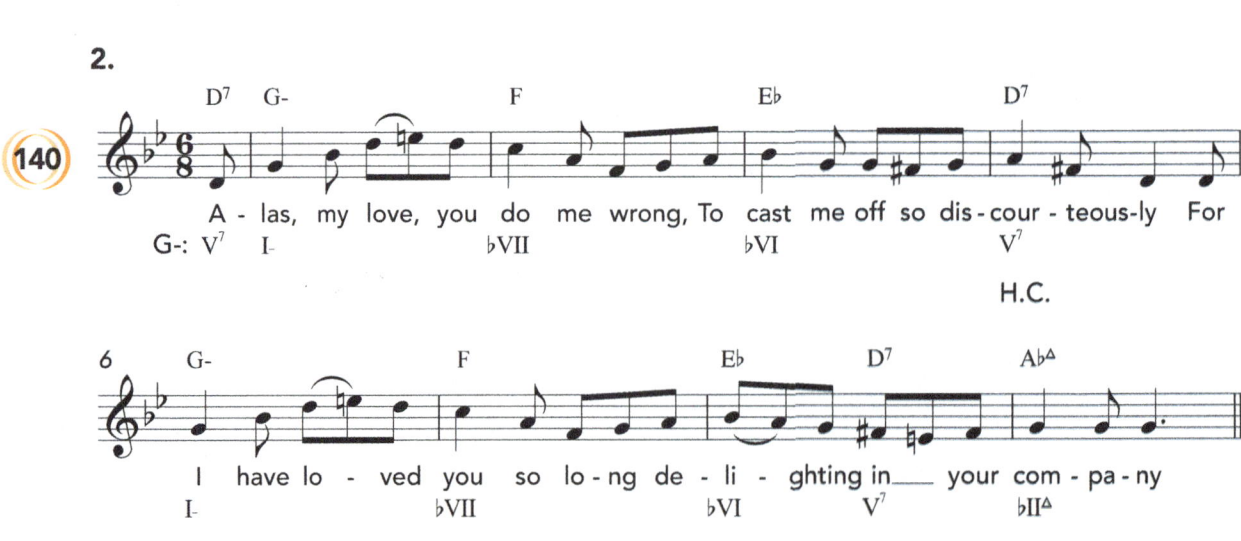

SD - D Cadence

Dominant Areas that resolve to Tonic Areas have an arrow that shows the movement from tension to resolution. The Subdominant Area can lead to the big moment of Dominant to Tonic tension and resolution.

- The Subdominant Area's job (function) is to create this moment of excitement, anticipation and leads to the tension of the Dominant Area.
- The Subdominant Area does not always lead to the Dominant Area.

Some ways to think about the Subdominant Area

1. Subdominant anticipation is like a baseball pitcher throwing a ball. This leads to a moment of tension. Will the batter get a hit? Will the batter miss? If the batter misses, will it be a strike or a ball?
2. Subdominant anticipation is like sitting in a restaurant after your food is ordered. You anticipate the meal you are about to have. You are hungry...you might even glance around to see if a waiter is carrying your food. You smell the food from other people's meals and this builds your excitement. When will the food come out? Will it be as good as you imagine? How long will you wait?

How to Show SD - D Cadence

The movement from Subdominant to Dominant Area is labeled with an upside down bracket, below the Roman Numerals for the chords in the Subdominant and Dominant Areas.

SD - D = ⌐‾‾‾‾‾‾‾‾‾‾¬

1. Major key SD to D
2. Minor key SD to D

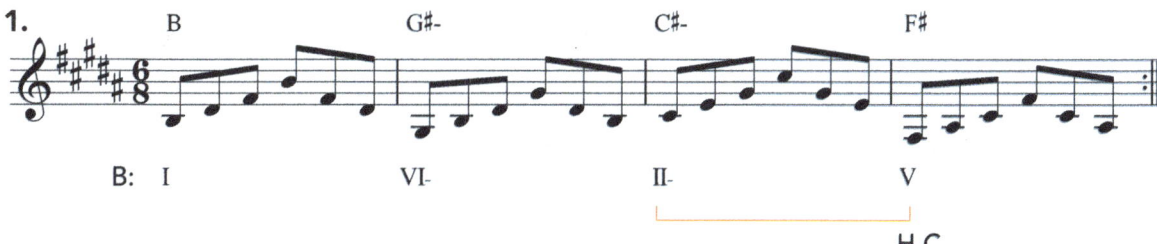

SD – D Possible Chords: Major Keys

SD	D
IV	V
IV△	V7
IV7	VII°
IV-	VIIø
IV-7	VII°7
II-	
II-7	

SD	D
IV	V
IV△	V7
IV7	VII°
IV-	VIIø
IV-7	VII°7
II-	
II-7	

SD	D
IV	V
IV△	V7
IV7	VII°
IV-	VIIø
IV-7	VII°7
II-	
II-7	

SD	D
IV	V
IV△	V7
IV7	VII°
IV-	VIIø
IV-7	VII°7
II-	
II-7	

SD	D
IV	V
IV△	V7
IV7	VII°
IV-	VIIø
IV-7	VII°7
II-	
II-7	

SD	D
IV	V
IV△	V7
IV7	VII°
IV-	VIIø
IV-7	VII°7
II-	
II-7	

SD	D
IV	V
IV△	V7
IV7	VII°
IV-	VIIø
IV-7	VII°7
II-	
II-7	

SD - D Possible Chords: Minor Keys

SD	D	SD	D	SD	D
II°	V	II°	V	II°	V
IIø	V7	**IIø**	V7	IIø	V7
IV-	VII°	IV-	VII°	**IV-**	VII°
IV-7	VIIø	IV-7	VIIø	IV-7	VIIø
IV	VII°7	IV	VII°7	IV	VII°7
IV 7		IV 7		IV 7	
VI		VI		VI	
VI △		VI △		VI △	

SD	D	SD	D	SD	D
II°	V	II°	V	II°	V
IIø	V7	IIø	V7	IIø	V7
IV-	VII°	IV-	VII°	IV-	VII°
IV-7	VIIø	IV-7	VIIø	IV-7	VIIø
IV	VII°7	**IV**	VII°7	IV	VII°7
IV 7		IV 7		**IV 7**	
VI		VI		VI	
VI △		VI △		VI △	

SD	D	SD	D
II°	V	II°	V
IIø	V7	IIø	V7
IV-	VII°	IV-	VII°
IV-7	VIIø	IV-7	VIIø
IV	VII°7	IV	VII°7
IV 7		IV 7	
VI		VI	
VI △		**VI △**	

SD - D When To Use It?

Use the SD to D bracket in all genres. It clearly shows movement from the Subdominant to Dominant Areas. In classical analysis you may only see "T SD D T" with lines below Roman Numerals.

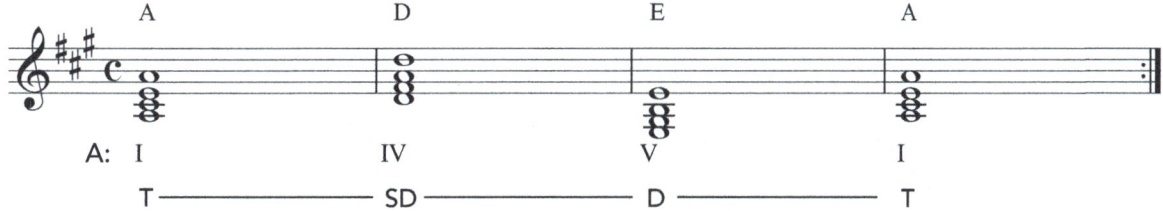

A: I — IV — V — I
T ——— SD ——— D ——— T

sus Chord Extra Tension Before Resolution

sus4 chords have been used for hundreds of years to create tension and resolution within the already existing tension of a **V** chord. sus4 chords are still used in this way in all modern genres.

- Can be used to create a mini SD - T tension resolution inside any **V** or **V7** chord.
- Can be used to extend the Dominant Area within a Perfect Authentic Cadence.
- Can be used to extend the Dominant Area within an Imperfect Authentic Cadence.
- Can be used to extend the Dominant Area within a Half Cadence.
- Can be used to extend the Dominant Area within a Deceptive Cadence.
- Does not have to be used in a cadence.
- Voicing and inversion does not matter. All that matters is the movement from Fourth to Third within the **V** chord.

V 4-3

We will think of the sus4 to triad or sus4 to seventh chord mini tension and resolution as happening inside one chord instead of two separate chords. Analyze this movement as 4-3 to show the movement from the Fourth of the **V** chord down to the Third of the **V** chord.

$$V\,4\text{--}3 \qquad V^7\,4\text{--}3$$

V 4-3 Triad And Seventh Chord

(141)

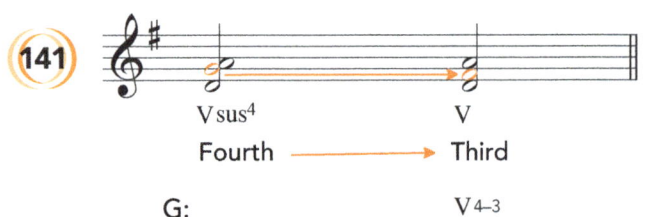

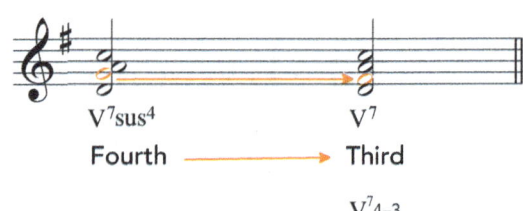

When a Phrase Does Not Line Up with Measures

Anticipation

When notes or chords start before a measure after the music has started, it is anticipation because we generally expect changes to happen at the start of new measures. If the anticipation breaks the expected pattern of the metric hierarchy, then it is also syncopation. Anticipation can create tension between melody and chords. When one pushes forward and the other stays in place.

> 1. Melody anticipation. m.1 melody starts before the double bar line (new section) in m. 2.
> 2. Melody and chord anticipation. m. 2 melody and guitar start before downbeat of m. 3.
> 3. Chord anticipation. m. 3 guitar plays eighth note early; vocals start on downbeat of m. 4.

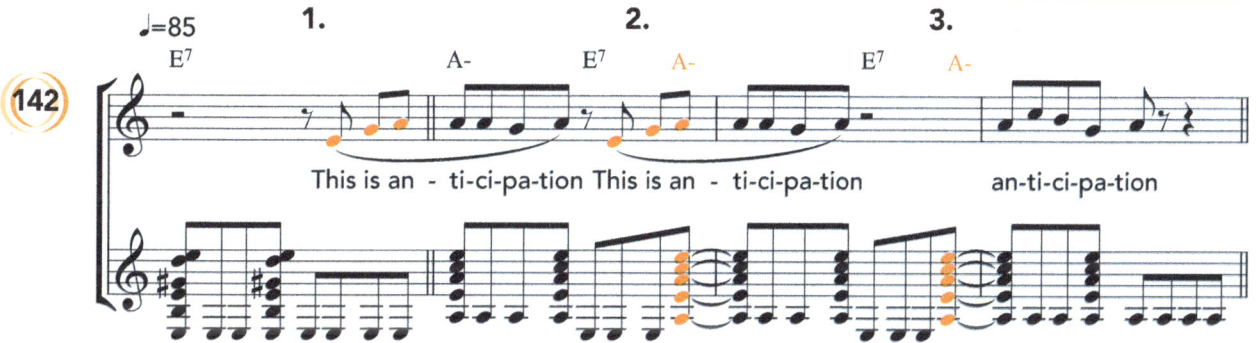

Delay

The opposite of anticipation is delay, when notes or chords change or start after the measure. How do we tell the difference between extreme anticipation and delay? Delay will be moved back from the start of a section of a song or back from the start of a phrase.

> 1. Melody delay. m. 2 melody starts after the double bar line (new section).
> 2. Melody and chord delay. m. 3 melody idea and guitar start after the downbeat.
> 3. Chord delay. m. 4 guitar starts after the downbeat.

How to Think About Anticipation and Delay

In analysis think of the anticipation and delay as a small shift away from the phrase or typical placement of a chord or cadence.. In general, no action is needed from you when an anticipation of a note, chord, or cadence is present. Think of the music as if the anticipation was not there to determine phrases, chords, and cadences. Below is the same rhythm, moved forward and backward by 1 beat to create anticipation and delay.

Anticipation

Delay

Review

- Cadence
- Perfect Authentic Cadence
    - P.A.C. major keys
    - P.A.C. minor keys
- Imperfect Authentic Cadence
    - I.A.C. major keys
    - I.A.C. minor keys
- Leading Tone Imperfect Authentic Cadence
    - L.T.I.A.C. major keys
    - L.T.I.A.C. minor keys
- Plagal Cadence
    - P.C. major keys
    - P.C. minor keys
- Half Cadence
    - H.C. major keys
    - H.C. minor keys
- Deceptive Cadence
    - D.C. major keys
    - D.C. minor keys
- SD - D Cadence
    - SD - D major keys
    - SD - D minor keys
- sus4 tension and resolution in a **V** chord
    - V 4–3
    - V^7 4–3
- Anticipation
- Delay

New Words You Should Know

1. Cadence
2. Perfect Authentic Cadence
3. Imperfect Authentic Cadence
4. Leading Tone Imperfect Authentic Cadence
5. Plagal Cadence
6. Half Cadence
7. Deceptive Cadence
8. Anticipation

Analysis 7: Borrowed Chords Bonanza

Buckle up for a borrowed chords bonanza!

Roman Numeral Reality Check

You can take any chord or chord quality and use it in any key. We will think of this as "borrowing" chords and qualities from other harmonized scales. Another way of thinking about this is called "mode mixture," and the next book covers this in more detail.

In some music all chords follow the quality formula of their harmonized scales. Songs that borrow different chords from different keys and scales are commonly found in pop, gospel, R&B, jazz, fusion, cinematic music, and video game music.

> **Be ready to find any quality of chord built on any scale degree.**

How to Recognize and Analyze a Key Change

A key change is when a piece of music changes key for more than a few measures. It is common to find a group of chords in a row that is outside the key. Chords that come from outside the key are generally creating or implying new Tonic, Subdominant, and Dominant Areas (more on this in upcoming pages). This is not a key change.

Key Change

You will see a double bar line and a new key signature for "real" key changes. For analysis, write the new key letter and quality under the staff of the first measure of the key change, like you do at the start of pieces of music. Then continue analyzing the music in the new key.

The key change below is a complete transposition of the notes and chords to a different key. The Roman Numerals stay the same because the chords and notes keep the same relationship to each other, moved up by M6.

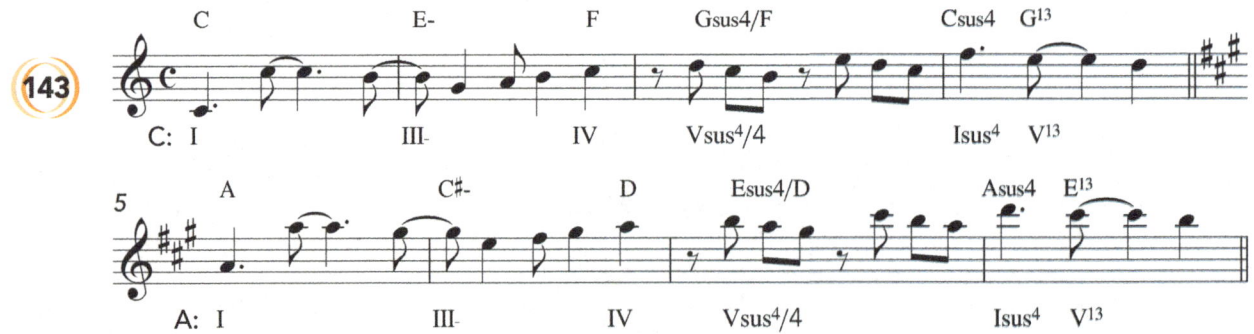

Borrowed Chords from Parallel Keys

Borrowed chords from parallel keys are common. Borrowed chords are not a key change.

> **Borrowed Chords From Parallel Keys Rules**
> 1. Use the scale degree system and write ♭ in front of any Roman Numeral that is harmonized from a note that is one half-step lower than it would be for the major scale.
> 2. If you are writing music, look to the Tonic Area chords to figure out if the key is major or minor. Also look for the chord built on $\hat{1}$ (the Tonic scale degree) because this chord is the most important to determine the key.
> 3. You can look at a key signature if performing an analysis.
> 4. There is no limit to the number of chords you can borrow or will find borrowed from parallel major and minor keys.

Borrowed From Parallel Minor

This is a common borrowed chord progression that is close to a common minor chord progression. The switch happens in m. 3. Typically we would see a C- here, but wow, the C creates a different emotional sound! Why is this progression not in the key of C- with a borrowed C major? C is the Tonic and is the Tonic Area, giving the major chord the defining power over the key. In cases where we already heard this progression a few times with the C-, then as a contrast we hear the C major, it would be correct to think of the music as being in the key of C- with the C is borrowed from the parallel major.

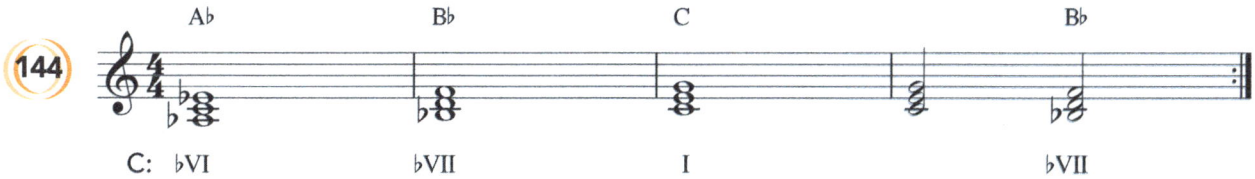

Borrowed From Parallel Major

This chord progression walks up a C minor scale...with a twist! In m. 2, the chord harmonized from $\hat{2}$ is not diminished; it is minor, borrowed from C major. In m. 4, the chord harmonized from $\hat{4}$ is major instead of minor. A jazzy, modern sound, borrowing 2 chords from the parallel major.

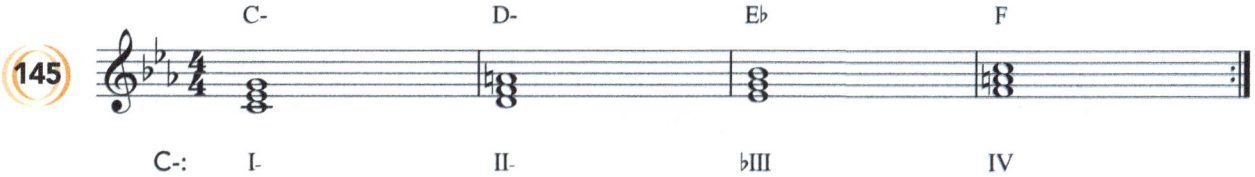

Secondary Dominants

- Secondary dominant chords are the quality of dominant seven.
- Secondary dominant chords can be altered chords.
- Secondary dominants are mini tension resolution movements that are not always cadences. It is a mini Dominant to Tonic Area movement.
- Secondary dominants serve the function of a mini Dominant Area that makes the next chord "feel" and "become anticipated" like a chord in a Tonic Area.
- Secondary dominants resolve to a "target" chord that is not built from harmonizing $\hat{1}$.

How Do Secondary Dominants Work?

- Normally, the only dominant chord in a key is built from $\hat{5}$. Secondary dominants are built from $\hat{5}$ of their target chords.
- Secondary dominants can be built on $\hat{5}$ of $\hat{2}$, $\hat{3}$, $\hat{4}$, $\hat{5}$, $\hat{6}$, **and $\hat{7}$**. This is why they are secondary. These chord are not created by harmonizing the scale of the key of the music.

You can pick any chord from a harmonized scale (besides the **I** or **I-** chord) and say:

1. "The Root of this chord is now the Tonic $\hat{1}$."
2. Then, walk up the major scale of that new Tonic from $\hat{1}$ to $\hat{5}$. (Whole, Whole, Half, Whole)
3. Then, build a dominant chord on the new $\hat{5}$ of the new $\hat{1}$.
4. You could also think forward one step in the circle of fifths to find the dominant of any chord. C to G, G to D, D to A, A to E, E to B, etc.

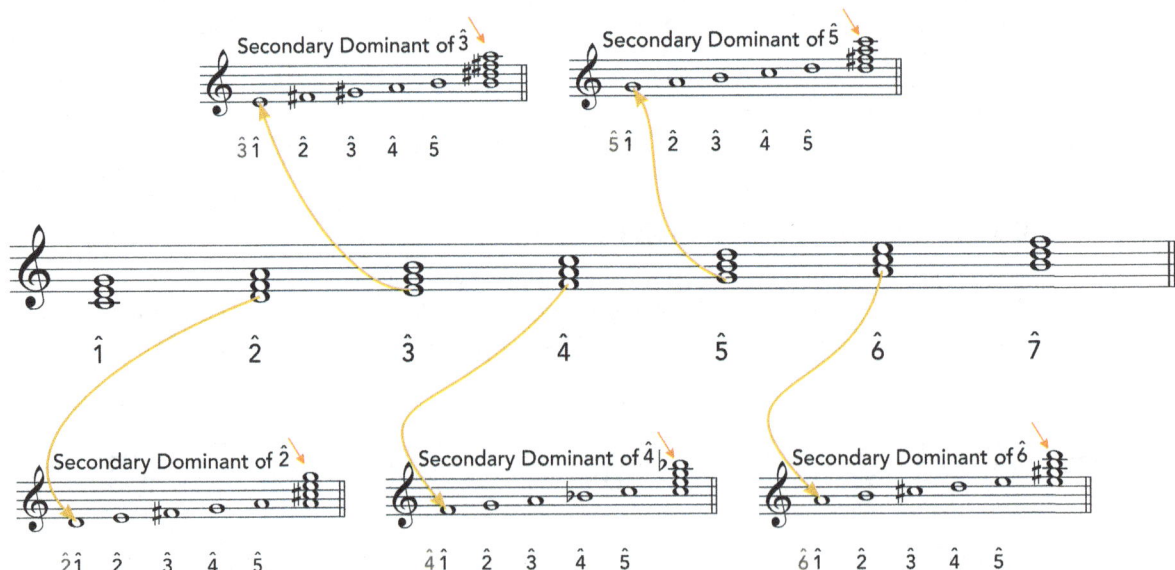

How to Recognize Secondary Dominants

> 1. Notation: a secondary dominant will have at least one accidental because it is being borrowed from another key and is usually followed by its target chord.
>
> 2. Lead sheet: a secondary dominant is a dominant seven chord that is not made from harmonizing the scale of the key and is usually followed by its target chord.

1.

2.

How to Talk About and Label Secondary Dominants

How to Talk About Secondary Dominants

Secondary dominants "belong" to their target chord. Because they are dominant, we start by saying "the five of..." followed by the Roman Numeral number of the target chord. See the example below for the five of two (A7 to D-), the five of three (B7 to E-), and the five of five (D7 to G7).

How to Label Secondary Dominants

To label secondary dominants, we use a slash between two Roman Numerals, kinda like slash chords. We show **V7/*Roman Numeral of the target chord***. Do not write full chord qualities like "**V7/II-7(add11)**," even if that is the quality of the target chord. **V7/II-** is enough to show the function of the secondary dominant and the target chord that it "belongs" to.

Secondary Dominant
V7/II-
Of The Chord

Analysis 7: Borrowed Chords Bonanza

Secondary Dominants: Major Keys

All the secondary dominants in a harmonized major scale.

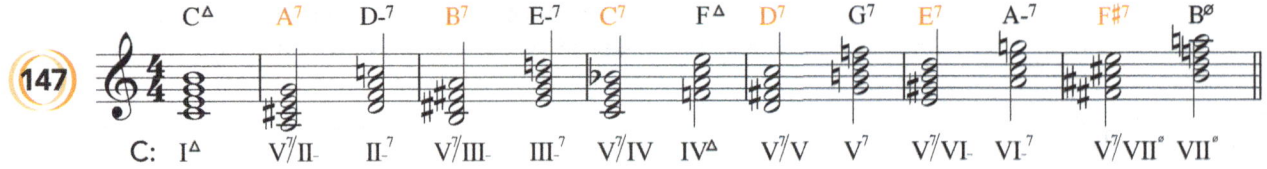

Secondary Dominants: Minor Keys

All the secondary dominants in a harmonized natural minor scale.

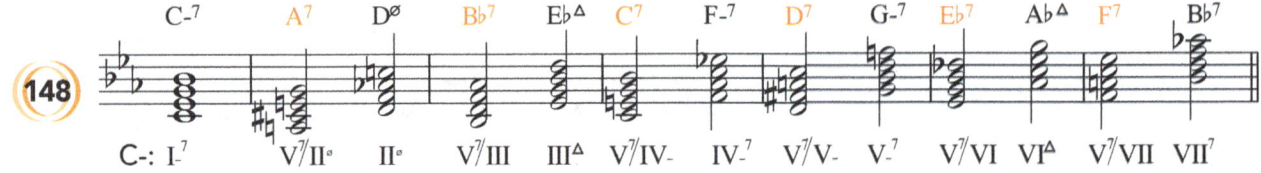

> If all these secondary dominants in a row sound like classical music to you, it is because classical composers love to use a bunch of secondary dominants in a row!

Secondary Dominants: Anything Goes

Secondary Dominants: Any Chord

A secondary dominant can lead to borrowed chords that are not from the key.

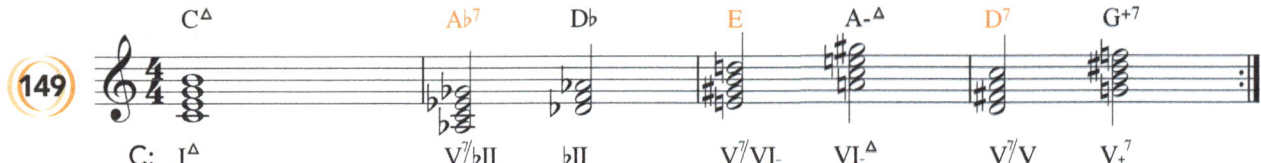

Secondary Dominants: No Resolution + Triads & Extended Chords

Secondary dominants do not have to resolve to their target chord (m. 2). Secondary dominants can be major triads (m. 3) and include any extension on a dominant chord (m. 4).

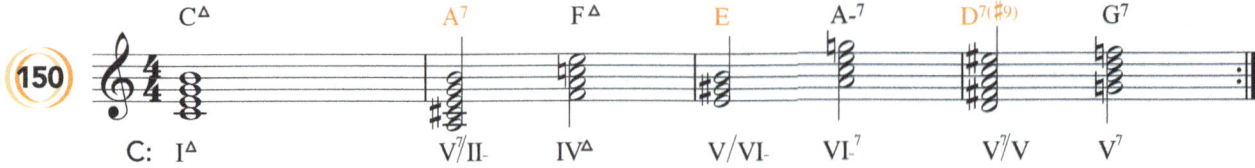

Borrowed SD - D

You can write and will find chords that add an SD Area onto the D - T relationship of a secondary dominant.

How to Analyze Borrowed SD - D Chords

It is common to find a few chords in a row that create new SD - D - T Area functions for target chords. Like secondary dominants, we show the Roman Numeral of the chords and how they are related to the "resolution" target chord.

SD - D Borrowed Chords Rules

1. The Subdominant Area chords get a / notation like secondary dominants.

2. The only time a chord that already exists in the key will be treated as a borrowed chord is when the chord's function is changed, like the C in m. 2. See the breakdown below.

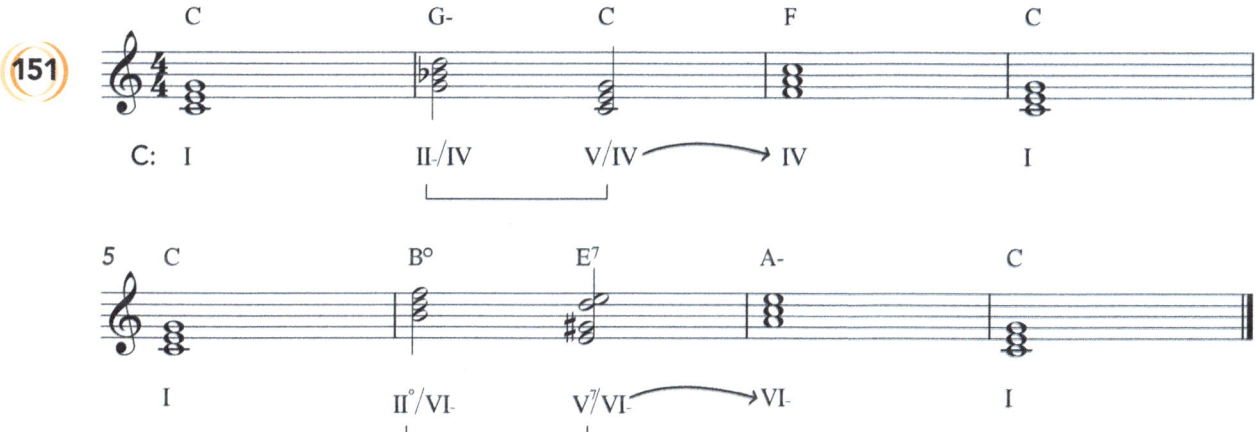

Example Breakdown

Harmonic Function

In m. 2 the C chord is no longer serving a Tonic Area function. It is now serving as a Dominant Area for the **IV** chord, F. How do we recognize this? It is very common to find **II- V I** chord progressions leading to major chords that already exist in the key.

In m. 6 the B° is not functioning as the leading tone of C, even though it normally does. Here, the B° is acting as a Subdominant Area for **VI-**. How do we recognize this? It is very common to find **II° V I-** chord progressions leading to minor chords that already exist in the key.

Roman Numerals

The Roman Numerals show the function of the chords. In m. 2 the G- is not a **V-**; it is a **II-/IV**, which is a SD that leads to the **V/V**, which leads to the **IV** chord. The same idea applies to m. 6. Mini SD - D - T, this time leading to **VI-**. Whenever you can make a connection between a possible subdominant and dominant chord that are next to each other, do it.

Analysis 7: Borrowed Chords Bonanza

SD - D Borrowed Chords 1

In m. 2 a G- and a C7 create a SD - D - T, which create a cadence to the **IV** chord (F) in m. 3. To show that the G- and C7 are related to the F, we write the Roman Numerals **II-/IV** and **V7/IV**. This is "the two of four" and "the five of four." We are not going to think about the G- and C7 as being part of the key of C major. We think of them as a mini-moment that drives us to the target **IV** chord that is already in the key of C major.

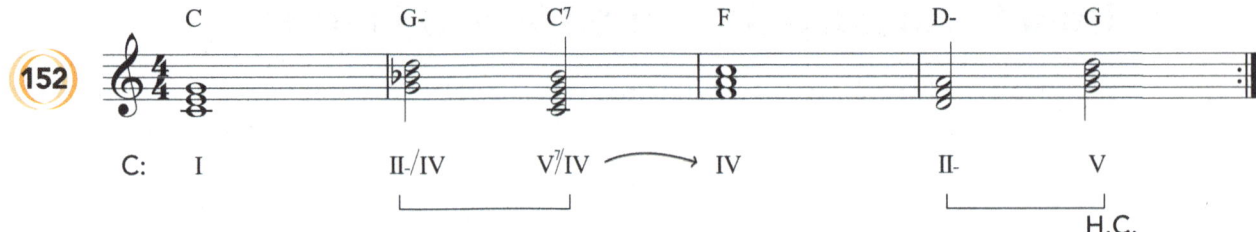

SD - D Chords 2

In m. 2 there is a SD - D - T **IV/IV** to **V7/IV** to **IV**. In m. 3 there is a SD - D - T with **II°/VI-** to **V7/VI-** to **VI**. Not to be left out of the fun, m. 4 has a **V/V** to **V**.

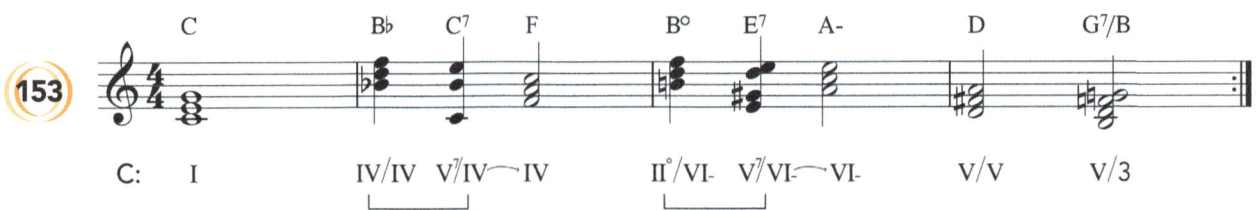

SD - D Chords 3

Here is a chord progression based on a real jazz song.

More Borrowed Chords

Any chord can be added to any key. Add a ♭ if the Root is one half-step lower than it would be in the major scale. Add a ♯ if the Root is one half-step higher than it would be in the major scale.

Borrowed Major Chords

If you create or analyze music with a lot of borrowed chords, it can be useful to use no sharps or flats in the key signature. In other words, use the key signature of C major, but only if you cannot find a tonal center in the music.

Borrowed Minor Chords

Borrowed Major Seven Chords

Analysis 7: Borrowed Chords Bonanza

Borrowed Minor Seven Chords

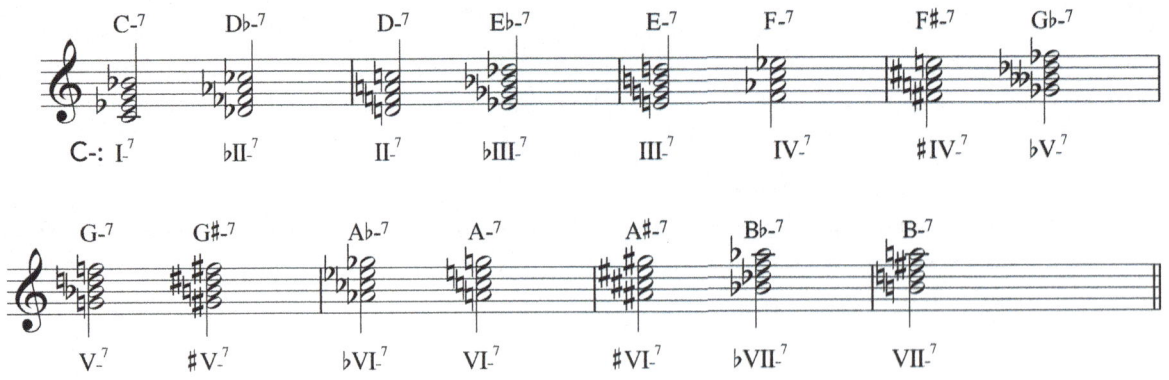

Borrowed Dominant Seven Chords

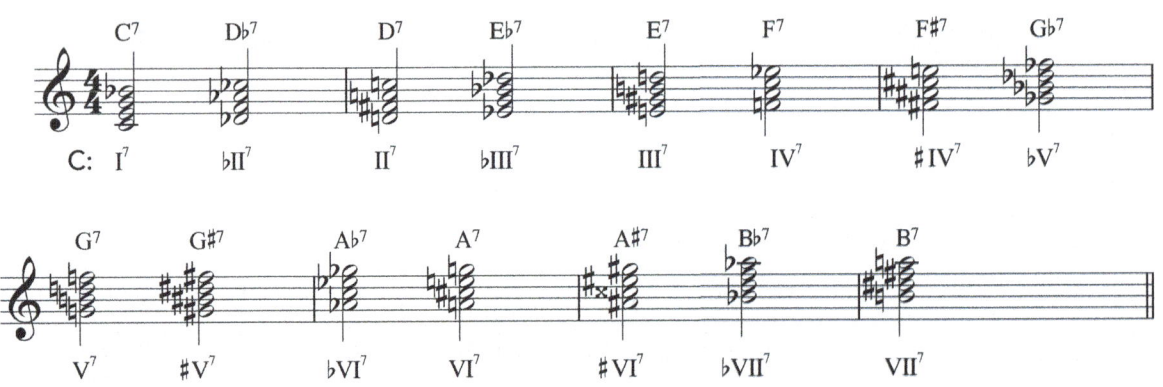

Borrowed Chords Rules

You just saw examples of only a few qualities of chords that can be borrowed. You also only saw the chords in the key of C major. Any chord, of any quality, can be used in any key.

> **Any chord, of any quality, can be used in any key.**

Borrowed Chords Thinking

Any type of borrowed chord can:

1. Resolve to a target chord from the key.
2. Resolve to a target chord which is also from outside the key.
3. Move to the next chord which is from the key.
4. Move to the next chord which is also from outside the key.

Borrowed Chord Examples

These examples are taken from real songs. The lesson from this page is: if it sounds good to you, use it!

Borrowed Chords 1

All major seven chords? Yes. Sounds great too!

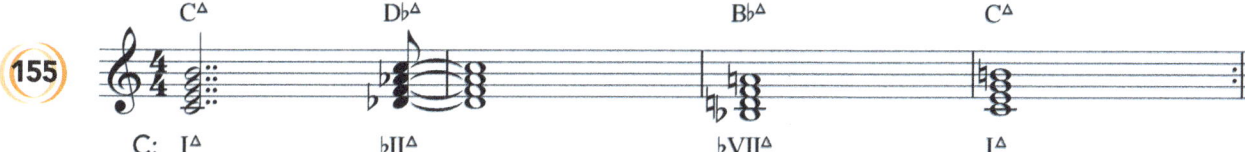

Borrowed Chords 2

Who cares if **IV** chord quality changes in the same chord progression?

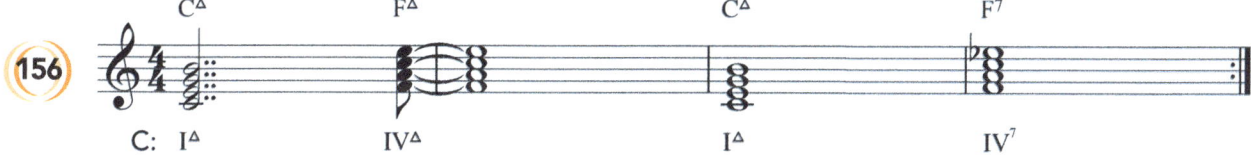

Borrowed Chords 3

Get heavy with this rock and metal riff.

Tritone Substitution

Tritone substitutions create a new color of tension and resolution by taking the place of any dominant seven chord or secondary dominant. You can be "cool" and say "tritone subs."

The Two Most Important Chord Tones In Modern Music

The two most important chord tones in most chords are the Third and the Seventh. The Third tells us if the chord is major or minor. The Seventh tells us if the chord is dominant, minor seven, major seven, and so on. The Third and Seventh are called "guide tones."

The Fifth is the least important chord tone and does not need to be present unless it is altered to create a diminished or augmented chord. The Root is important but not as important as the Third and Seventh because we can guess the Root based on the Third and Seventh.

How Tritone Substitution Works

1. Remove the Fifth of any dominant chord. This also works for secondary dominants.

2. Raise the Root of the chord by a tritone (A4/d5), fix the note spelling, and you have a new seventh chord. For correct spelling you must pick an asc. d5 as the new Root note.

3. The guide tones are now reversed. The Third of the dominant chord is now the Seventh of the tritone substitution chord. The Seventh of the dominant chord is now the Third of the tritone substitution chord.

Example 1

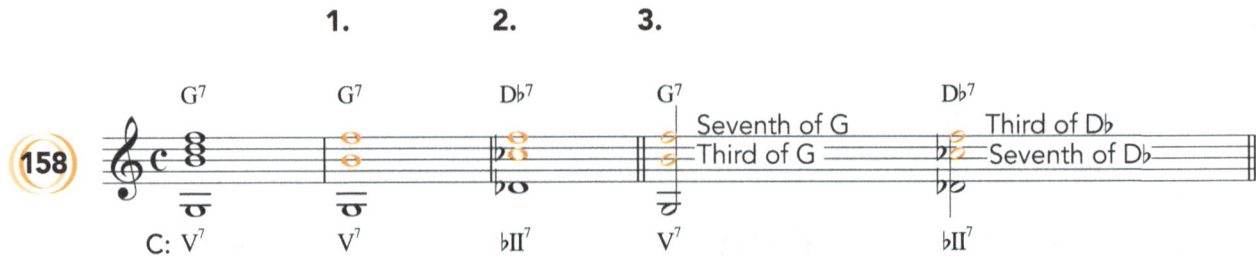

Not counting the Fifth, the chord tones of a G7 chord are G, B, F.
Not counting the Fifth, the chord tones of a D♭7 chord are D♭, F, C♭.
Common notes between the two chords: F and B (C♭). B and C♭ are enharmonic equivalents.

F is the Seventh of G7. F is also the Third of D♭7.
B is the Third of G7. C♭ (B) is also the Seventh of D♭7.

By omitting the Fifth, these chords have only one note that is different between them, which is their Root note. The Roots of both chords are a Tritone apart. This is tritone substitution. This means D♭7 can be used at any time instead of G7.

Example 2

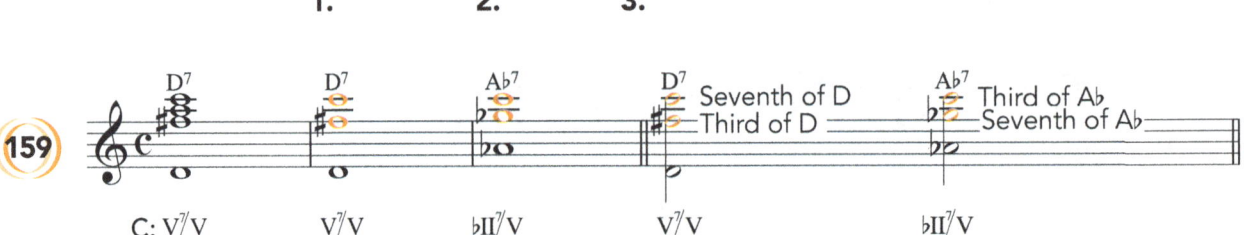

Not counting the Fifth, the chord tones of a D7 chord are D, F♯, C.
Not counting the Fifth, the chord tones of an A♭7 chord are A♭, C, G♭.
Common notes between the two chords: F♯ (G♭) and C. F♯ and G♭ are enharmonic equivalents.

F♯ is the Third of D7. G♭ (F♯) is also the Seventh of A♭7.
C is the Seventh of D7. C is also the Third of A♭7.

By omitting the Fifth, these chords have only one note that is different between them, which is their Root note. The Roots of both chords are a Tritone apart. This is tritone substitution. This means A♭7 can be used at any time instead of D7.

Tension And Resolution: Tritone Substitutions

Tritone Sub To Major Seven

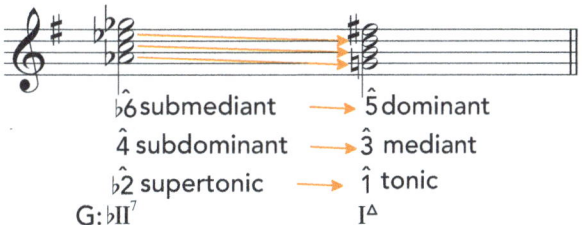

Tritone Sub To Minor Seven

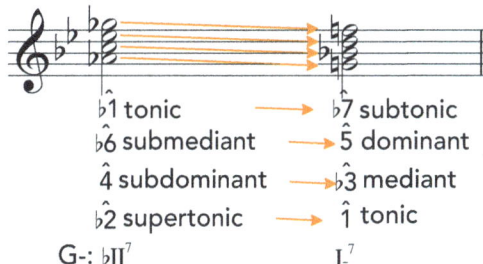

Tritone Sub To Dominant Seven

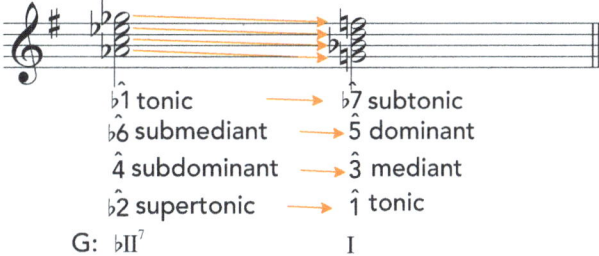

Tritone Substitutions: Major Keys

All the tritone substitutions that replace secondary dominants in a harmonized major scale.

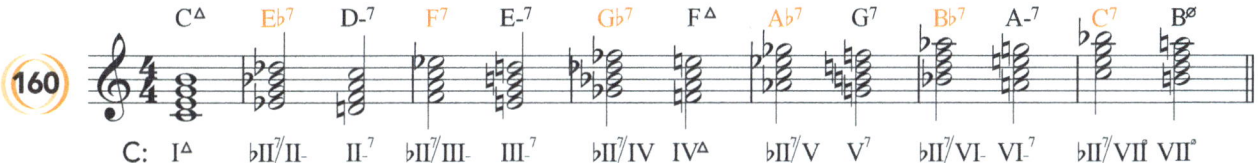

Tritone Substitutions: Minor Keys

All the tritone substitutions that replace secondary dominants in a harmonized natural minor scale. It is more common to find tritone substitutions with common enharmonic spellings. For example, F♭7 is usually written as E7, and B♭♭7 is usually written as A7. For the sake of clarity, all tritone subs here are written to show the ♭II relationship to the chord they resolve to. It is rare to find this "correct spelling" using uncommon enharmonic equivalents in the real world.

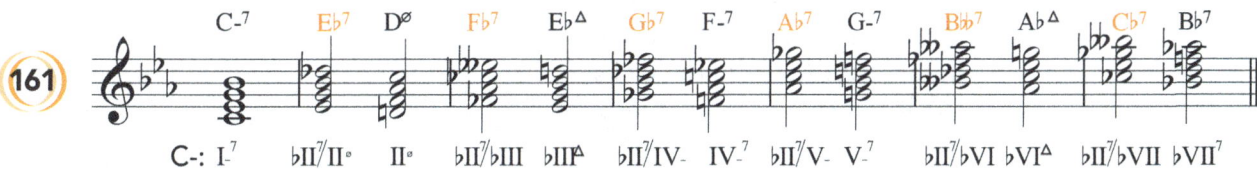

How to Label Tritone Substitutions

Like a leading tone cadence, we use a dotted arrow to show that a cadence is resolving by one half-step. The arrow is exactly the same as the L.T.I.A.C. arrow.

- Only use the dotted arrow when a tritone substitution resolves from ♭II of a chord to the target chord.
- In the example below, F7 resolves to E7, even though E7 is really functioning as the **V/III-**.

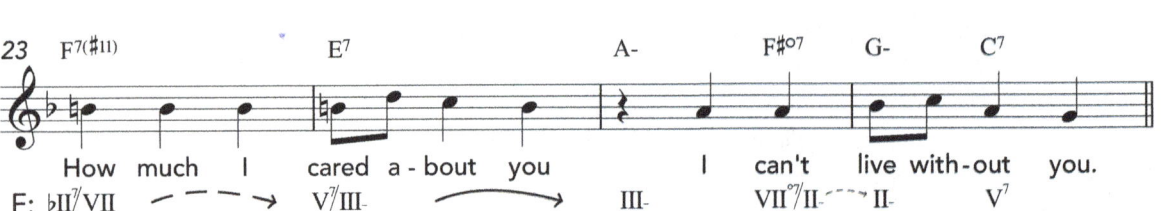

Review

- How to recognize and analyze a key change
- Borrowed chords from parallel keys
- Secondary dominants
    - How to recognize secondary dominants
    - How to talk about and label secondary dominants
    - Secondary dominants in major keys
    - Secondary dominants in minor keys
    - Secondary dominants not connected to the key
- Borrowed SD - D
    - How to analyze SD - D
    - How to find SD - D
- More borrowed chords
- Tritone substitution
    - How tritone substitution works
    - Tension and resolution in tritone substitutions
    - Tritone substitutions in major keys
    - Tritone substitutions in minor keys
    - When tritone substitutions resolve

New Words You Should Know

1. Borrowed chords
2. Secondary dominants
3. Tritone substitution

Analysis 8: Phrase & Advanced Lead Sheet Analysis

In this chapter you will discover how to analyze phrases and cadences so you can see how music is constructed. Then, use that understanding to write your own music (if you want to).

Musical Form Hierarchy

Form hierarchy is based on the time it takes to complete each part of the song or piece.

Form Hierarchy: Shortest To Longest Duration

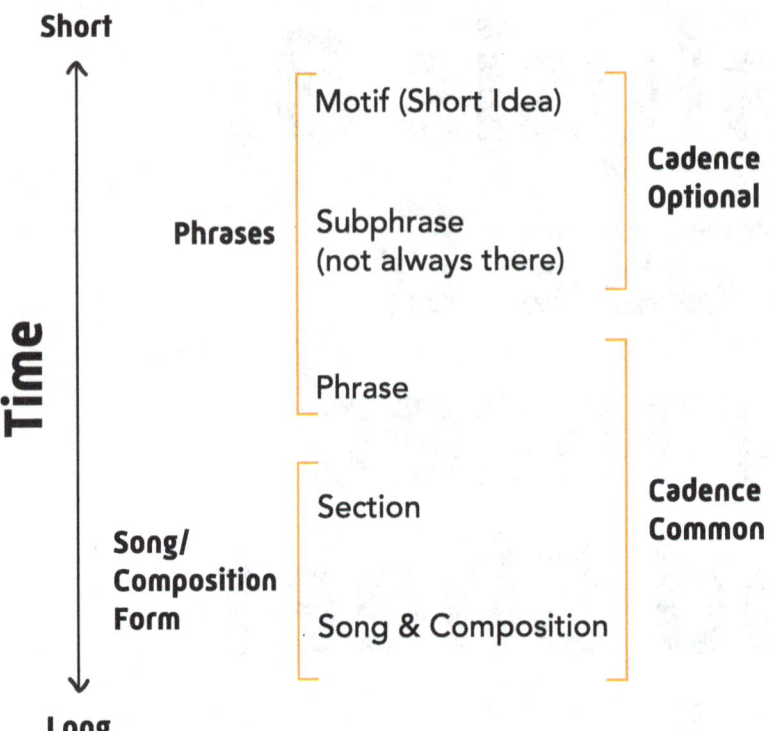

Advanced Lead Sheet Analysis

Steps to Analyze Lead Sheets

1. Identify and label the key.
2. Perform a Roman Numeral analysis and identify cadences and harmonic functions.
3. Perform a phrase analysis.
4. Perform a form analysis.

You already know how to identify and label keys. You also know how to perform a Roman Numeral analysis and form analysis. We will do a new way of performing a form analysis.

We do phrase analysis after the Roman Numeral analysis, because we can use the information from the Roman Numerals and cadences to help identify phrases.

How to Write a Cadence & Harmonic Function Analysis

Types Of Cadences

Perfect Authentic & Imperfect Authentic Cadence
- **V** chords that lead to any quality of **I** or **I-** chord.
- Write an arrow between RNs.

Leading Tone Imperfect Authentic Cadence
- **VII°** chords that lead to any quality of **I** or **I-** chord.
- Diminished, half diminished, and fully diminished chords that resolve up by 1 half-step.
- Write a dotted arrow between RNs.

Plagal Cadence
- Any quality of **IV** chord that leads to any quality of **I** or **I-** chord at the end of phrases.
- Write P.C. below RNs.

Half Cadence
- Phrases or subphrases that end on a **V** chord.
- Write H.C. below the staff.

Deceptive Cadence
- **V** chords that lead to any quality of chord that is not **I** or **I-** in a way that is surprising and made you think a **I** or **I-** chords was expected at the end of the phrase.
- Write D.C. below RNs.

SD - D Cadence
- Any movement from a Subdominant to a Dominant Area at any point in a phrase.
- Can lead to:
    Perfect Authentic Cadence
    Imperfect Authentic Cadence
    Half Cadence
    Deceptive Cadence
- Can also lead to another SD - D Cadence or any other chord.
- Write an upside down bracket below RNs.

Cadence Example 1

Angels We Have Heard On High - Harmonic Analysis

Cadence Example 1 Breakdown

Authentic cadences have been used less often in modern music since the 2000s. You can find pop songs where there are no cadences. Instead, there are chord progressions that create some tension and resolution using chords from Tonic, Subdominant, and Dominant Areas. This is partly because authentic cadences have been used so much in the past. To find a "new" sound, songwriters use fewer authentic cadences. To give you an example of cadences in action, we look to an older piece of music.

We could think of mm.1-9 as being a two-part phrase with two subphrases each. There are subphrases that end in authentic cadences in mm. 2 and 6.

Interestingly, we could also think of mm. 1-4 as being a phrase and also mm. 5-9 as being a separate phrase, each with two subphrases. Each pair of subphrases acts as kind of antecedent and consequent. We can think this because of the authentic cadences that happen 2X in each of the first two lines.

Starting in m. 9, an SD - D movement creates an authentic cadence in the middle of the phrase, and it does not stop there. A half cadence in m. 12 is followed by a subphrase with another half cadence. One half cadence is enough to build up tension and excitement. The repetition of the half cadence increases tension and anticipation for the next phrase of the chorus.

One could call mm. 9-14 a 6-measure antecedent. Indeed, you might say that mm. 13-14 is an extension of the phrase. You could further back up this idea by pointing out that the second time through the "chorus" ends with an authentic cadence in m. 21. This creates a perfect antecedent and consequent relationship with mm. 9-14 asking the question, ending on a half cadence, and mm. 15-21 giving the answer, ending on an authentic cadence.

The point of going through these analyses is not to be "right." It is to see how the music is working, how the notes of the melody are highlighted by the chords and cadences, and then take ideas to use for your own music...or just have fun and see how it all works.

How to Find Cadences

1. Because the function of cadences is to highlight the notes in the phrase, and it is common for phrases to be 4 or 8 measures long, check the ends of 4- and 8-measure groups.

2. Because phrases can be any length and cadences can be found in subphrases and motifs, check for cadences throughout any piece of music you are analyzing.

3. In genres like jazz, The Blues, R&B, fusion, and gospel, you will find cadences everywhere, not just at the ends of phrases.

4. You can find SD - D cadences anywhere in all genres.

Cadence Example 2

"All Alone" - Irving Berlin - Harmonic Analysis

How to Perform a Phrase Analysis

Form Hierarchy In Time

Not all subphrases have two motifs or ideas. Not all phrases have two subphrases. Not all sections have two phrases. This is a general way of "seeing" how songs and pieces work.

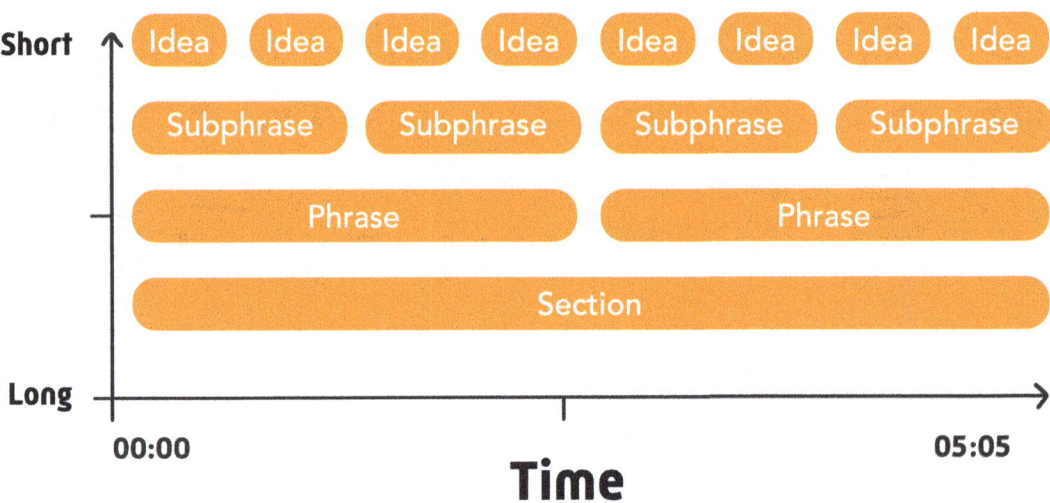

How to Identify A Phrase

- A phrase is like a sentence, a full idea with a beginning, middle, and end.
- There can be a question (antecedent) subphrase and an answer (consequent) subphrase within the phrase.
- Subphrases can be smaller ideas in the phrase.
- Phrases can end with a cadence. If you find a cadence that lines up with groups of 4 or 8 measures, it is likely that the phrase ends on this cadence.
- Phrases can end with a resolution, like a sentence that ends with a period.
- Phrases can end with tension, like a sentence that ends with a question.
- Phrases can take place over T - D - T and T - SD - D - T chords, but do not have to be tied to harmonic function. In many modern genres, it is rare to find phrases tied to functions and cadences.
- Look for the contour, which is the general shape of the melody notes on the staff. Spotting shapes that look similar or the same will be easier and faster than going one note at a time.

How to Label Phrases

Each phrase is given a lowercase letter that will identify the phrase.

> 1. The first phrase is "a," the next phrase that is different is "b," and so on, down the regular alphabet. We only count rhythms, notes, and chords. Ignore lyrics.
>
> 2. Phrases that have the same notes, rhythm, performance marks, and dynamic marks receive the same letter "a." This typically happens when an idea is repeated later on in a piece of music. It is rare to have two phrases that are exactly the same one after the next, because this can become less interesting and too repetitive (not pictured).
>
> 3. Phrases that start with the same notes and rhythm but end differently are labeled with a letter number combination "a1, a2."

How to Perform A Phrase Analysis

1. Look at the contour, which is the general shape of the melody notes on the staff. Spotting shapes that look similar or the same will be easier and faster than going one note at a time.

2. Look for similar rhythm patterns. These are ideas or motifs that are used in the phrase.

3. Because we can run out of space to perform all types of analysis on sheet music, it is easier to write a phrase analysis on a separate sheet of paper.

4. Write your phrase analysis (see walkthrough on this and the next page).

How to Perform A Phrase Analysis: Walkthrough

1. Write a "m." for measure. Leave a space below the below the "m." then write the key of music, followed by a colon (like for Roman Numeral analysis).

2. Write the measure number each phrase starts and ends on with a slur between the measure numbers.

3. Below the slur, write the total number of measures each phrase takes up, using "mm." for measures.

4. Above the slur, write the phrase letter and phrase letter number labels.

5. Write the subphrases below the phrases with their own slurs and measure duration numbers. This may be the antecedent and consequent.

6. Write cadence arrows and dotted arrows, along with the abbreviations P.C. (plagal), and D.C. (deceptive) in line with the key. When you can tell exactly the type of cadence, write abbreviations below the arrows.

1.

m.

C-:

2.

C-:

3.

m. 8mm. 8 9 8mm. 16 17 8mm. 24 25 8mm. 3 2

C-:

4.

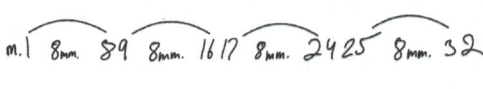

m. 8mm. 8 9 8mm. 16 17 8mm. 24 25 8mm. 3 2

C-:

5.

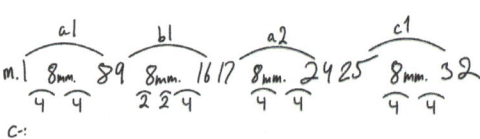

6

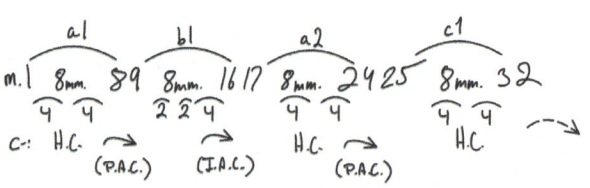

It can become impossible to write all cadences when more than 2 happen in a single phrase or subphrase. In these cases, write the cadence that happens at the end of the phrase or subphrase. The rest of the cadences will be shown in your harmonic analysis.

Phrase Analysis - "All Alone" (Verse) - Irving Berlin

(m. 11) The first phrase has an easy antecedent to spot because it ends in a half cadence. The second half of the phrase ends in an authentic cadence, which makes it a consequent (m. 19). The second phrase starts out using the same notes and rhythms as the first phrase until beat 3 of m. 20. The first part of the second phrase ends with a descending half-step movement that starts in m. 22, ending in m. 24. The second half of the phrase ends with a half cadence, which creates tension to launch us into the chorus.

Form Analysis 2

Now that you know all about verses, choruses, bridges, and other parts of songs, it is time to understand the universal language of form!

You won't always find verses, refrains, and choruses. If a song has no words, how can we figure out the section? We will simplify different sections by labeling, writing, and talking about them with capital letters.

In the same way we analyze lyrics and phrases, we start with A, then B, then C, and so on. Just like phrases, we will label repeated sections with a letter number combination like A1, A2, and so on.

> **Form Analysis Rules**
> 1. Do not pay attention to lyrics other than to see where sections end and begin.
> 2. Do not pay attention to variations in the melody other than when the melody is different enough that we know we are in a new section.
> 3. Do not pay attention to the chords other than to make sure the general chord structure or progression stays similar between matching sections.
> 4. Look for general connections between sections. They do not need to be perfectly identical. You are looking for the general "idea" of the section to be "about the same."

Form Analysis Examples

Look at a few song maps from Level 2 to see how the sections are translated into letters!

Wabash Cannonball - Johnny Cash

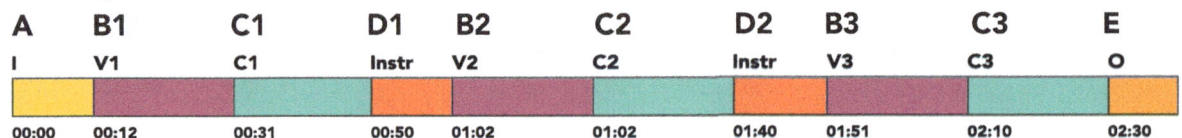

American Pie - Don McLean

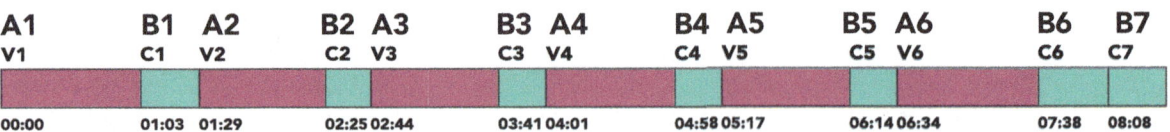

Stayin' Alive - Bee Gees

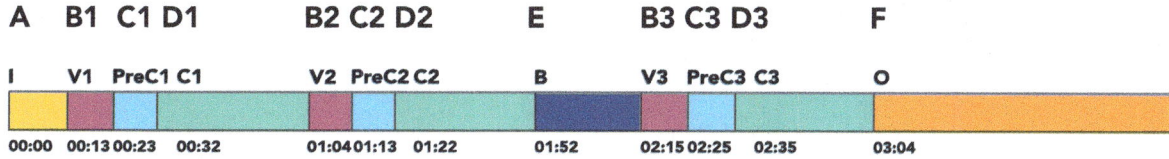

Another Brick in the Wall (Part 2) - Pink Floyd

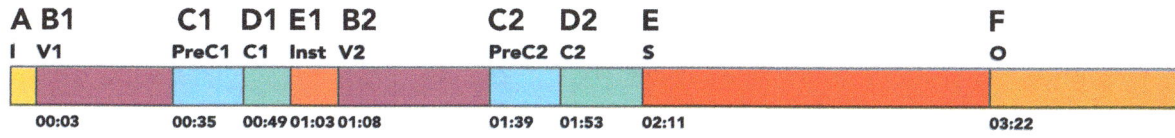

Eye of the Tiger - Survivor

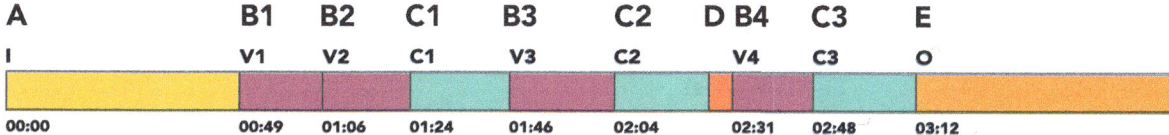

> **How to Identify Parts of Songs**
>
> 1. Look for breaks in phrases, double bar lines, and changes in the motifs, subphrases, chords, chord progressions, and any other musical elements. We will explore instrumental music form more in the next books.
> 2. Write the letter or letter number combination for the section.

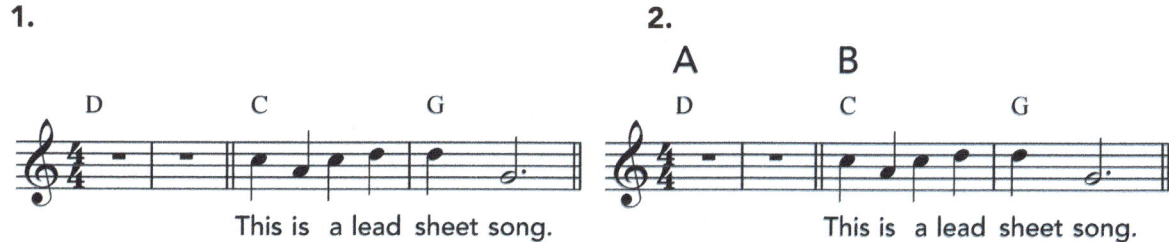

Analysis 8: Phrase & Advanced Lead Sheet Analysis

Review

- Musical form hierarchy
    - Motif
    - Subphrase
    - Phrase
    - Section
    - Song & Composition

- Roman Numeral Analysis
    - Label Roman Numerals
    - Label cadences

- Phrase Analysis
    - Identify phrases
    - Label phrases
    - How to write a phrase analysis

- Form Analysis
    - Alphabet letters
    - Section names

Analysis 9: The Blues

In this chapter you will see a unique American art form called The Blues. You will discover how The Blues works, its history, and how to write "a blues" song if you want!

The Blues

The Blues is a unique American art form born out of American slavery, which existed in the United States from 1776 until 1865. Slaves' work songs eventually led to the creation of The Blues. The Blues grew in a movement of individualism, during which Black musicians began to travel and perform. The Blues is an aural music tradition, meaning that it is mainly passed down without writing any of the music. Each blues musician learns to play the music through trial and error using only their ears and teachers. That being said, we can confidently write down some parts of The Blues to learn from this incredible American art form.

Work Songs And Rhyme Scheme

The songs that give The Blues its form were call-and-response songs sung by slaves in places they worked, including fields. A leading singer would sing out a line, everyone else would respond, then the leader would finish the form with a second musical idea. This creates the following form/rhyme scheme.

"Sweet Home Chicago" - Robert Johnson - Lyrics

A (lasts for 4 measures) Short

Oh, baby, don't you want to go?

A (lasts for 4 measures) Short

Oh, baby, don't you want to go?

B (lasts for 4 measures) Long

Back to the land of California, to my sweet home Chicago

> The rhyme scheme is A, A, A in this example. The form of the lyrics gives us the A, A, B. Short (A), short (A), long (B).

12-Bar Blues Harmony

- 12 measures long, that is the 12 "bars."
- Repeats over and over for the duration of the song.
- Features only dominant seven chords.
- Can be in any key.

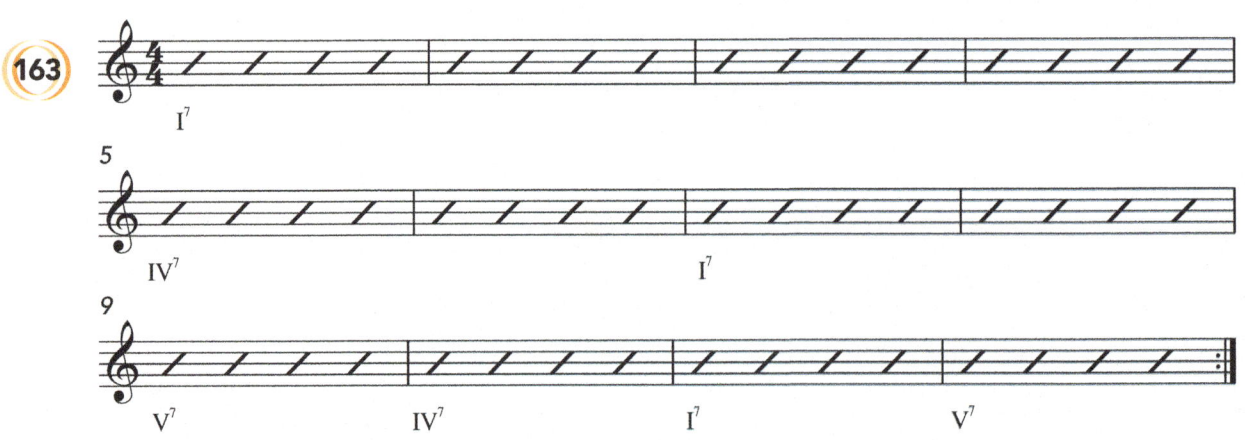

Blues Rhythm

- Can be in any time signature, traditionally The Blues is in $\frac{4}{4}$.
- Can be straight, swing, or shuffle.
- Can be in $\frac{12}{8}$. You will hear drummers play all three divisions of the beat on the hi-hat.

Turnaround

The turnaround is the last two measures of a 12-bar blues. It is called a turnaround because…it turns us around back to m. 1. The form repeats over and over for the duration of the song, including any instrumental solos. The song will typically end with a "walk down" or "walk up" that outlines something close to an authentic or plagal cadence in a coda section.

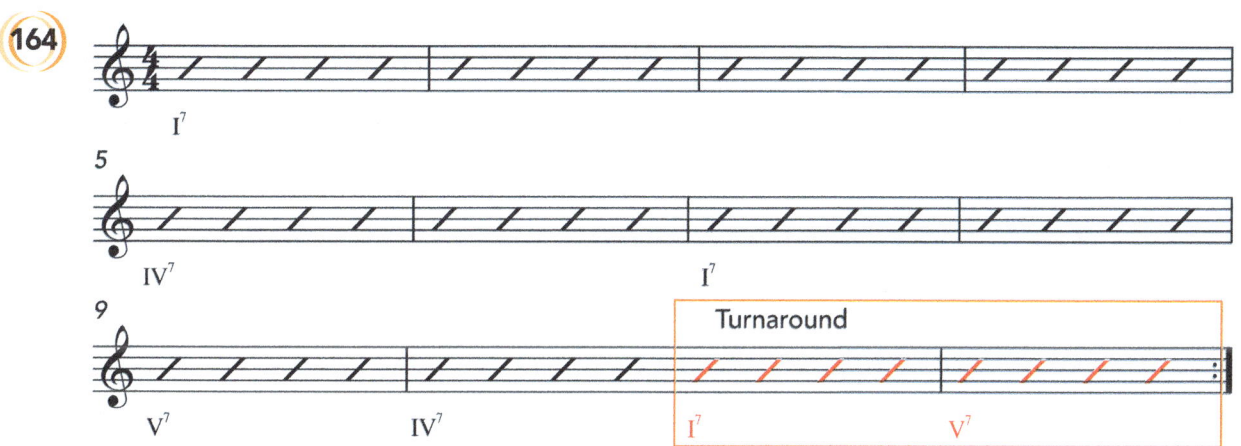

Quick Change

A 12-bar blues can have a **IV7** chord in m. 2. This "quick" chord change is called the "quick change."

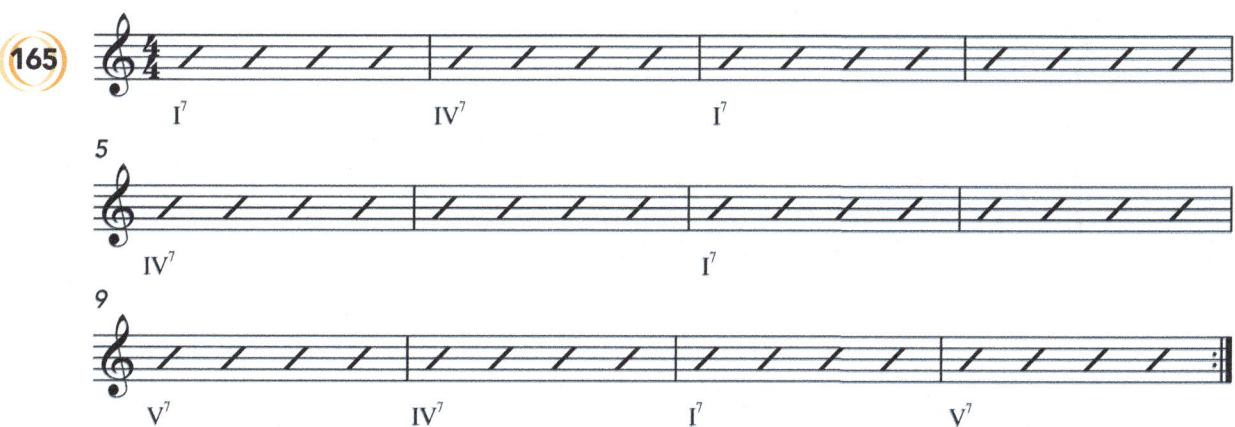

12-Bar Minor Blues Harmony

- 12 measures long, that is the 12 "bars."
- Repeats over and over for the duration of the song.
- Can be in any key.

All Minor Chords

A minor version of the 12-bar blues. Chords could be minor or minor 7.

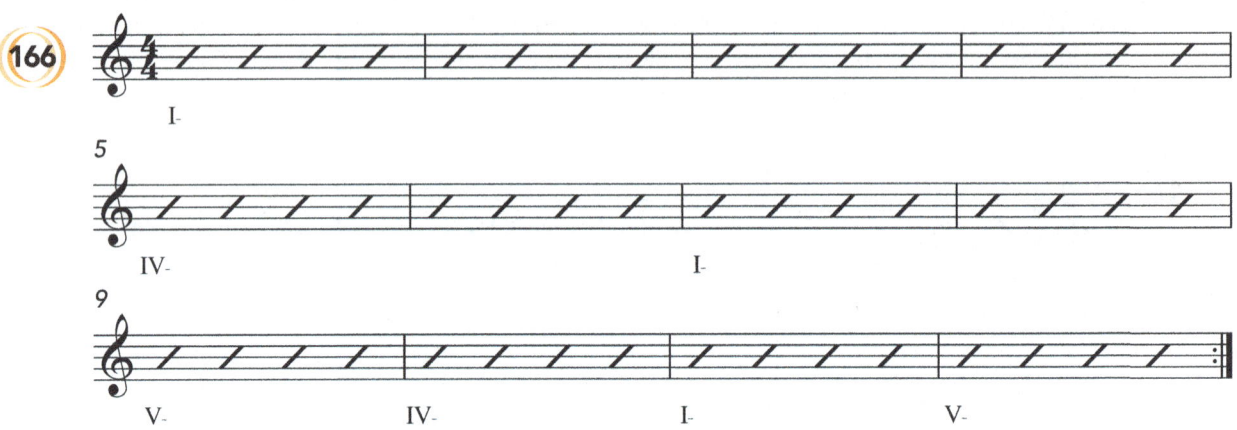

Quick Change and Borrowed V

A minor version of the 12-bar blues with a quick change and a **V7** in the turnaround.

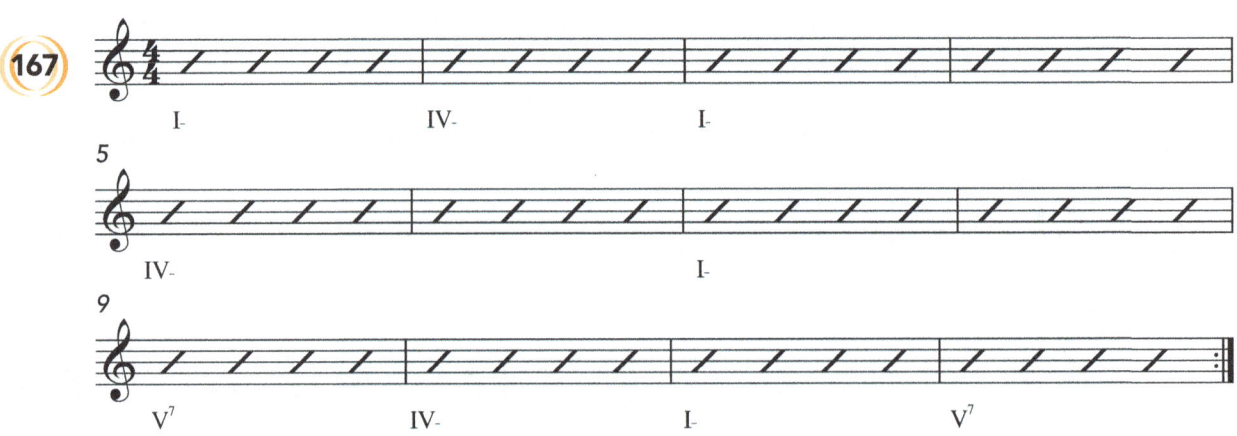

Borrowed V And More Complex Turnaround

A minor version of the 12-bar blues. Chords could be minor or minor 7. More complex harmony starts in m. 9 which creates a half-step approach in harmony down to **V7** in m.10. We could also think of the ♭VI in m. 9 as being the ♭II/ **V**, which is a tritone substitution leading to the target chord of **V**.

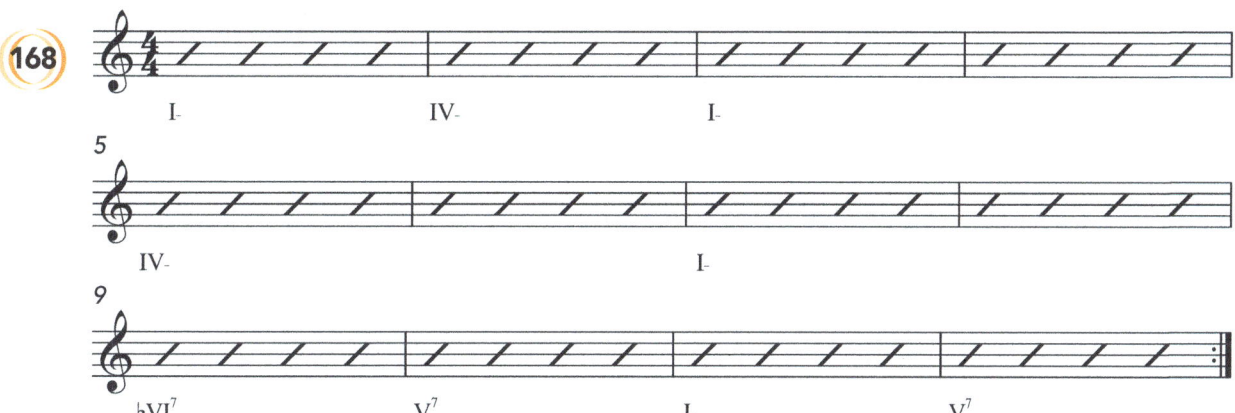

Borrowed IV, V, And More Complex Turnaround

A minor version of the 12-bar blues. Chords could be minor or minor 7. All **IV** chords could also be minor or minor seven instead of dominant.

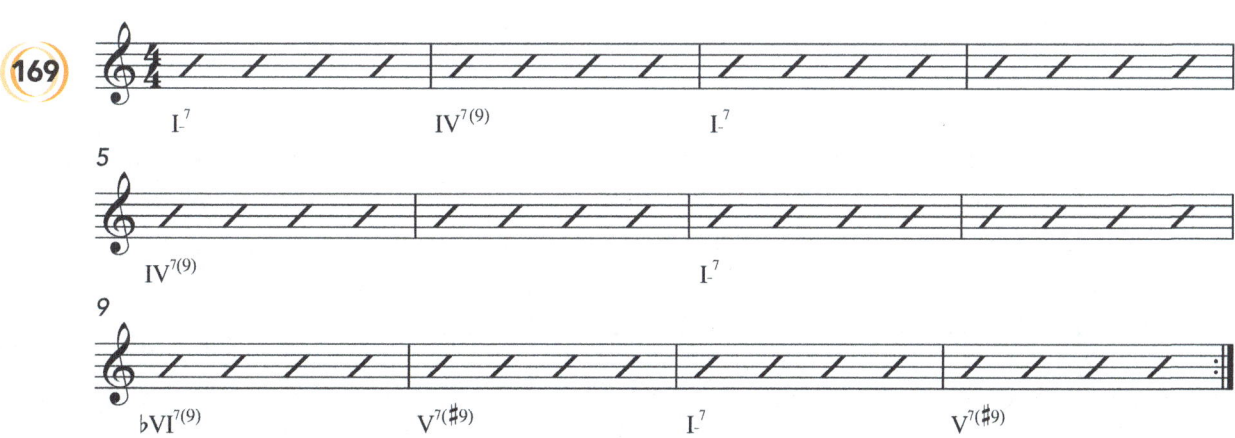

Blues with a B Section

Many blues songs use the 12-bar form as an A section. After a certain number of repetitions, the music will change to a B section that functions as a bridge. Typically the music returns to the A section after the B section.

No "rule" exists for which chords should be played in the B section. The example below is a common chord progression for the B section. Secondary dominants are everywhere.

12-Bar Jazz-Blues

Jazz takes The Blues, and adds SD - D, secondary dominants, and half-step descending movements to increase harmonic complexity.

Less Harmonic Complexity

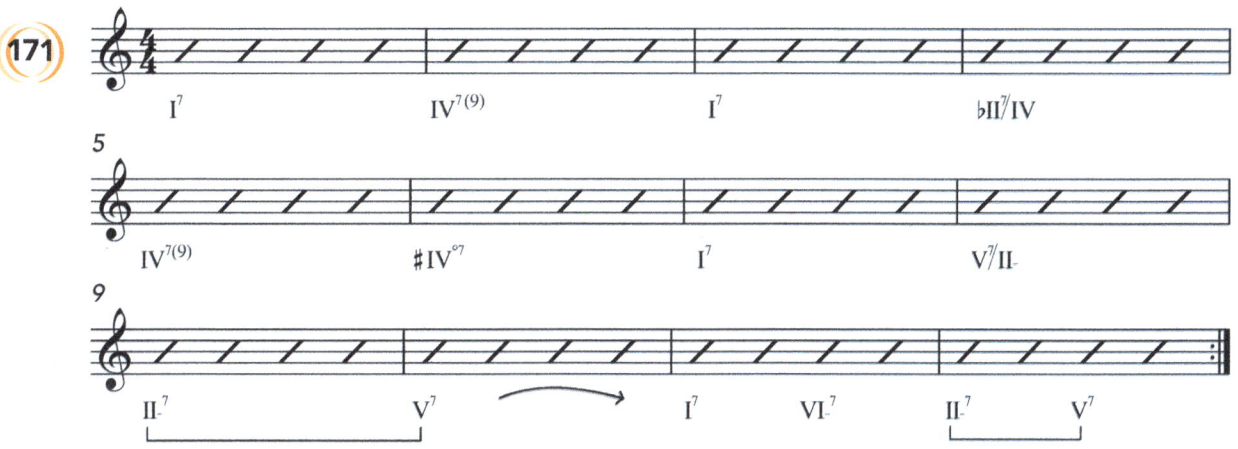

A tritone substitution drives us from m. 4 to m. 5. In m. 6, the #IV°7 chord could also be thought of as a half-step approach, because it contains ♭$\hat{3}$, ♭$\hat{5}$, and $\hat{6}$, which all resolve up by one half-step back to **I7** as $\hat{3}$, $\hat{5}$, and ♭$\hat{7}$. A secondary dominant in m. 8 brings us to an SD - D - T movement. The turnaround uses more chords than a blues turnaround. Finding new ways to navigate through chord changes and harmonic Areas is one of the fun parts of jazz!

More Harmonic Complexity

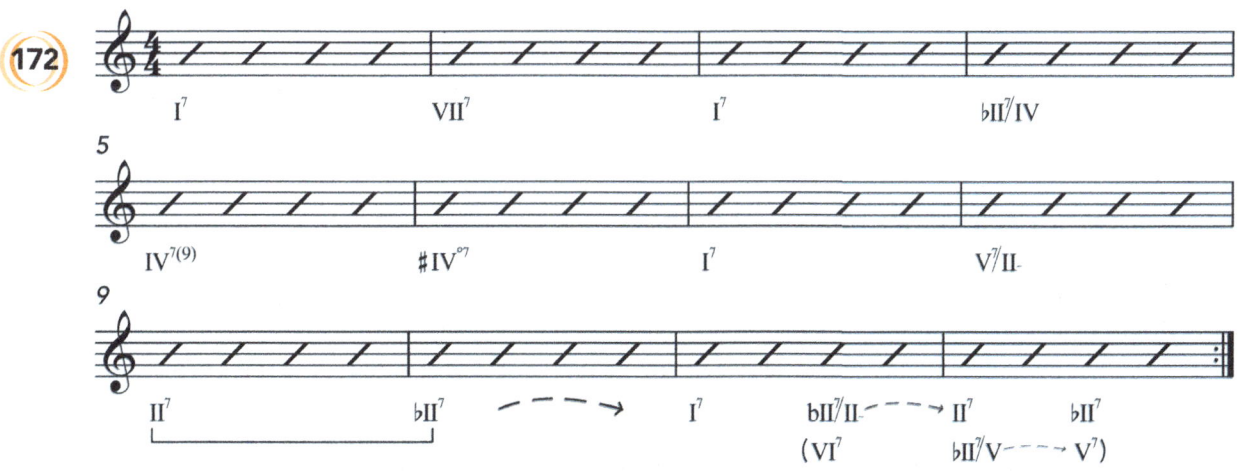

m. 2 features a tritone substitution for the **IV7** chord. Everything remains the same as in the "Less Harmonic Complexity" version until m. 9. In m. 9, instead of going to a **II-7**, a **II7** highlights a change in chord quality. This **II7** could also be thought of as **V/V**. Instead of SD - D going to **V7** in m. 10, a tritone substitution leads us back to **I7**. In the turnaround, there are two different options for tritone substitutions! Both tritone substitution turnarounds use a descending chromatic bass line.

Blues Melody

Blues Scale: Is It Real?

A "blues scale" is not really a blues scale. The "blues note" in the "blues scale" is not really a blues note. The blues note is actually a microtonal expression. A microtone is a pitch between half-steps. In the blues, the microtone can shift up and down on a continuum with no set starting or stopping point. The movment up and down through several notes is made through singing or bending guitar strings. Other instruments can perform these bends like trombones. Listen to the following artists to hear microtones and real blues in action.

Buddy Guy	Albert King	Robert Johnson
Freddie King	B. B. King	Jimi Hendrix
John Lee Hooker	Howlin' Wolf	Muddy Waters
Lightnin' Hopkins	T-Bone Walker	Elmore James

The Blues Scale

Below is the "blues scale." "Blues scales" are created by adding a "blues note" to a major or minor pentatonic scale. You will hear the blues scale used like this in Rock, Hard Rock, Metal, and other genres. You will also hear this scale in The Blues, but bends and microtonal expressions close to the "blues note" are used more often.

Major Blues Scale (Add ♭$\hat{3}$)

Microtonal expression beween $\hat{2}$ and $\hat{3}$

Minor Blues Scale (Add ♭$\hat{5}$)

Microtonal expression between $\hat{4}$ and $\hat{5}$

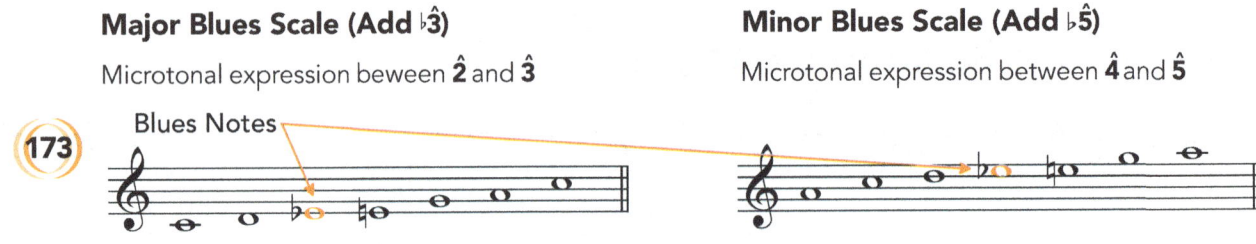

Major And Minor Mix

The Blues uses both major and minor pentatonic scales, and changes back and forth between the two. One of the hallmarks of the blues is the beautiful, tension-filled sound of $\hat{3}$ over a I- and ♭$\hat{3}$ over a I chord.

It is more common to hear and find the minor pentatonic and minor blues scale in major and minor blues. It is less common to hear a major pentatonic scale in a minor blues, though it has been done by some of the greats. The only notes from a major pentatonic that you will find in a minor blues will be the occasional microtonal expression to and around $\hat{3}$ and $\hat{6}$. These borrowed notes from parallel major and minor show up in guitar solos and singing.

This is the signature sound of the blues, that carries over into pop, country, jazz, R&B, gospel, rock, metal, and other modern genres. In other genres, it is common to hear the mix of parallel major and minor pentatonics in a melody.

174

Example Breakdown

In this example of a 12-bar blues, a minor pentatonic and blues note are used for the melody. This minor melody has "appropriate" friction and tension with the dominant chords of the harmony. The phrases of the melody are a a b, like the A A B of blues lyrics. The first a phrase starts on beat 2 of m.1. The second a phrase starts on beat 2 of m. 4. The bass guitar is playing an arpeggio with an added Sixth. This is a typical (but not very cool) way of playing a bass line for a Blues. The guitar and bass lay a foundation for a major sound, but the melody insists on a minor pentatonic, completing "the sound."

Analysis 9: The Blues

A Blues Solo Mixing Parallel Major and Minor Pentatonics and Blues Scales

Black noteheads = Minor Pentatonic

Orange noteheads = Major Pentatonic

Red noteheads = Blues Notes

- Solos do not need to follow the a a b phrase.
- Solos do not need to use only pentatonic and blues scales. They can use any notes.

To go deeper into The Blues, analyze guitar solo transcriptions that are "official," "note for note," or "as heard on X recording." You can also analyze full blues songs, from melodies, solos, chords, lyrics...the whole thing! Use your skills!

Review

- Blues rhyme scheme
- 12-bar blues harmony
    - Major blues
    - Minor blues
    - Jazz blues
- Blues rhythm
- The turnaround
- Blues melody
    - The "blues scale"
    - The "blues note"
    - Mix major and minor

New Words You Should Know

1. The Blues
2. Turnaround
3. Quick change

How to Write Music 3: Cycles of Tension, Resolution, & Reharmonization

Reharmonization is the perfect step to writing more music. All you need to think about are the chords and how they relate to the melody. This might sound too easy at first glance, but like most things in music, there are layers of complexity.

Melody Making Maps

The notes in every motif, subphrase, phrase, and melody can be seen in two different ways.

> 1. **Horizontal:** As scale degrees from the scale associated with the key of the music. This includes major pentatonic, minor pentatonic, major, natural minor, harmonic minor, real melodic minor, and classical melodic minor scales. Up until now, this is how you have been thinking, reading, and writing music.
>
> 2. **Vertical:** As chord tones or non-chord tones related to the chord that is happening in the same measure as the notes. Chord tones are the Root, Third, Fifth, and Seventh of each chord symbol above the staff. Chord tones include extensions, ADD notes, and sus notes.

1. Horizontal: Scale Degrees

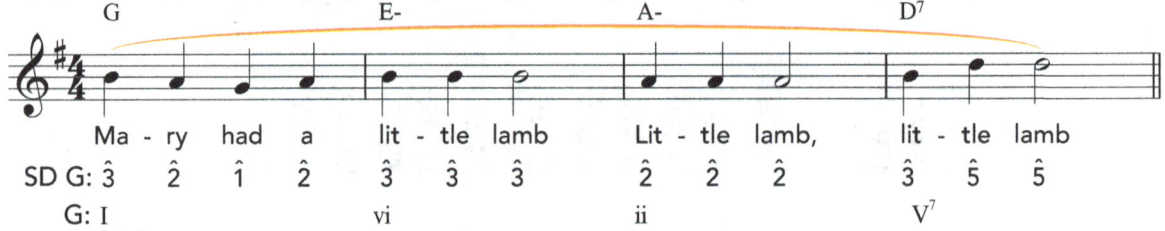

2. Vertical: Chord Tones

- **Orange** notes on the second staff show when the note in the melody is also a chord tone in the triad or seventh chord that is in the same measure.

- **Red** notes on the second staff show when the note in the melody is not a chord tone.

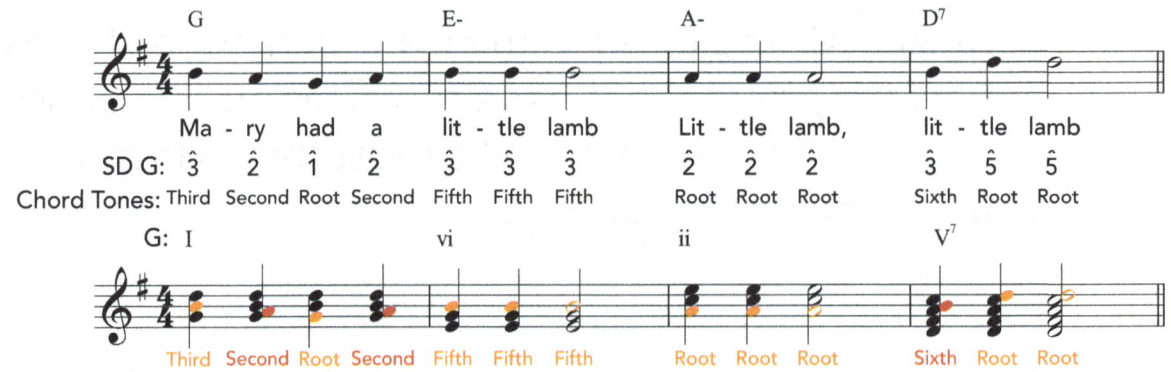

Chord-Melody Relationship

- Also called the "chord-scale" relationship, the chord-melody relationship breaks down each melody note's relationship to the harmony (chord) that is present for that melody note. This is the "vertical" way of thinking about notes and chords.
- Melodies that mix chord tones and non-chord tones are generally more interesting, especially when paired with syncopation and motivic development, because they create an extra layer of tension and resolution in each measure between melody and harmony.

Chord-Melody Relationship: Tension and Resolution

- When we think and write melodies from a vertical perspective, we will think about all the notes as being "part" of the harmony. Use the same system as chord tones (Third, Fifth Seventh) to think about these notes: Second, Fourth, Sixth.
- The Second, Fourth, and Sixth create tension and that tension resolves as the melody moves to the Root, Third, Fifth, or Seventh of the harmony in each measure.
- We can also think in terms of Traditional Consonance and Dissonance.

    Each time the melody note creates dissonance with the Root of the chord, there is tension.

    Each time the melody note creates a perfect consonance or imperfect consonance with the Root of the chord, tension is resolved.

Perfect Consonance (PC)	Imperfect Consonance (IC)	Dissonance (D)
1. PU	1. m3	1. m2
2. P5	2. M3	2. M2
3. P8	3. m6	3. A2
4. P4	4. M6	4. A4
		5. d5
		6. m7
		7. M7

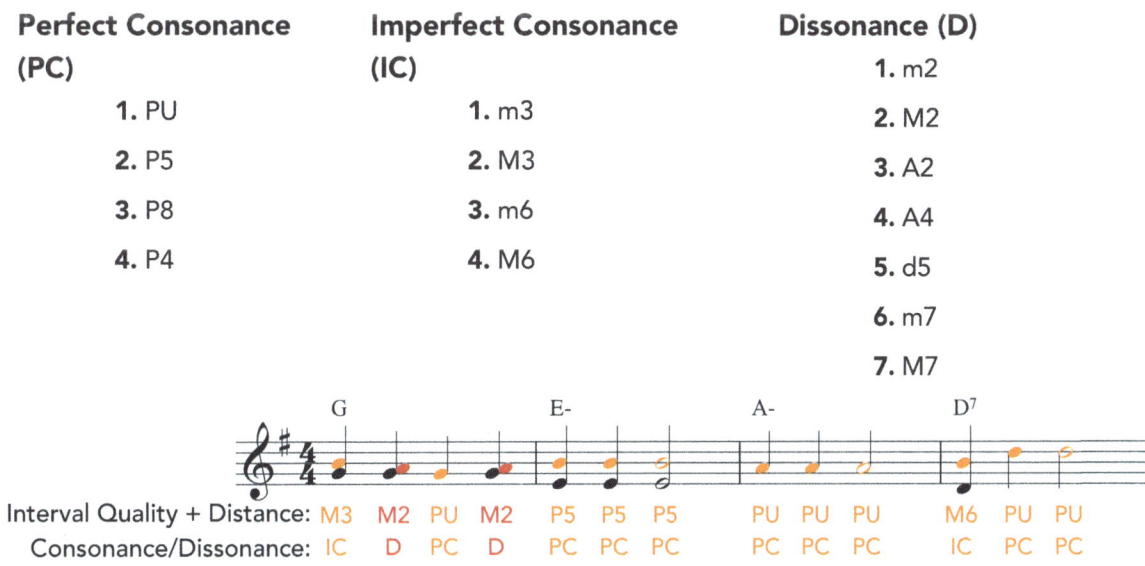

Part of what makes "Mary Had a Little Lamb" sound so basic and childish is that almost every chord has matching Root, Third, and Fifth chord tones in the melody on strong and weak beats. It is "too obvious" and that makes it sound cheesy and easy. This is partly because too little tension exists between the melody and harmony.

> **Melodies that have a mix of chord tones and non-chord tones are much more effective, especially when paired with syncopation and motivic development.**

Types of Tension and Resolution

In any song or piece of music, there are many types of tension and resolution that are all happening at different speeds and at different times. These are the fundamental parts of any song or piece of music that alternate between tension and resolution.

Rhythm

Rhythm Tension
Syncopation

Rhythm Resolution
Non-syncopated rhythms

Notes

Note Tension
Non-chord tones

Note Resolution
Chord tones

Intervals

Interval Tension
Dissonant intervals

Interval Resolution
Consonant intervals

Chords

Chord Tension
Borrowed chords
Dominant + Subdominant Area chords
sus chords
ADD chords with dissonant intervals
Altered chords

Chord Resolution
Major + minor chords
Tonic Area chords

Chord Progressions

Chord Progression Tension
End in half cadence
End in deceptive cadence
End with tension or "unfinished business"

Chord Progression Resolution
End with any kind of authentic cadence
End on Tonic

Phrase

Phrase Tension
Antecedent

Phrase Resolution
Consequent

Cycles of Tension and Resolution

The cycles of tension and resolution created by rhythm, notes, intervals, chords, chord progressions, cadences, and phrases happen at different speeds at the same time. This is the powerful machine that drives music. Here are a few ways that tension and resolution cycle back and forth in music.

> 1. Note to note + rhythmic figure to rhythmic figure
> 2. Motif to motif + idea to idea
> 3. Subphrase to subphrase
> 4. Phrase to phrase: melody
> 5. Phrase to phrase: chord progression + harmony + cadences
> 6. Section to section
> 7. Start of music to end of music

T = Tension   R = Resolution

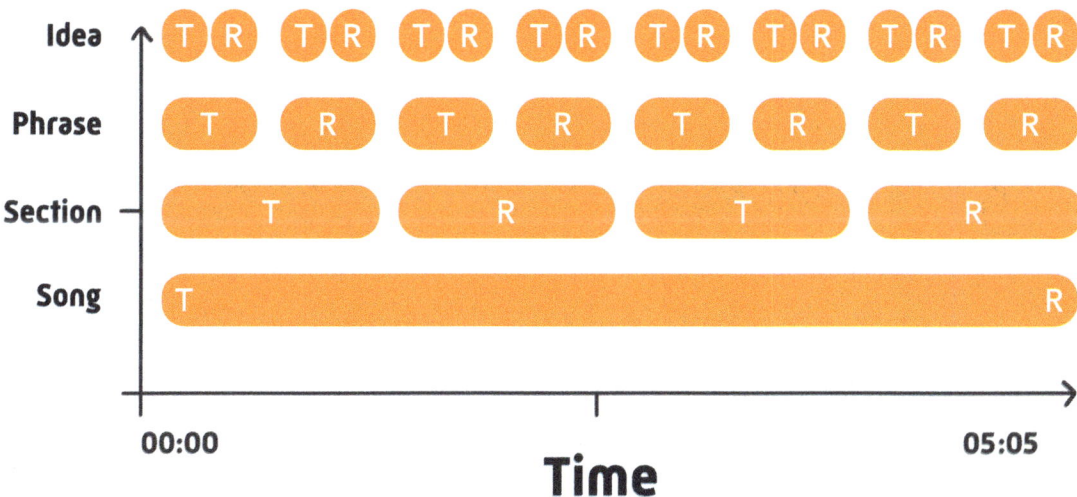

Meta-Cycles Of Tension And Resolution

Because it is typical to have cycles of tension and resolution in a song or piece, any break from this pattern creates an artist (composer or songwriter) cycle of tension and resolution. As an artist, you can cycle between creating music with expected patterns of tension and resolution and other music with unexpected patterns of tension and resolution.

When songs and pieces follow a mostly predictable pattern of tension and resolution, we can think of this way of creating art as resolution because it is expected; it is home base. Anytime a song or piece does not follow expected tension and resolution overall, it is tension because it is not expected and makes any song after it that does follow the typical patterns of tension and resolution feel like home.

At a smaller level, within a song or piece, breaking the expected pattern of tension and resolution creates another meta-cycle of tension and resolution at a song level.

Harmonic Rhythm

Harmonic rhythm is how fast chords change in a song. You could also think about harmonic rhythm as how long each chord lasts.

> - Harmonic rhythm can change from section to section. This is common in all modern music with singing.
> - Harmonic rhythm can change within a section.
> - Harmonic rhythm can change at the end of a section to create resolution or tension to lead into the next section.

Harmonic Rhythm: New Chord Every 1 Measure

Harmonic Rhythm: New Chord Every 2 Measures

Harmonic Rhythm: A Pop Song

You Belong With Me - Taylor Swift

Intro	(0:00 - 0:07)	1 chord every 4 measures.
V1	(0:08 - 0:21)	1 chord every 2 measures.
	(0:21 - 0:23)	Transition to V2 2 chords every 1 measure implied.
V2	(0:24 - 0:37)	1 chord every 2 measures.
PreC1	(0:38 - 0:49)	1 chord every 1 measure.
	(0:49 - 0:52)	Transition to C1 chord every 2 measures.
C1	(0:53 - 1:07)	1 chord every 2 measures.

The pace for the harmonic rhythm is set by the intro with a single chord. Anything that happens with more chords after this is going to feel like a jump in interest and energy. The transition from V1 to V2 has an implied 2 chords in 1 measure. The silence in the first half of the measure carries the intention of the previous chord, and the bass line implies a Dominant Area, creating an authentic cadence that pushes us into V2. The change from 1 chord every 2 measures in the verse sections to the 1 chord every one measure in the pre-chorus section highlights the "speeding up" and "tension" of the pre-chorus that launches us into the chorus, which is back to our "home" "resolution" of 1 chord every 2 measures. The transition from pre-chorus to the chorus features the dominant chord of the key in the Dominant Area for 2 measures, which really builds expectation and anticipation for the chorus with a half cadence.

Phrase Rhythm

Phrase rhythm is how fast phrases change and how many subphrases are in each phrase (if there are any subphrases).

- Phrase rhythm can change from phrase to phrase.
- Phrase rhythm can change from section to section.
- Phrase rhythm can change at any time and does not need to stay the same in all song sections and in all phrases.
- Phrase rhythm can follow and include anticipations and anacrusis.

Most phrases are 2, 4, or 8 measures long in modern music. For this reason it is more interesting to explore what happens when this pattern is broken in an effective way. What is the difference between a 2-measure phrase and 2-measure subphrase? The subphrase is part of a larger idea like an antecedent.

Phrase Rhythm: A Pop Song

Yesterday - The Beatles
Intro............ (0:00 - 0:04)......................No phrase = 4 measures.
a phrase.......(0:04 - 0:12)......................1 phrase = 3 measures.
b phrase.......(0:12 - 0:16)......................1 phrase = 2 measures.
c phrase.......(0:16 - 0:21)......................1 phrase = 2 measures.

It is uncommon for modern popular music to have a variation in phrase length and it is also uncommon to find an odd number of measures in the verse. It is also uncommon to have such short phrases! There are a total of 7 measures in V1, because the first phrase (a) is 3 measures in length!

Reharmonization

Reharmonization is when a melody stays the same, but the chords under the melody change. Any existing melody can be reharmonized. Reharmonization will show you a path for adding chords to any song you write. This is called harmonizing a melody.

- Use reharmonization ideas to create chords and chord progressions for your own melodies, compositions, and songs.
- Use reharmonization to create "covers" and remixes of other people's songs and compositions.
- Use reharmonization to build and change a melody inside your own songs and compositions.

How to Begin Reharmonization

Tip: use music notation software so you can hear what your chords sound like with the melody. This means that your first step would be to write the melody into a notation software, then add an extra line of staff to write the chords on in notation form.

1. Identify the relative major and minor keys that are linked to the key signature and notes.
2. Perform a scale degree analysis for both relative major and minor keys. If you already know you want the song to be major or minor, do the one you will use.
3. Decide if you want to start making the reharmonization in a major or minor key. You can create as many harmonizations of a single melody as you want in major and minor keys. Pick one to start for now. You can start new reharmonizations later.
4. Based on the scale degrees and how they relate to chord tones, where would you guess the Tonic, Subdominant, and Dominant Areas work well with the melody? You do not need all three Areas.
5. Roughly determine where the different Areas of harmonic function will be and write them down as T, SD, and D wherever you think they should happen, in classical style.
6. Write the chord symbols above the staff that line up with your idea of where the Tonic, Subdominant, and Dominant Areas should be. Use any harmonic rhythm.
7. Add more chords to create cadences if you want.
8. You can use a modern chord progression instead of T - D - T and T - SD - D - T. This is a great idea for making melodies sound like pop, R&B, or more modern songs. This is an equally valid way of harmonizing a melody..
9. Go back and adjust your chords and harmonic function Areas until you have a series of chords you like accompanying the melody. You may need to adjust chord voicings, inversions, and rhythms to get the whole thing to sound the way you want.
10. You are done! Congratulations on harmonizing your first song!

1., 2., 3.

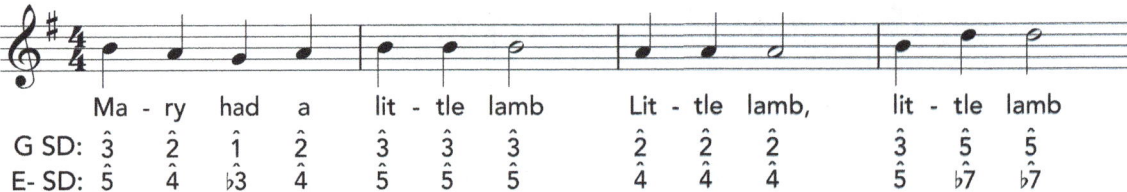

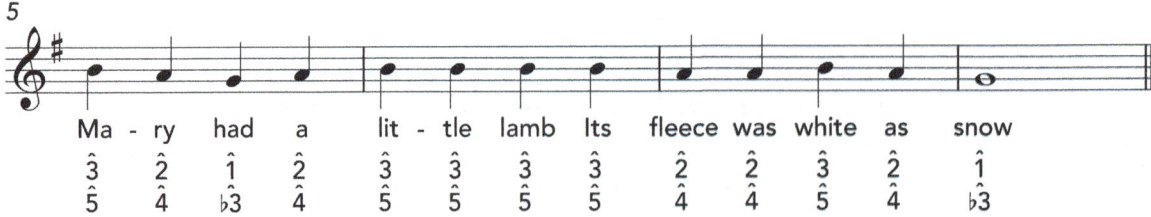

Choice: I will make a major reharmonization.

4., 5.

In this song you can spot the change from Tonic Area to Dominant Area that happens in m3. The scale degrees change from the notes on strongest and strong beats being the Root and Third chord tones of the tonic chord (mm.1-2) to "something else" in m3. Looking at m3, we could think of this as being a Subdominant Area with the notes in the melody being the Root of **II-**. Indeed, you could create an SD - D cadence here with a **II-** to **V7**. The same ideas apply in the second line.

6., 7., 8.

The first line is straightforward. It maintains a harmonic rhythm of 2 chords per measure. The Tonic Area uses only Tonic Area chords, the Dominant Area uses only Dominant Area chords, half cadence in m. 4 launches us into m. 5. In the second line, a secondary dominant with ♯5 to match the melody note on beat 3 brings us to the **VI-**. In m.6 a chromatic movement from E to D♯ to D takes place in the chord tones from the E- to the E-△ to the D in m. 7. The song ends with a plagal cadence.
Because harmonizing melodies can get complex, we will break down harmonizing into 3 levels.

Level 1 Reharmonization

1. Pick a key and perform a scale degree analysis of the melody.
2. Identify or pick Tonic, Subdominant, and Dominant Areas.
3. Fill in the Tonic, Subdominant, and Dominant Areas using only Root position triads and seventh chords from the harmonized scale of the key. You can borrow **V** and **V7** in minor keys.
4. You can increase or decrease the harmonic rhythm (add or take away chords per measure).
5. Think about the relationship of the melody to the chord tones and listen to how the music sounds by writing your melody and chords into a notation software like Noteflight, Sibelius, or Finale.

Level 1 Reharmonization: Major

Level 1 Reharmonization: Minor

Deciding to break from "the rules" and start in a Dominant Area "feels" much better in my subjective opinion. It makes the first measure "feel" like an anacrusis, a launching pad that pushes us with tension into the resolution of m. 2. It is fun - a little meta tension and resolution from what your ears might expect. Everything else for the rest of the song follows the T - D - T with an added SD - D cadence in m. 7 that drives us back home to m. 8.

> You can also throw T - D - T and T - SD - D - T out the window and use a chord progression instead. This is a great idea for making melodies sound like a pop, R&B, or more modern song. This is an equally valid way of reharmonizing a melody.

Level 2 Reharmonization

1. Pick a key and perform a scale analysis of the melody.

2. Identify Tonic, Subdominant, and Dominant Areas.

3. Fill in the Tonic, Subdominant, and Dominant Area with any chord of any quality from the key of the music. This includes inversions, slash chord, sus, and ADD chords. You can borrow **V** and **V7** in minor keys.

4. You can increase or decrease the harmonic rhythm (add or take away chords per measure).

5. You can "invent" new chord progression to go under the melody. Have fun and create sounds that make your heart happy.

6. Think about the relationship of the melody to the chord tones and listen to how the music sounds by writing your melody and chords into a notation software like Noteflight, Sibelius, or Finale.

Level 2 Reharmonization: Major

The harmonic rhythm of line 1 pushes and moves! This contrasts with the harmonic rhythm in line 2. It is not always a good idea to shift harmonic rhythm this much, but this sounds fun. If it works and makes your heart happy, keep it! A descending bass line follows the G major scale starting on beat 3 of m. 5 and completes its "walk" down to the Subdominant chord on beat 2 of m. 8.

Level 2 Reharmonization: Minor

Adding to the harmonic complexity of this harmonization, a little "fun" rhythm has been added to the treble clef of the piano part. To continue the fun, we have a "007 James Bond" moment in mm. 5-6.

> **You can also throw T - D - T and T - SD - D -T out the window and use a chord progression instead. This is a great idea for making melodies sound like a pop, R&B, or more modern song. This is an equally valid way of reharmonizing a melody.**

Level 3 Reharmonization

1. Pick a key and perform a scale degree analysis of the melody.
2. Identify Tonic, Subdominant, and Dominant Areas.
3. Fill in the Tonic, Subdominant, and Dominant Areas with any chord of any quality from any key. This includes inversions, any slash chord, sus, ADD, extended chords, altered chords, borrowed chords, secondary dominants, and tritone substitutions.
4. This can change the sound of the overall song from major to minor or make it impossible to define the key of the music.
5. You can increase or decrease the harmonic rhythm.
6. You can invent new chord progression to go under the melody.
7. Think about the relationship of the melody to the chord tones and listen to how the music sounds by writing your melody and chords into a notation software like Noteflight, Sibelius, or Finale.
8. You can make melody notes align with alteration, ADD notes, and tensions in chords.

(See next page for the reharmonization).

Level 3 Reharmonization: Major

Yes, this is in the key of G major. The song still follows T - D - T in both lines, but there sure are a few more chords than before. The Subdominant Area in m. 6 moves into the Dominant Area of m. 7 with a secondary dominant.

A lot of these chords "make sense to your ear" because they have chord tones that align them with the melody, like the E♭ on beat 3 of m.1, and the Eadd4 in on beat 3 of m. 3.

An ascending chomatic (a sequece of half-steps) bass line from m. 5 to m. 6 "walks" our ears up to the Subdominant Area.

A desencing chromatic bass line from beat 4 of m. 6 to beat 3 of m. 8 "walks" our ears down to the G/D. The G/D functions as a kind of gentle dominant, because $\hat{5}$ is the lowest note in the chord. This gentle inversion tension guides us home to the I in beat 4 of m. 8.

You do not need to write music this harmonically complex...but it can be a lot of fun.

> You can avoid T - D - T and T - SD - D - T and use a chord progression instead. This is a great idea for making melodies sound like a pop, R&B, or more modern song. This is an equally valid harmonize a melody.

How to Show There Is No Chord

In your reharmonizations, original songs, and compositions, you may feel that in certain measures you you only want melody without chords. All you need to do is write N.C. above the staff instead of a chord symbol to show that only the notes on the staff should make sound.

N.C. = No Chord = Silence = Chord Instrument(s) Rest

Review

- The two ways of thinking about melody
    - Horizontal (notes)
    - Vertical (chord tones)
- Chord-melody relationship
- Types of tension and resolution
- Cycles of tension and resolution
    - Idea
    - Phrase
    - Section
    - Song
    - Artist
- Harmonic rhythm
- Phrase rhythm
- Reharmonization
- No chord (N.C.)

New Words You Should Know

1. Harmonic rhythm
2. Phrase rhythm
3. Reharmonization

How to Write Music 4: Art

In this chapter, you will get a complete outline and step-by-step process to write a song and see how to write more complex music, too!

What Makes "Good" Art?

Art is not good or bad. We must leave these simple words behind.

Use other words to express how art makes you feel when you come in contact with it at any level.

How does the art make you feel when you:

- Hear it
- See it
- Touch it
- Smell it
- Taste it
- Think about it

Communicate to yourself and other people how art makes you feel using different adjectives than "good" and "bad."

We cannot measure or quantify all parts of art.

What we can measure in music is called music theory. We use music theory to measure the measurable parts of other people's art so we can learn the frameworks, tools, and tricks they use.

What Is Needed to Create Art?

There are three things every piece of art needs.

1. Your imagination of the completed art (or as far to completion as you can imagine it). This is called your "vision."
2. Figuring out how to achieve this vision or change the vision along the way. Every decision you make when creating art is your "artistic choice."
3. Doing the work or the steps that you choose to do to create your art. This is called "execution."

In art there are no mistakes. There is only your vision, your choices, and your execution.

The Dichotomy of Art

A dichotomy is when something is split into two parts that are opposite from each other. Everything in art has at least two options that are opposites and both of the two options are true and real.

- You can make art without any intention by using a blank mind, software, or physical randomizers or algorithms.
- You can make art without first having a vision...just start and see what happens!
- You can outsource artistic choices to randomizers, algorithms, sequences of numbers, and more!
- No form of execution is better than others. Art is art. It is about you expressing yourself, not how you do the expressing...but it could also be about how you express yourself.

There Are Answers, But There Are No Answers

Like a painter has brushes, canvases, and paints, music theory is the tools you will use to create your unique (or not unique, if you want) art. Both paintings below are made with paint, brushes, and canvas. They were both created using the same types of tools.

Vincent van Gogh - Starry Night

Claude Monet - Bridge over a Pond of Water Lillies

All people who make music have the same 12 notes (the full musical alphabet) to use in whatever way they want. What will you create?

How to Write a Song 2

How to Start A Song

There is no right way to start or finish a song. Try starting a few different ways and you will find an order of creation that works for you. You could start a song with:

1. A concept
2. Lyrics
3. Melody
4. Chords
5. Song form
6. Any combination of concept, lyrics, melody, chords, or song form

Just pick something and start with that. Adjust as you go.

Example: Write A Song

This example is JUST AN EXAMPLE. You can follow these steps or go in a different order by starting with a melody or a chord progression as your idea.

1. Define concept.
2. Write lyrics.
3. By looking at the lyrics, create the song form. You may need to add or remove lyrics.
4. Pick one part of your lyrics that will be the chorus, if your song has a chorus.
5. Write the rhythm of the lyrics in notation until you have a flow with the rhythm that makes your heart happy.
6. Add notes from a scale to your lyric rhythm to create a melody that makes your heart happy.
7. Shape the feeling of your music with performance, dynamic, and articulation marks.
8. Harmonize your melody. Pick a chord progression for each section of the song. It can be the same for each section, or it can change. A good rule is to keep all the Verse and Chorus progressions the same. You could write the chords in lead sheet style above the staff, or with notation in a separate line of staff, like we did in *The Best Music Theory Book for Beginners 1 pp.138-139* .
9. Adjust or change anything you don't like or think could be better.
10. Done. You have written a song.

1. Start With Why

Why are you writing this song?
- Is it for your own enjoyment?
- Is it for a release like a single, EP, or album?
- Is it for a special or specific event or occasion?
- Is it to pay tribute to someone, some place, or something?
- Is it for an exercise?

2. Concept

A concept is a plan or original idea for something. Concepts can come from:

- Inspiration/the universe/God/love.
- An idea or theme you pick.
- Your experience.
- The experience of someone you know or love.
- Imagining someone else's experience.

How to Dive Deep Into A Concept

In this example of a concept, we start with the idea of writing a song about "traveling through space."

1. Start with the concept.
2. Dive deep into the concept and consider it from many angles to find more ideas and fuel for your lyrics and musical inspiration.

Concept: Traveling through space

Ideas:
- Exploration of universe and self - purpose.
- Continuation of love - love survives after Earth is gone because we go to other planets.
- Continuation of family.
- The human experience, a journey through time.
- Hope for a better future.
- The human body is a space and time machine used to travel through time and space.
- Legacy, bittersweet, excitement + fear of the unknown.
- Repeat actions.
    Dynamics in relationships can stay the same in different spaces + change through time.
    We can repeat patterns.

Wow! Those are a lot of ideas that all work with the concept of "traveling through space." Now we have a bunch of topics and ideas for lyrics and the emotions of the music. With this number of ideas, it is likely you will not get stuck for a lack of ideas when it comes to writing lyrics.

3. Lyrics

Lyrics tell the story of the song. If you have a long list of ideas from your concept, you have fuel for many verses, pre-choruses, choruses, post-choruses, bridges, and any other section you want to write.

- If you are inspired, don't think about rules and write what you hear or feel. The rules and structure will be waiting to help you craft your music when you are done with your inspiration.
- Allow yourself to break any ideas of rhyme scheme in your first burst of creativity. Get the ideas down.
- If you are inspired, keep writing lyrics until you feel that the inspiration has passed and you are "empty" or "done."
- After you have finished writing, look over all your lyrics.

    Are there words you can change to improve the story?
    Are there lines you can change to improve each stanza?
    Are there stanzas you can move forward or backward in the order of the song?
    Which stanzas work best as verses?
    Which stanzas work best for a chorus or refrain?

- You can change the order of the lyrics of a song after writing them. Sometimes, a stanza you planned to have as a verse works better as a chorus. The opposite can be true.
- Give yourself time and space to go back and reconfigure your lyrics so that the story will be told at the speed, emotional intensity, and order of information you want.

4. Melody

There are 2 parts of every melody. Rhythm and notes. Focus on both in shaping and crafting your melodies, like we did in Book 2.

- If you are inspired, write what you hear or feel. The rules and structure will be waiting for you when you are done with your inspiration.
- Allow yourself to break any ideas of motifs and phrases in your first burst of creativity.
- Keep writing until you feel the inspiration has passed and you are "empty" or "done."
- Create the melody from an idea or motif or by combining notes and rhythms into phrases.
- What scale or scales and time signature will you use for the melody? Will there be borrowed notes from other keys?
- Revise and change the melody if you feel you can make it more compelling.
- Think about only the rhythm of the melody. Is there anything you can improve?
- Think about only the notes of the melody. Is there anything you can improve?
- How will you complement the story with the melody? A melody that is too big and bold in a verse may not leave room for growth and progress in a pre-chorus or chorus.
- What is the phrase rhythm? Does it change from section to section? Does it stay the same for the whole song? There is no wrong answer.
- Give yourself time and space to go back and reconfigure your lyrics and melody so that the story will be told with the emotional intensity and order of information you want.

5. Chords

- If you are inspired, don't think about rules and write what you hear or feel. The rules and structure will be waiting to help you craft your music when you are done with your inspiration.

- When writing, crafting, or picking chords you can:

    Write the melody first, then harmonize the melody.
    Write a chord progression or series of chords, then write a melody to fit the chords.
    Change one or more chords in a "common" chord progression.
    Use different chords or progressions for different sections of a song.
    Create your own chord progressions.
    Use a non-repeating or partially repeating series of chords.
    Any combination of all the options above.

- If things sound cheesy, you might have too many chord tones in the melody. Use different chords, more syncopation, and fewer authentic cadences. You may need to revisit the melody to make your song sound less predictable.

- Will you use cadences? If yes, where, when, and how often?

- What is the harmonic rhythm? Does it change from section to section? Does it stay the same for the whole song? There is no wrong answer.

- Give yourself time and space to go back and reconfigure your lyrics, melody, and chords so that the story will be told with the emotional intensity and order of information you want.

> **In general, the melody is a higher priority.
> Shape the harmony to make the melody shine in its best light.**

6. Structure

- If you are inspired, don't think about rules and write what you hear or feel. The rules and structure will be waiting to help you craft your music when you are done with your inspiration.

- You can pick your song structure before, during, or after concept, lyrics, melody, and chords.

- You can change your structure at any time.

Songwriting Dichotomies

- You must take your time and make good choices every step of the way, but not so much time that the song is never completed.

- You must have structure and use the tools of music theory, but also be creative and break the rules using the tools of music theory when it sounds good to you.

- You must seek out advice and opinions on your songs from experienced producers or people who write "better" songs than you. You must also know when you are on the right track and not listen to anyone.

Ideas: Mix and Match

For songwriting and composition, you can use most combinations of the 13 ways to develop a motif. This creates HUNDREDS of ways you can take a single musical idea and develop it. Here are some examples.

1. Retrograde + Diatonic Sequence

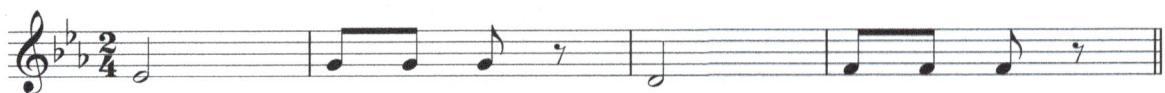

2. Original + Retrograde + Diatonic Sequence

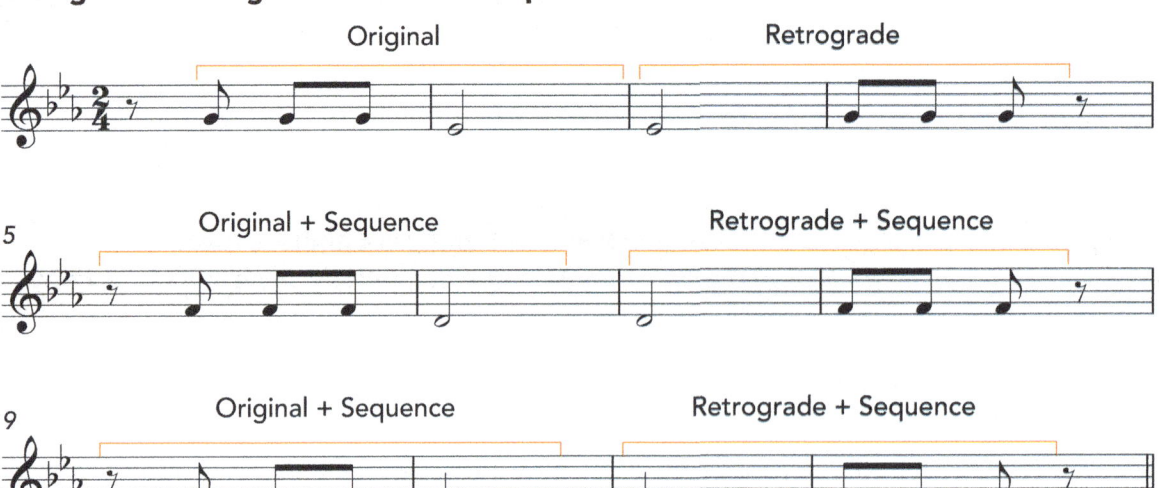

3. Original + Inversion + Chromatic Sequence

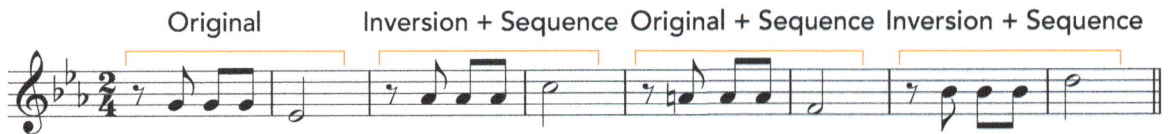

What Is the Next Step?

Many of the skills you have gained up to this point involve understanding and using music theory concepts at a high level. For this reason, songwriting has been emphasized. This is because songwriting at its most fundamental level is a melody. On a musical level, songwriting is less complex than composition, if only because there are fewer instruments that need to have parts written for them.

Levels 1-3 prepare you to write songs with lyrics, a melody, and chords.

If you can write a melody, add chords to it, and make that sound good to your heart and your ears, you have mastered the fundamental act of creating an idea.

The art of composition steps in at this point and asks, "Yes, but **how** are we going to get the chords and melody to work with each other in a dynamic way?"

This is what we will answer in the next books, where we will explore (among many other things):

- A deep dive into the inner workings of melodies, motifs, phrases, and subphrases.
- Counterpoint
- 4-part harmony
- Score analysis
- Modes of scales
- Advanced music theory ideas and applications

These skills that are waiting for you allow you to take a melody and chords and intertwine and shape them together in the most intimate and artistic way. These skills also give you the tools to write all the music for a rock band, chorus of voices, orchestra, and smaller groups of instruments like duos, trios, quartets, quintets, sextets, septets, octets, big bands, and more.

Dive deep in book 4 so you can create arrangements of songs, bring many instruments together to create melodies, harmonies, and take your ideas, songs, and compositions to the next level!

You Are Invited

To join me and other Music Makers in our community!

- Free lessons
- Q&As
- Community support
- New music opportunities

Scan the QR code or go to:

facebook.com/groups/musicmakersofficial

Made in the USA
Las Vegas, NV
17 December 2024